The Story of America

for Elementary Schools

Albert F. Blaisdell

Alpha Editions

This edition published in 2024

ISBN : 9789362923813

Design and Setting By
Alpha Editions
www.alphaedis.com
Email - info@alphaedis.com

As per information held with us this book is in Public Domain.
This book is a reproduction of an important historical work. Alpha Editions uses the best technology to reproduce historical work in the same manner it was first published to preserve its original nature. Any marks or number seen are left intentionally to preserve its true form.

Contents

PREFACE. ....- 1 -

CHAPTER I. AMERICA IN THE OLD DAYS. ....- 2 -

CHAPTER II. COLUMBUS AND THE DISCOVERY OF AMERICA. ....- 7 -

CHAPTER III. SIR WALTER RALEIGH AND CAPTAIN JOHN SMITH. ....- 17 -

CHAPTER IV. THE STORY OF THE PILGRIMS. ....- 25 -

CHAPTER V. MORE ABOUT THE PILGRIMS. ....- 33 -

CHAPTER VI. THE INDIANS AND HOW THEY LIVED. ....- 40 -

CHAPTER VII. THE DUTCH IN NEW YORK; THE QUAKERS IN PENNSYLVANIA. ....- 48 -

CHAPTER VIII. THE FRENCH AND INDIAN WARS. ....- 58 -

CHAPTER IX. EVERYDAY LIFE IN COLONIAL TIMES. ....- 68 -

CHAPTER X. THE BEGINNING OF THE REVOLUTION. ....- 75 -

CHAPTER XI. LEXINGTON AND CONCORD. ....- 85 -

CHAPTER XII. THE BATTLE OF BUNKER HILL. ....- 91 -

CHAPTER XIII. THE DECLARATION OF INDEPENDENCE. ....- 98 -

CHAPTER XIV. THE BURGOYNE CAMPAIGN. ....- 106 -

CHAPTER XV. WASHINGTON AND THE REVOLUTION. ....- 118 -

CHAPTER XVI. THE WAR OF THE REVOLUTION IN THE SOUTH. ....- 132 -

CHAPTER XVII. THE STORY OF ARNOLD'S TREASON. ....- 143 -

CHAPTER XVIII. JOHN PAUL JONES: OUR FIRST GREAT NAVAL HERO. ....- 150 -

CHAPTER XIX. BENJAMIN FRANKLIN: HIS HIGHLY USEFUL CAREER. ....- 155 -

CHAPTER XX. EVERYDAY LIFE ONE HUNDRED YEARS AGO. ....- 163 -

CHAPTER XXI. WHAT OUR NAVY DID IN THE WAR OF 1812. ....- 169 -

CHAPTER XXII. THE SETTLEMENT OF THE PACIFIC COAST. ....- 177 -

CHAPTER XXIII. LINCOLN AND THE WAR FOR THE UNION. ....- 184 -

CHAPTER XXIV. MORE ABOUT THE
WAR FOR THE UNION..- 192 -

CHAPTER XXV. OUR NAVY IN THE
WAR FOR THE UNION..- 202 -

CHAPTER XXVI. THE WAR WITH
SPAIN IN 1898..- 212 -

APPENDIX..- 221 -

PREFACE.

SOME sort of a first book on American history is now quite generally used in schools as a preparation for the more intelligent study of a larger and more formal text-book in the higher grammar grades.

For beginners, a mere compilation of facts is dry and unsatisfactory. Such books have now given place, for the most part, to those prepared on a more attractive and judicious plan. The real aim in a first book should be to interest boys and girls in the history of their country, and to encourage them to cultivate a taste for further study and reading.

This book is intended for use in the earlier grammar grades and to be preliminary to the study of a more advanced work in the higher grades. The author has also kept in mind the fact that the school life of many children is brief, and that all their instruction in American history must come from a text-book of this kind.

The author has not aimed to cover the whole range of our country's history. Of many noted men and important affairs no mention is made. Only the leading events of certain periods and the personal achievements of a few representative "makers of our country" are treated in any detail. The subject is approached through biographical sketches of a few of the more illustrious actors in our nation's history. Some prominence is given to exceptional deeds of valor, details of everyday living in olden times, dramatic episodes, and personal incident.

The schoolroom test demonstrates the fact that such a treatment of the subject is more attractive and profitable to children of the lower grades than the mere recital of minor matters and petty details of public events.

The author would acknowledge his indebtedness to Dr. Homer B. Sprague of New York City for editorial help in reading and revising the manuscript. Thanks are also due to Dr. John E. Sanborn of Melrose, Mass., for editorial assistance.

A. F. BLAISDELL.

NOVEMBER, 1900.

CHAPTER I.
AMERICA IN THE OLD DAYS.

1. The Story of our Country.—We are sure that every intelligent and patriotic American youth must like to read the story of our country's life. To a boy or girl of good sense no work of fiction can surpass it in interest or power.

How delightful to let the imagination summon up the forms and the deeds of the fearless Norse sailors who dared to cross the unknown seas in their frail and tiny vessels without compass and without charts! How interesting the oft-told but ever-fresh narrative of the intrepid Columbus and his memorable first voyage into and across the "Sea of Darkness"! What romance was ever more exciting than the stories of the fierce struggles between the white men and the Indians for existence and supremacy on this continent?

How deep the pathos of the simple tales that tell of the patient sufferings, the severe toils, the ever-present dangers, and the heroic self-denials of the early colonists in making for themselves homes in the New World! How richly suggestive are those pages that record the glorious events of our American Revolution—the splendid and immortal deeds of Washington and his illustrious associates!

Then there is the thrilling account of the most tremendous civil war in all history, with its four million soldiers, its two thousand battles, and its preservation of the Union.

And to come down to a time within the memory of every schoolboy, the echoes of the Spanish-American conflict have hardly yet died away. The story of this short war in the summer of 1898 still rings in our ears—with its astounding naval victories at Manila and Santiago, the freedom of Cuba, and the destruction of the last vestige of the once mighty Spanish supremacy on this western continent!

2. Lessons of Wisdom and Inspiration to be learned.—But beyond and above all mere gratification and pleasure to be derived from the study of our country's history, there are in it lessons of wisdom to be learned, there is inspiration to noble living, there is an uplifting of the soul to a higher plane of thought and sentiment, there is constant aid in the development and upbuilding of manly and womanly character.

And when we think of the marvelous growth of less than three centuries which, beginning with the infant colonies of Jamestown and Plymouth, has made us a nation of more than seventy millions; when we think of the wonderful record of trial and triumph and unceasing progress, and of the great and good and wise men that have laid the foundations and reared the superstructure of this mighty temple of liberty,—we must be blind indeed and ungrateful beyond expression not to recognize with devout thankfulness the guiding hand of a beneficent Providence.

America, under God, stood at Plymouth for religious freedom; in the Revolution, for independence; in our civil war, for the preservation of the Union. She now stands for humanity, civilization, and the uplifting of the whole race.

3. The People of Ancient America.—Wise men who have made a special study of the subject tell us that this country has been continuously inhabited by generations of men for many thousands of years. Rude tools, and human skulls, intermingled with bones of animals of species long extinct, have been found in caves or dug out of deep layers of earth; and they indicate that in the Mississippi valley and on the Atlantic and Pacific slopes there lived, perhaps hundreds of ages ago, men of a low grade of culture.

In the great museums—as the Smithsonian Institution at Washington, the Peabody Museums at Cambridge and New Haven, and the natural history rooms at New York and elsewhere—may be seen thousands of the relics of vanished races of men and animals that once inhabited this continent.

4. The Red Men or Indians.—The Indians constitute a race by themselves. Whether they are descended from some of those prehistoric inhabitants of whom we have just spoken no one can say; but they make up an American type with marks as clearly recognized as those that distinguish the Mongolians and the Malays. For long ages the red men had spread themselves over the two continents, from Hudson Bay to Cape Horn. With few or no exceptions, all had the same copperish or cinnamon color, deep-set and intensely black eyes, high cheek-bones, straight black hair, with little or no beard; but the long lapse of time, the great varieties of environment, and perhaps other causes, brought about striking differences of appearance, of manners, customs, dialects, and the like.

5. Three Principal Divisions of the Indians.—The eminent historian, Dr. John Fiske, groups the Indians in three leading divisions,—as savage, barbarous, and half-civilized.

ANCIENT CLIFF DWELLINGS.

The savage Indians ranged to the west of Hudson Bay, and southward between the Rocky Mountains and the Pacific, to the northern part of Mexico. They lived by catching fish or game. They knew little or nothing of tilling the soil. They did not dwell in permanent villages, but roamed from place to place like Bedouin Arabs.

The barbarous Indians inhabited the country east of the Rocky Mountains. They did not depend wholly upon hunting or fishing, but knew how to upturn the soil slightly with rude tools, and raise squashes, beans, tomatoes, and, most important of all, Indian corn. They lived in villages, and made houses that would last several years. They had dogs of an inferior breed, but no other domestic animals. Some tribes were able to weave coarse cloth and make weapons of polished stones. They had strange social customs and singular religious beliefs. Fighting was their principal occupation.

The half-civilized Indians once lived in New Mexico and the adjoining region. They have had almost nothing to do with the history of the United States. They are the Pueblo Indians, so called from the pueblos or strongholds, dwellings which they built of stones or of sun-dried brick. Some of these strongholds, story above story, would accommodate at least three thousand inhabitants! They were built oftentimes in situations almost inaccessible, like eagles' nests on cliffs, apparently that they might be defended more easily against the attack of an enemy.

6. The Northmen and their Discoveries.—The real contact between the eastern and western halves of the world practically began in 1492, the year of the first great voyage of Columbus. Occasional visitors may have sailed before that date directly across the "Sea of Darkness" from the Old World to the New. The subject is shrouded for the most part in the mists of vague stories and obscure traditions.

It seems quite certain, however, that in the year 986 a daring Scandinavian navigator, Eric the Red, founded on the southwestern coast of Greenland a colony that lasted four or five hundred years. In the same year, as the Iceland Sagas (heroic legends) tell us, another Norse sailor, voyaging from

Iceland to Greenland, was driven by storms far out towards the southwest, and was perhaps the first white man to behold the American coast.

NORSE RUINS IN GREENLAND.

Many interesting ruins of stone-built houses and of a church are still to be seen on that desolate Greenland shore. In those ages the Northmen, or Norsemen, as the people of Norway, Sweden, and Denmark were called, were the most skillful sailors in the world. Eric the Red had several sons, bold sailors like their father. The oldest of these (whose statue stands on Commonwealth Avenue, Boston), Leif the Lucky, with thirty-five hardy men, sailed south from Greenland in the year 1000, to explore these lands that had been discovered fourteen years before. He landed at several points along the coast. In a place which he called "Vinland the Good" (land of vines), he found an abundance of luscious wild grapes. Just where this sturdy Norse sailor feasted on the grapes is, of course, uncertain, but good authorities are inclined to think it may have been not far from Plymouth, on the coast of Massachusetts Bay. He returned home in the spring. Two years later Leif's brother, Thorwald, came on a voyage of discovery, but was killed by the natives in the summer of 1004.
In the spring of the year 1007 an Icelandic chief, accompanied by his wife and a crew of one hundred and sixty men, in three vessels, came to this Vinland. He remained here three years, and had many dealings with the Indians.

A NORSE SHIP.

The Norsemen went home and gave vivid and accurate descriptions of the land they visited. They described the Indians, the fish, the animals, and the plants, all of which are given in the Icelandic chronicles. No real relic, however, of these people has yet been found upon our own coast.

Columbus, who visited Iceland in the year 1477, may have had access to the Icelandic archives, and have learned of the discoveries of these rovers of the deep. But we have no evidence on that point. After the eleventh century America remained as much unknown as if the bold Northmen had never steered their dragon-prowed ships along our shores. The waves that incessantly rolled upon its sands or dashed against its rocks brought no vessel from the far-away lands of the East. Nearly five hundred years were to come and go before, in the fullness of time, the hour struck for the real and fruitful discovery of the New World. It was left for Columbus, the great Genoese navigator, to open wide its gates!

LANDING OF THE NORSEMEN.

CHAPTER II.
COLUMBUS AND THE DISCOVERY OF AMERICA.

7. Commercial Activity in the Fifteenth Century.—In southern Europe, the last half of the fifteenth century was a period of great commercial activity. Then, for the first time, many voyages of exploration were made in various directions, to find new riches, new markets, or new routes of travel and transportation. Merchants were turning their attention more and more to enterprises in far-off regions beyond the seas.

Venice and Genoa became rivals for the vast and valuable trade of India. With other Italian cities they grew rich and powerful. They kept great fleets of merchant vessels plying back and forth across the Mediterranean.

They sent out to India large quantities of copper, iron, pitch, wool, hides, and the like, and brought back cargoes of drugs, spices, silks, pearls, and other luxuries. But the path of this commerce between the Mediterranean and India required both ships and caravans; and whether by way of the Isthmus of Suez and the Red Sea, or by Damascus and the Persian Gulf, or by the Black Sea and the Caspian and thence across the eastern plains, the journey was long, tedious, costly; always hazardous, and often, by reason of the Turkish wars, positively dangerous.

And so it became important, especially for the merchants of Spain and Portugal, the would-be rivals of Venice and Genoa, to find a shorter and safer route. In many a country, people were asking, "Is there no easier way to get to India?"

In the attempts to solve this problem Portugal took the lead. Her sailors boldly ventured farther and farther down the coast of Africa until, about twenty years before Columbus discovered America, they crossed the equator. But it was not till five years after the memorable exploit of Columbus, that Vasco da Gama, a Portuguese captain, rounded the Cape of Good Hope and crossed the broad Indian Ocean to India. Two years later he returned home with his vessels full of rich merchandise from that country.

8. The Shape of the Earth—Spherical or Flat?—The learned men of that age, for the most part, believed the earth to be round like a ball. But the common people, and doubtless many of high rank, thought the land surface to be flat, with a flat ocean flowing around it on every side. Now if the earth were really a sphere, and no larger than was commonly supposed, it would seem that the easiest way to get to India, unless unforeseen obstacles intervened, would be to strike out to the west and sail straight across the "Sea of Darkness," as the sailors called the Atlantic. To embrace so startling a theory and deliberately to risk his life in testing its truth, required a man of keen sagacity, of lofty faith, of unbending resolution, and of the most heroic daring. Such a man was Christopher Columbus.

9. Columbus; his Early Life as a Sailor.—He was born at Genoa, in or about the year 1445. He was the son of a poor wool-comber, and while yet very young he helped in his father's daily toil. We find him a studious boy, early able to write a good hand and to draw maps and charts for mariners visiting his home. He loves the sea, listens eagerly to old sailors' "yarns," weaves their fancies and legends into his day-dreams, and is fired with ambition to go in search of strange lands. How shall he realize his visions? Who will believe in him?

At the age of fourteen he becomes a sailor. He sails south along the African coast, and north as far as England, and even to Iceland. Always observing, studying, planning, the ardent, thoughtful boy grows up an earnest, thoughtful man. He is convinced that the earth is a globe, and that, if he sails west far enough, he will reach India by a route shorter than any to the east. Nothing can shake his faith in this belief. It becomes the inspiration of his life.

But like that of many learned men of his day, his estimate of the distance is widely wrong. He supposes it to be only a few thousand miles, requiring but a few weeks' sail. Little does he imagine that directly in his westward path lies a vast continent, and beyond this rolls an ocean far wider than the Atlantic!

10. Curious Things from the Unknown West.—To reflecting minds many facts gave hints of lands in the distant west. Curiously carved wood had been washed ashore by westerly gales; far out on the sunset sea an old pilot had picked up a quaintly wrought paddle; cane stalks of tropic growth, and huge pines that could not have come from the east, had drifted to the Azores. It was believed that these articles, strange to European eyes, had floated across the broad ocean from the eastern coast of Asia.

Meditating much upon all these and kindred facts, and upon the teachings of science, Columbus conceives himself to be divinely commissioned to open up this new route to India, incidentally discovering unknown lands and showing that the earth was round. But this stupendous project calls for ships, men, and vast sums of money. He is poor, and he has no rich patrons.

11. Columbus seeks Aid from Foreign Governments.—For ten years Columbus tried to persuade some European government to send him on this voyage across the Atlantic. First he sought help from his own people, the republic of Genoa; then from Venice, and afterwards from Portugal. For seven years he had patiently and persistently endeavored to interest Ferdinand and Isabella, the king and queen of Spain, in his scheme of a shorter route to India than that which their rivals, the Portuguese, were hoping to find by sailing down the western coast of the dark continent. After years of waiting and seeking, the long-sought help at last came. Isabella had faith in Columbus, and proved herself a firm friend. She listened patiently to his plans; and she finally decided to fit out an expedition at the expense of her own kingdom of Castile.

By the terms of the agreement, Columbus was to be admiral of all the oceans he sailed and viceroy of all the lands he discovered, and to have one-eighth of all the profits of the expedition—the pearls, diamonds, gold, silver, and spices.

It was hard work to get a crew willing to go on this long voyage into the mysterious western seas. It was indeed a strange and hazardous project, and prudent sailors, though stout-hearted, might well shrink from taking the risk. Some, badly in debt, consented to ship on condition that their debts should be paid. Others, convicted culprits, promising to join the expedition, were released from jail.

12. Columbus sails on his Wonderful Voyage.—Finally, in August, 1492, after a delay of several months, three vessels with ninety men sailed from Palos, a little port of Spain, on the most wonderful voyage the world has ever seen—the voyage which ended in the discovery of the great New World. What a heroic venture,—to sail out into an unknown ocean!

VESSELS OF COLUMBUS CROSSING THE OCEAN.

Every day and every hour took them farther from home. Onward and still onward they were sailing, across the trackless and boundless deep, with nothing in sight but sky and ocean.

No wonder they became angry with themselves for having started upon what seemed so foolhardy an enterprise. When at first the land sank from sight on the eastern horizon, many of them lamented their sad fate, and cried and sobbed like children. Columbus, fearing trouble, took the precaution to keep two different reckonings as to the distance sailed, a true one for himself and a false one for his men.

To add to their fears, the needle of the compass no longer pointed, as usual, a little to the right of the north star, but began to sway toward the left. Columbus did not know what to make of this variation of the compass needle, but by giving an ingenious astronomical explanation he managed to satisfy his men.

"This day we sailed westward, which was our course," were the simple but grand words which the brave commander wrote in his journal day after day. The sailors, in despair and rebellion, threatened to throw him overboard; but he stood firm in his hope and courage, gazing almost incessantly towards the ever-receding western horizon.

13. The Great Problem at last solved.—Many times the eager sailors thought they saw land, and many times they were disappointed. At last birds began to circle around the ships. A bush covered with fresh red berries floated by, and a piece of carved wood. Presently the birds were seen to fly southward. By these signs Columbus felt sure that they were approaching land. "We shall see land in the morning," he said to his men. All was excitement and activity. No one could sleep. All waited impatiently for the dawn.

COLUMBUS'S FIRST VIEW OF THE NEW WORLD.

The day broke, and a beautiful island appeared before them. Columbus was the first to step upon the beach; the others followed; all knelt as the great discoverer kissed the ground and gave thanks to God. He rose from his knees, drew his sword, unfurled the great flag of Spain, gorgeous with its red and gold, and in the name of Spain he took possession of the land, calling it San Salvador. From his sublime purpose the mighty navigator had not swerved a hair's breadth! He had solved the great problem! He had earned a name that should never die!

14. The New World and its Strange People; the Homeward Voyage.—The island on which Columbus first landed was one of those we now call the West Indies, the name given by him. The voyagers were wild with delight at the new country. They gazed in wonder at the rare and lovely flowers, the bright-colored birds flashing through the sunlight, the lofty palms, the strange trees bearing abundant fruits; but most of all at the singular people, whom of course they called Indians.

Not less were the natives astonished. They thought the strange visitors divine beings from the sky, and the ships unearthly monsters from the deep. Columbus found the natives kindly and generous with gifts. Maize or Indian corn, potatoes, cotton, and tobacco were found; but neither gold nor diamonds.

Columbus felt sure that this land was some part of Asia. After a stay of twelve weeks he decided to sail back to Spain with the news of his great discovery. He took with him a number of the natives and a vast store of curiosities. On the voyage a terrific storm raged for four days, and it seemed as if the frail vessels must be destroyed. The peril being very great, Columbus wrote upon parchment two brief accounts of his discoveries; each of these he wrapped in a cloth, enclosed it in a large cake of wax, and securely packed it in a tight cask. One of these kegs was flung into the sea, and the other was lashed to the vessel.

The two frail vessels, however, rode out the storm and at last put into one of the Azores to refit. On the homeward way another storm overtook the weary voyagers, and Columbus was glad to reach at last a port in Portugal. From thence in March, 1493, he arrived safe in the harbor of Palos.

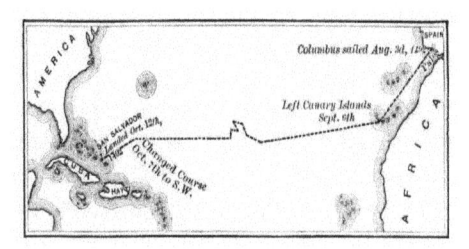

MAP OF COLUMBUS'S ROUTE ON HIS GREAT VOYAGE ACROSS THE OCEAN.

15. Columbus receives a Royal Welcome on his Return.—A royal welcome was given Columbus on his return. The man who had been laughed at for his strange theories, now returning from a newly discovered world beyond the sea, was regarded as the greatest of men. Ferdinand and Isabella received him with royal pomp and asked him to tell them his story. Marvelous it must have seemed, and all who heard it must have listened with breathless attention. The highest honors were bestowed upon him. His discovery of course excited intense interest throughout the civilized world.

COLUMBUS REBUKING THE COURTIERS.

But the high honors paid to him aroused the jealousy of the courtiers. Once, while sitting as a guest of honor at table, one of the courtiers said with a sneer that it was not such a great thing after all to discover the New World; any one else could have done it. By way of reply Columbus took an egg from a dish before him, and handing it to the courtier, asked him to make it stand on end. The man tried but could not do it. Others tried but failed, and the egg came back to Columbus. He struck it upon the table with slight force, cracking the shell a little, and then it stood upright.

"Oh, any one could do that," said the courtier. "So any one could discover the Indies after I have shown the way," was the reply of Columbus.

16. Columbus sails on Other Voyages across the Atlantic.—In spite of the joy among the Spanish people over the great discovery, there was general disappointment that Columbus brought back no gold or precious stones. It was believed that another voyage might bring better success. Accordingly he soon prepared to sail again across the ocean. There was no trouble now in obtaining crews; multitudes wished to go.

In September, 1493, he started—this time with seventeen ships and fifteen hundred men! He landed among the Caribbean Islands. The natives were frightened at the horses which were brought over, thinking the rider and the steed all one; they were doubly terrified to see the man dismount and the strange being come to pieces, making two separate animals!

Columbus coasted along the south side of Cuba, and being sure it was India, tried to find the mouth of the Ganges! Seeing traces of a gold mine that had once been worked, he concluded that in that region must have been found the gold of Ophir, which had been used for Solomon's temple, and that probably the great temple itself was not far off!

17. Queen Isabella proves a Friend.—After a great deal of trouble during his absence of nearly three years, Columbus returned home in 1496. Serious disputes followed his arrival. Much disappointment was felt that he had found no gold or diamonds; many denounced "the foreign upstart" as a fraud and a tyrant, saying that he cost more than he was worth. Jealousy, intrigue, disappointed greed, hatred for fancied slights, every motive to hostility took shape against him. Yet as Isabella was still his friend, and as he hoped for better fortune in another trial, he prepared for a third voyage. In May, 1498, with six vessels and two hundred men he again set sail.

On this voyage Columbus touched the mainland of South America and passed the mouth of the river Orinoco. The broad flow of the great river, the magnificent scenery, and the charming climate delighted him. "This must be the river," he said, "that flows through the Garden of Eden."

Meanwhile, many of the Spaniards that had been left on the islands rebelled against him. Evil-minded officials in Spain sent out a sort of inspector to examine into the rebellion. Prompted by malice, he exceeded his authority and caused Columbus to be chained as a criminal. With stern fortitude the stout-hearted mariner endured the cruel irons, and he was thus taken back to Spain. The captain of the vessel offered to free him from his chains. The brave discoverer answered sadly but proudly: "No: I will wear them as a memento of the gratitude of princes!"

18. The Fourth and Last Voyage.—His firm friend, the queen, justly indignant, received him with tears. Then the much-enduring old man broke down, and with sobs and weeping threw himself at her feet. The great-hearted Isabella encouraged him to go on still another expedition. In May, 1502, with four vessels and one hundred and fifty men, he sailed on his fourth and last voyage.

He skirted the south side of Cuba, touched at Honduras, and coasted along the northern shores of South America. Many of his men were killed by the Indians, his company was short of food, his ships began to leak, the vessel on which he sailed was wrecked, and the voyage was every way disastrous. In November, 1504, old, feeble, and broken-hearted, Columbus returned to. Spain. His royal patron and best friend, Isabella, was dead. His constitution was shattered by the labors and perils he had undergone. His last year was passed in sickness and poverty. In 1506 he closed his eyes in death.

19. Columbus and his Mighty Achievement.—After all his four eventful voyages, this prince of explorers died in the belief that he had reached the eastern shores of Asia, and that, too, by the best and most direct route. He never imagined that he had found a new continent. Although self-deceived as to the true nature of his discoveries, he yet well deserved all the honors that have crowned his memory. His own time was not worthy of him; but after-ages have paid him due and ever-increasing reverence. His name will forever be linked with lofty ideas and magnificent achievements.

Columbus was a man of noble and commanding presence, tall, and powerfully built. He had long-waving hair, a fair, ruddy complexion, and keen blue-gray eyes that easily kindled and glowed. He inspired strong affection and deep respect. He always carried himself with an air of authority, as became a man of great heart and lofty thoughts.

Why was this continent not named for Columbus? Let me tell you. Because in his life it was not known as a new world, and hence had no need of a new name. It already had the names India and Cathay (China). In 1501 Americus Vespucius, a Florentine merchant and a mariner already familiar with the western waters, sailed on his third voyage far southward along the eastern coast of South America. The vast size of that country thus became partially known. He wrote an account of his voyages to the "New World," and in his honor it was named "America." Gradually this name was applied to the northern continent also.

LANDING OF COLUMBUS.

20. The Cabots and their Voyages.—We need not be told that these expeditions made a great sensation in Europe, and that many bold mariners started out from Portugal and Spain. The sovereigns of other nations, too, as England and France, soon sent navigators to make claims for their own countries. Among the most notable of these were the Cabots, John and his son Sebastian. Though natives of Genoa, they lived in England and had entered the service of King Henry VII. They had permission from him to sail across the Atlantic and to take possession, in his name, of any lands which were not known to Europeans.

In May, 1497, with one ship and eighteen men, John Cabot with his son Sebastian left England. The first land he saw is supposed to have been either Cape Breton Island or the shores of Labrador. He did not remain long on that cold and dismal coast, but returned home to England after an absence of about three months. John Cabot was probably the first European since the days of the Northmen to set foot upon the mainland of North America.

On his return he was received with much honor by the king. He was called "The Great Admiral," and he went about the streets richly dressed in silk, followed by a crowd of admirers. The next year the Cabots set out upon a second voyage. This took a wider range. The exact limits of these explorations are not clearly known; but it is believed that they discovered the coast of Labrador, sailed along to Newfoundland, thence probably as far south as Cape Cod, and perhaps to Cape Hatteras. Inasmuch as Columbus never set foot upon the mainland of North America, the Cabot discoveries are of importance. It is claimed that they gave England a right to the settlement and ownership of this northern continent.

Sebastian lived to be a very old man, and to the last was full of enthusiasm about the new-found world He was known as "The Great Yeoman." It was said of him: "He gave England a continent—and no one knows his burial place!"

21. A Spanish Knight seeks the Fountain of Youth.—A singular expedition was that of Ponce de Leon, a brave knight who had sailed with Columbus on his second voyage. The Spaniards had heard somewhere in eastern Asia the old, old legend, of a fountain whose water gave perpetual youth to any one who drank of it. In 1513 Ponce de Leon sailed from Porto Rico, where he had been governor, with three vessels, in search of this wonderful "Fountain of Youth."

On Easter Sunday (which in Spanish is Pascua Florida, flowering Easter) he first came within sight of a coast to which he gave the name Florida, partly in honor of the day and partly because it was indeed a region of flowers. He took possession of it in the name of the King of Spain. Never before had he seen so beautiful a region. It seemed the land of eternal summer.

He landed not far from what is now St. Augustine, and followed the coast south to its western shore; but he went back disappointed. If he or any one else ever saw this spring of magic power, it was only in dreams. In 1521 our romantic knight sailed again in search of the hoped-for fountain; but by reason of a severe wound from an Indian arrow he was forced to return to Cuba. There he died of his painful injury.

22. How De Soto sought in Vain for Gold.—Another adventurous Spanish knight was Ferdinand de Soto. He attempted to explore and conquer the country across the waters to the north of Cuba. In 1539, with nine vessels and five hundred and seventy men, he left Havana. Landing on the eastern coast of Florida, De Soto marched north to the Savannah River, thence going westward. Dangers beset him on every side. Sometimes the natives, who had learned to fear and hate the Spaniards, sent poisoned arrows flying through the air. Sometimes they purposely led their greedy foes into swamps in the search for gold. The Spaniards in turn treated the Indians with extreme cruelty.

DE SOTO'S FIRST VIEW OF THE MISSISSIPPI RIVER.

A number of dreadful battles were fought in which De Soto lost many men. Through tangled forests and swamps the Spaniards, suffering from hunger and sickness, plodded on their weary march. De Soto would not turn back. He was determined to find gold. The proud Spaniard could not endure the thought of failure. He had promised his followers an abundance of treasure, and he resolved to keep that promise.

At last they reached the banks of a mighty river. Compared with other streams it was like the sea. It was the great Mississippi. De Soto was probably the first white man that ever gazed upon it. Under his direction the men built rafts, crossed the "Father of Waters," and pushed far on to what is now Arkansas and Missouri, in search of the fabled land of gold. They never found it. Instead of gems and gold, they found hunger, sickness, and death.

23. Death of De Soto.—At last, a little group exhausted and emaciated, they turned their steps southward and toward the great river again. De Soto was broken-hearted. A fever seized him, and he soon died.

The Indians stood in great awe of De Soto. They called him a "child of the Sun," and believed he would never die. His men therefore wished to conceal the fact of their leader's death. They wrapped his dead body in a mantle and sank it at night beneath the waters of the Mississippi. The wretched remnant of his followers managed to build a few boats, and in these they floated down the stream. A few of them at last reached friends to whom they told the story of their failure.

CHAPTER III.
SIR WALTER RALEIGH AND CAPTAIN JOHN SMITH.

SIR WALTER RALEIGH.

24. Sir Walter Raleigh: Soldier, Sailor, and Courtier.—Not until many years after the voyages of the two Cabots did the English begin to make settlements in the New World. For more than three-quarters of a century no one seemed to comprehend the vast importance of the discoveries of those explorers, or to dream of the wonderful changes that would follow during the coming ages. But there was at last one man in England of high rank who foresaw that a great nation would some time people the realm beyond the Atlantic. That man was Sir Walter Raleigh. He was a skillful sailor, a daring soldier, an accomplished scholar, an elegant poet, a learned historian, a graceful courtier—in fact, a prince among men. He became a great favorite with Queen Elizabeth. He was very rich, and when he asked permission to fit out ships and establish colonies in America, the queen readily granted his request.

The first two vessels sent out by Raleigh reached the coast of North Carolina in 1584. No attempt at colonization was then made, and they soon sailed back to England. When Queen Elizabeth heard of the wonders of the new country—its luscious fruits, its "sweete-smelling timber trees," its rich soil, whereon the natives seemed to live "after the manner of the golden age"—she said: "This place shall be named Virginia in honor of me." For the great queen was called the "Virgin Queen," and she used to boast that she was wedded to her kingdom alone.

25. First Attempts to colonize Virginia.—Soon afterwards Raleigh sent out vessels on a second voyage "to plant an English nation in America." It had been planned to make a settlement on Roanoke Island; but the Indians were warlike, food was scarce, and the colonists instead of planting corn searched for gold. After they had nearly died of starvation a vessel arrived, which carried the homesick men back to England. Two years afterwards a third company was sent out by Raleigh. This company included men, women, and children. These also settled at Roanoke Island. There, in August, 1587, was born Virginia Dare, the first American child of English parentage.

This colony also fared hard. The governor sailed back to England for supplies, and when he returned to America, after being delayed for three years, every trace of the colony had disappeared. It was never known whether the colonists had gone far away, to live with the Indians, or had somehow perished. They were never heard of again.

26. How Tobacco and Potatoes came into Popular Use.—And thus it was that in the first colonizing of this country Sir Walter Raleigh had as much to do as any other one man. Although his various attempts at settlements proved failures, yet he opened the way, set the example, and made it less difficult for others to come to America.

One of the most wholesome and nutritious of vegetables, the common white potato, had never been seen in Europe until some of the Virginia settlers sent to Sir Walter as a present several of the "roots," as they were called. He showed the poor how easily potatoes could be raised. Thus they first came into use as a staple article of food.

The settlers in Virginia soon found that the Indians took great comfort in smoking the dried leaves of a certain fragrant herb. This was the now well-known tobacco plant. The English colonists tried smoking,—and liked it. They sent some of the plant across the ocean as a present to Sir Walter. He tried smoking, and he also liked it!

At first it seemed a strange sight in England to see a man smoking. The story is often told that as Raleigh was one day enjoying his pipe, a servant came into the room. As the man had never before seen any one smoke, he was much astonished; he thought his master was on fire. He rushed out of the room, seized a pitcher of water, and running back threw it over Sir Walter!

RALEIGH'S SERVANT INTERRUPTS HIS MASTER'S SMOKE.

From that time till now tobacco has been most extensively used. The settler who raised tobacco could buy with it whatever he needed. Large crops of it were carried to England and sold. It did much to establish the commercial prosperity of the Virginia colony.

27. Captain John Smith and his Early Career.—In the year 1607 there came to Virginia a remarkable man by the name of John Smith. He plays an important part in the early history of that colony.

This the most famous John Smith that ever lived, was born in England in 1580. While yet a boy he was fond of wild and daring adventures. When thirteen years old he sold his school books and ran away from home. When he became a young man he went to the continent, and for two or three years fought in the Dutch and French armies.

Once, when Smith was a sailor on a ship going from Marseilles to Italy, a terrible storm arose; the sailors, believing that he was the cause of their bad luck, threw him overboard. But, swimming "with lusty sinews," he managed to reach an island near by, and thus his life was saved. He was rescued from the shore and was taken on board a French man-of-war. Soon afterwards the ship met an enemy, and a battle ensued. In that conflict the young English sailor fought so hard that the ship's officers gave him a share of the plunder of the captured vessel.

28. His Romantic Adventures.—Our bold adventurer now went farther east and enlisted in the Austrian army to fight against the Turks. In that service he soon became well known as a brave and dashing fellow, and before long he was made a captain of cavalry. After a battle in which the Austrians were defeated, Smith, badly wounded, lay a while among the dead. But he was found and cared for. After his wounds had healed, he was taken to Constantinople and sold to the Turks as a slave. A Turkish lady showed him great kindness.

CAPTAIN JOHN SMITH.

Then he was sent to Russia. There, at a place about a mile from the house of his cruel master, he was set to threshing grain. One day his owner rode up and shamefully abused him. Stung by his insolence, Smith killed the man with a flail, exchanged his own slave garments for his victim's clothes, hid the body in the straw, mounted a horse, and started off. He traveled over Russia, Austria, France, and Spain, and at last, after many stirring adventures, drifted back to his old home in England again.

All these stories and many more Captain John tells us in his book of travels. Perhaps they are true, and perhaps we may conclude with some other persons that Smith was a daring fellow at telling stories as well as at fighting Turks!

29. Captain John begins his Career in the New World.—When our adventurer arrived in England, all the talk was about the wonderful western world. Although he had roamed so widely and had fared so hard, he was then less than thirty years old and was ready for new adventures. All of his previous life seemed a preparation for a career of romance and heroism in the New World. So he joined an expedition which sailed for Virginia in the early part of 1607.

On the voyage his superior talents and experience were so evident that his comrades became jealous of him, and on some pretext caused him to be put in chains. They had a long and stormy voyage. It was as late as April when they reached Chesapeake Bay. They were so glad to leave the stormy ocean and find a place of rest that they named the land near their first anchorage Point Comfort, a name it still bears.

They entered between two capes, which they called Charles and Henry from the king's two sons. From their king, James the First, they named the river up which they sailed the James, and they called the village that they built Jamestown. Thus was laid in the year 1607 the foundations of the first permanent English settlement in the New World.

30. How Smith managed the Virginia Colonists.—These Virginia colonists were not suited to the rough, hard work of making a settlement in this new country. They had not been accustomed to earn their living by manual toil. They liked to call themselves "gentlemen," as if that title somehow made an excuse for shiftless idleness. The real need was for farmers, carpenters, blacksmiths, masons—useful mechanics and willing laborers. These genteel settlers expected to find in this wonderful region plenty of gold; their sole purpose was to get enough of the precious ore, and then go back to England and remain there.

But Captain Smith was the saving spirit of the colony. He showed the immigrants the necessity of labor, and told them plainly that if they would not work they must not expect to eat. He taught them to fell trees and build huts. Their voyage had been so long, and so much of their provisions had been spoiled, that, when they landed, their stock of food was almost gone. Something must be done, and that soon, or they would starve.

Then was shown the courage, skill, and good sense of an energetic leader. The corn that a few friendly Indians brought to the settlers was not enough to feed so many. Therefore Smith took some companions, went in his boat up and down the rivers, made friends of the Indians, and bought from them corn and game, giving in payment shiny trinkets, beads, and little mirrors.

But the river lands were low and unhealthful; the water was bad; very many of the settlers became sick; and, before the autumn frosts came, more than half of them had died. Smith worked hard to help the survivors and to teach them to help themselves. Meanwhile, in his boat, he made long excursions up the James and the Potomac rivers, hoping perchance to find a way to the South Sea, as every one then called the Pacific Ocean.

SMITH EXPLAINING THE COMPASS TO THE INDIANS.

31. Captured by the Indians.—On one of these exploring expeditions a gang of natives attacked Smith and killed all his men. He seized an Indian and holding him as a shield, shot down three of the savages. The place being swampy, he suddenly sank to his knees in the oozy soil and was captured by the enemy. Then the quick-witted prisoner, taking out his pocket compass, showed the vibrations and use of the needle, and spoke of the sun, moon, and stars. He interested his captors so deeply that they were sure he must be a supernatural being from some far-off world. They were afraid to kill him.

He persuaded them to send to the colony a piece of paper on which he had written. The result surprised them all the more! This strange being could make paper talk!

32. How Pocahontas saved Captain John's Life.—At last Captain John was sent to the great chief Powhatan, and by him was held captive during several weeks. These Indians, too, he amused with his compass and his writing; but after a while they grew tired of him, and Powhatan concluded to kill him.

So one day they gathered around the victim; he was stretched on the ground, his head was placed on a stone, and all was ready. A savage was just raising his club for the fatal blow, when forth rushed the bright young Pocahontas, the pet daughter of the old chief. Throwing her arms around

Smith's neck, she turned her face to her father and begged him to spare the captive's life. "Kill me," she cried; "kill me; you shall not kill him!" It seems that Smith had been improving his time in making whistles and rattles and strings of beads and shells for the Indian girl, and so had won her affection; and she in return saved his life! Indian chiefs do not often indulge in pity; but for the sake of his beloved daughter Powhatan released Smith and soon after let him go back to Jamestown. Such is the story of his romantic rescue as Captain John told it years afterwards. While there is nothing improbable about it, yet some people believe that he invented the story to magnify his own importance.

33. The Romantic Story of Pocahontas.—Pocahontas was at this time only about twelve years of age. Ever afterward she continued to be very friendly to the colonists, and often visited them at Jamestown, sometimes bringing baskets of corn to the hungry white men. Once the faithful girl came stealthily by night long miles through the dark forests to inform Smith of an Indian plot to murder all the whites.

As Pocahontas grew up, one of the young Englishmen, John Rolfe, became much attached to her. He said he had had a marvelous vision telling him that he ought to make her a Christian and marry her. That was nothing so very wonderful, for then as now tender-hearted youths often dreamed at night of what they were thinking of by day. In 1613, in the rude little church at Jamestown, Pocahontas gave up her Indian religion, accepted the Christian faith, and was baptized. She took the name Rebecca. The next year she was married to Rolfe. This romantic marriage was very fortunate for the colony, for it made her father, Powhatan, a warm friend to the feeble settlers, who at this time were in sore need of help.

34. The Indian Princess receives a Warm Welcome in London.— Three years afterwards the fair Indian girl, "Lady Rebecca," went with her husband to England, where of course she attracted a great deal of attention. The people came in crowds to see her. They cheered as she rode through the streets of London.

Pocahontas became a great favorite with the nobility, and was even received at court by the queen. But, for all that, she soon became homesick. Even amid the splendid novelties of London life, she longed to be once more among the noble forests and the lovely wild flowers of her old Virginia home. It was in the year 1617 that she prepared, with many pleasing anticipations, to return to the scenes of her childhood. But she suddenly sickened and, after a brief illness, died. She was only twenty-two years old. She left an infant son who came eventually to Virginia, and there grew to a worthy manhood. Many excellent families of Virginia are today proud to claim him as their ancestor.

35. The Troubles of the Colonists increase.—When Captain Smith, after his romantic rescue, returned to the colonists, he found them in a pitiful condition. During his absence the prospect had become in every way gloomy. Hunger and sickness had reduced their number from over a hundred men to only forty, and these were planning to go back to England. At this distressing time another vessel arrived from England bringing one hundred and twenty immigrants. This event brightened the darkly drooping spirits of the colonists. But the sunshine did not last long. These newcomers, like the old, were mostly idlers and "vagabond gentlemen," as the settlers called them. "We did not come here to work," they said. "Then you shall not eat," said the brusque leader. He was as good as his word. They soon found they must work or starve.

36. The Greed of the Colonists for Gold.—One trouble that annoyed Captain Smith very much was this: the English people kept urging the colonists to send home gold. Those that arrived later, like those that came before, had no idea of working for a living, but only the hope of shoveling up gold to carry away.

They were so ignorant of minerals that, finding in the soil small yellow scales of shining mica, they sent home bushels and bushels of it, believing it to be gold. Another group of men supposed the little glittering crystals of iron ore were really gold, and they spent weeks in collecting the worthless stuff to send to England. No wonder Captain Smith, although the leader of the colony, had hard work to manage and feed men who would far rather dig "fool's gold" than raise corn.

37. The Starving Time in Virginia.—All this happened while Smith was using the utmost wisdom and skill to guide the colony for the best. On one unhappy day a bag of gunpowder exploded near him, burning him so badly that he had to return to England for surgical treatment. This was in September, 1609. After he had gone, the colonists fell into still greater trouble, and the "starving time" followed. The people were compelled to eat dogs, rats, snakes, and toads; many died of starvation; four hundred and ninety men were reduced to sixty; but, by the fortunate arrival of more vessels, help finally came.

Within the next few years the colony was set upon its feet, and the foundations laid of a prosperous commonwealth. An energetic governor, Sir Thomas Dale, made the idlers till the ground and promptly hanged the criminals. The soil was found the best in the world for growing tobacco. Hundreds of skilled farmers came over to Virginia to make their fortunes by the cultivation of this fragrant weed.

38. Further Explorations along the Coast.—Having at length recovered from his wound, Smith scorned to remain idle, and became anxious to undertake another maritime enterprise. There was at that time a great deal of excitement in England about North Virginia, then so called. In 1614 he sailed again with two vessels on a voyage of discovery in that region.

He touched first the shores of Maine, the nooks and corners of which he explored; he then sailed along the ocean fringe from Penobscot Bay to Cape Cod. He examined the coast carefully, entered the bays and rivers, and named a number of prominent islands and capes. He sailed around Cape Ann. To the three islands off the end of the cape he gave the queer name of Three Turks' Heads. He prepared very carefully a map of the whole country, as far as he had seen it, and he called it NEW ENGLAND.

On his return to England Smith presented his map to the king's son, Prince Charles, who confirmed the name that had been given to it. Next year he started out again. His object was to found a colony in New England, a region of which he had great hopes. But his vessel was captured by a French man-of-war, and he was taken to France. With a return of good fortune this hero of surprising deeds escaped, and finally got back safely to England.

39. His Last Days; the "Father of Virginia."—Our bold explorer now gave up all plans of founding another colony in America. But he lived to know and rejoice in the success of the Pilgrims and the Puritans in Massachusetts. He wrote several books describing his travels and his wonderful adventures.

He had shown himself vigorous, quick-witted, far-seeing. He had been the ruling spirit and the preserver of the Virginia colony. In fact, he has often and justly been called the "Father of Virginia." His strong hand had also opened wide the door of New England.

We must think of Captain John Smith as the hero of the first struggle of English civilization with the wilderness of America. Wherever he was, his genius and resolute will had made him a leader. There was never a braver man. After a life full of romantic adventures and daring exploits, he died in London in 1631 at the age of fifty-two.

CHAPTER IV.
THE STORY OF THE PILGRIMS.

40. The Old-Time Idea about Kings.—We shall do well to remember that in England, about three hundred years ago, the sovereign's will commonly had the force of law. Many people really thought there was such sacredness about a royal ruler that whatever he commanded must be right, whatever he forbade must be wrong. Indeed, there was a proverb, "The king can do no wrong." He had his own kind of church and his own mode of worship. Everybody must attend that sort of church and practise that form of worship, or be punished.

41. Sturdy Englishmen dare to disobey the King.—But there were, after all, many honest, sturdy people in England who did not accept this notion about the king. They did not like his style of religion, and they would not pretend to like it. Besides, they felt that they had a right to meet quietly by themselves, publicly in their own churches, or privately in their own homes, and worship in their own way.

But these people were regarded with suspicion. Presently a number of them were seized and thrown into loathsome jails; not a few were heavily fined or made to suffer bodily harm; some died on the gallows; and all this because, in spiritual affairs, they had dared to disobey the monarch.

42. The Pilgrims seek a Home in Holland; the First Attempt a Failure.—Those who were brave enough to oppose the king's despotism in religious matters were at first styled Separatists, because they separated from the "established church." Afterwards some of them came to be called familiarly Pilgrims, because they wandered from place to place on the way "to heaven, their dearest country," as they said. They longed to go where they could be free to worship God as they pleased.

At last a company of them hired a vessel to take them just across the North Sea to Holland. They chose Holland, because in that country all people were allowed to worship as they thought best.

But just before the hour at which they had intended to embark, watchful officers found them, seized most of their money and goods, dragged them back, and put them in prison. It was indeed a pretty hard lot, punished if they stayed in the country, and punished if they tried to get away!

43. The Second Attempt Successful.—The next year the Pilgrims again tried to leave their native land. This time they succeeded. Taking their wives and little ones, these resolute men, led by their pastor, the good John Robinson, went as strangers and pilgrims to Holland. From time to time the same refuge was sought by other persecuted people, till many hundreds had settled in the old city of Leyden. Here they first exercised that freedom of faith which had been denied them in the land of their birth, and now they first experienced the delight of holding their religious meetings without fear.

They were so industrious and honest that their Dutch neighbors took very kindly to them.

A PILGRIM COLONIST.

But when they had lived in Holland about twelve years, they decided to remain no longer. Their children were learning the Dutch language, and they themselves were slowly becoming foreigners. They were not pleased with such results, for they still regarded themselves as Englishmen, still loved the English people, the English ways of living, and the glorious memories of their mother country.

About this time people were beginning to go to the New World beyond the ocean, and these Pilgrims made up their minds to leave Holland and seek a dwelling place in far-off America.

There were then about a thousand of them living in Holland. Nearly a hundred of the young and strong were selected to go in advance and make a beginning in the New World. They managed to charter for this purpose two small vessels, the Speedwell and the Mayflower. In July, 1620, the Speedwell sailed from Delftshaven; the Mayflower was chartered to sail from an English port.

A very pathetic parting it was for these poor exiles upon the shore of Holland, clasping their friends' hands for the last time, and looking upon the dear faces they were to see no more. With their beloved minister, Elder John Robinson, they knelt upon the sand while he prayed earnestly for God's blessing upon their perilous undertaking. The Pilgrims stopped at Plymouth, England, on the way, and as the Speedwell seemed to be unseaworthy, they all, with others of the same faith who joined the company there, went on board the Mayflower. In this one vessel, after many delays, the one hundred and two people that finally made up the Pilgrim company sailed from Plymouth in September, 1620, on their long and dangerous voyage.

44. The Pilgrims' Voyage across the Stormy Atlantic.—Crowded upon their little craft, this devoted company of men, women, and children had a dreary and anxious voyage of nine weeks. During severe weather the seas sometimes ran so high that for days the Mayflower was driven at the mercy of wind and waves, while all of the company, except the sailors, were compelled to remain, shivering and seasick, below the deck. In the foul air were bred the germs of quick consumption, the disease which carried off so many of this "Pilgrim band" during their first winter on the wild New England shore.

45. An Incident of the Voyage.—During one of these storms a lively young man named Howland fell overboard and would have been lost had he not seized a rope which was trailing in the sea. Bradford quaintly says in his journal that the young fellow "was sundry fathoms under water," but that he held on until "he was hauled up by the same rope to the brim of the water," and with the aid of a boat-hook was at last safely landed on deck. Howland was none the worse for his cold bath. He lived to sign the compact at Cape Cod, and became a most useful citizen of the new commonwealth, and the ancestor of many families.

46. Arrival on the Bleak New England Coast.—How often, in the last days of that dismal voyage, did the Pilgrims gaze far into the west, always hopeful, but no doubt sometimes dreading the future! As the weeks passed by, the weather became very cold, and they had scanty means for warming their cabin. When they neared the coast a driving storm compelled them to change their course, so that instead of going up the Hudson River as they had intended, they were forced into Massachusetts Bay, as it is now called, and along the icy shores of Cape Cod.

All the coast was white with snow, and the future looked cheerless and dark. There were no light-houses to warn them of dangerous shoals, no life-saving men patrolling the beach to help shipwrecked mariners. No one stood on the barren sandy shore to welcome them; they felt that they were indeed strangers in a strange land.

PILGRIM ELDER ASKING A BLESSING.

47. They sign a Compact in the Mayflower's Cabin.—Inside the curved point of Cape Cod, in a small bay which is now the harbor of Provincetown, the Mayflower first dropped anchor. While there, John Carver and William Bradford wrote a formal agreement for the government of the company, and all of the forty-one men signed it.

This compact was drawn up and signed on a chest belonging to Elder Brewster, which afterwards served as a table in his family. During the first winter, when food was very scarce and the Pilgrims were obliged to live almost entirely upon clams, the good Elder never failed to ask a blessing upon their scanty meals, and to thank God, "who had yet given them of the treasures hid in the sand."

By the compact it was agreed that all were to have equal rights. They pledged themselves to help and to defend each other, and to obey such laws as they might make for the good of the colony. They then chose John Carver for their first governor.

48. They explore the Cape Cod Shore under the Lead of Captain Miles Standish.—A small party soon landed and tramped along for miles looking for a suitable place to make a home. They could nowhere find good drinking water. For three or four weeks the Mayflower with its precious cargo sailed along the inner coast, trying to find a safe and inviting harbor. Small parties often went ashore to explore the country.

One day a company of sixteen, led by Captain Standish, went ashore to spend a number of days exploring a little way inland. This Captain Standish, although one of the company, was not really a Pilgrim in his way of living, nor in his religious views. His business was that of a soldier, an employment more common then than now. He had met some of the Pilgrims in Holland and was much pleased with their simple habits and honest ways. When they were preparing to sail to the New World, he thought it likely that they would need a soldier to show them how to fight. So he came with them, and they soon were glad to have just such a man. It was indeed well he did come, for he was often the most useful member of the whole colony.

While the Mayflower lay at anchor in Provincetown harbor, and the explorers were searching for a landing-place, a baby boy—the first New England child of English parentage—was born on board of the vessel. They gave him the quaint name of Peregrine. At Plymouth you may still see the cradle in which little Peregrine White was rocked.

THE MILES STANDISH HOUSE.

49. Their Travels along the Shore of Cape Cod Bay, and what they find.—They discovered the remains of a hut which seemed to have been recently occupied. So they surmised that Indians were living somewhere in the vicinity. They came upon some piles of roasted acorns, and the next day they caught a glimpse of a few savages and a deer. Soon afterwards they saw a dog and more Indians. "The wild men ran away and whistled the doggie after them." One day they discovered two or three mounds of earth. One of these contained rude mats and an earthen dish. They dug into other mounds and unearthed the skeletons of a grown person and a child, a box containing Indian bows and arrows and spears with flint points.

50. They find Baskets of Indian Corn.—In another place they noticed heaps of sand freshly smoothed over. On scraping away the earth, what should they find but Indian baskets full of corn! They had never seen any such grain. They were delighted with the sight of the bright-colored kernels, some red, some yellow, and others blue. The baskets were round, narrow at the top, and contained about three bushels each. They carried to the vessel all the corn they found, for they were in sore need of food; but they were careful to save enough for seed in the spring. They were honest men, and when long afterwards they found the Indians who had buried the corn, they paid them a fair price for it.

LANDING OF THE PILGRIMS AT PLYMOUTH.

One day these Pilgrim wanderers shot three fat geese and six ducks. These they ate with wonderful relish, or "with soldier stomachs," as their story says. At another time, as they were tramping through the woods, William Bradford, not very careful, perhaps, as to where he was stepping, suddenly found his foot entangled in a queer way. When his companions came to help him out, they found he had been caught in a deer trap set by the Indians!

51. First Attack by Indians.—One morning, just after their night's sleep by a camp fire, and while engaged in their prayers, the weary men were startled by a wild cry, very different from anything they had ever heard. For a moment even Captain Standish was alarmed. It was an Indian war-whoop; and the cry was followed by Indian arrows. Standish and his men now fired their guns at the Indians. The firing caused the savages to run away in great astonishment. They had never known of guns, and were greatly afraid of these strangers who could instantly make thunder and lightning. The Pilgrims had never before been targets for arrows, so they kept these strange weapons, which were pointed with eagles' claws or sharp pieces of deer's horn, as curiosities.

52. The Search for a Home.—The Pilgrims were very anxious to get settled as soon as possible; yet when Sunday came they stopped all work and spent the day in reading the Bible, in singing their hymns, and in prayer. For nearly a month they sought, with much weariness and in bitter cold, a place suitable for settlement. It must have been a cruel and pitiful work for those poor men. They waded knee-deep in the snow; slept unprotected under the wintry sky; often suffered from hunger; and, for fear of Indians, were always compelled to keep anxious watch.

FIRST ATTACK BY THE INDIANS.

After a tedious search along the shore of what is now Massachusetts Bay, these stout-hearted wanderers at last found a sheltered place where, not far from the shore, there was an abundant spring of good water. Near by were some old cornfields that had formerly been used by the Indians. Here they decided to land. The water being shallow, the vessel was anchored nearly a mile from the beach. The Pilgrims were brought in their boat, a few at a time, from the vessel to the landing-place. To reach the shore, it is said that they found it convenient to step upon a large stone. This is now known as Plymouth Rock. It is claimed that the first English woman to set foot upon this stone on the Plymouth shore was Mary Chilton.

53. The Famous Plymouth Rock.—Plymouth Rock is not very large; but it is sacred in the eyes and the hearts of every American. Every year thousands go to look upon "the stepping-stone of New England"; to linger by the graves of the Pilgrims; and to see in Pilgrim Hall the many curious interesting things which once belonged to those pioneers of western civilization.

CANOPY OVER PLYMOUTH ROCK.

From the name of the last town they had left in England, the Pilgrims named this, the first spot in Massachusetts settled by white men, New Plymouth. The date of the landing was December 21, 1620, and its anniversary is now celebrated as "Forefathers' Day."

CHAPTER V.
MORE ABOUT THE PILGRIMS.

54. The Hardships caused by the Winter Season.—We may think it unfortunate, and so indeed it was, that the Pilgrims had not come to this country in the spring or summer. They would have had a much pleasanter voyage, and on their arrival might have found the forests green, the birds singing in the trees, and the ground adorned with flowers. If they could have come in April or May they would probably have had warm, pleasant weather for landing or exploring, and could have built their houses at their leisure. They could have planted their fields as soon as they landed, and in a few months could have gathered sufficient crops for their support.

55. The Toil and Perils of the First Winter.—As it was, our Pilgrim fathers found the landing very tedious. In a single small boat they had to come and go, and bring all their provisions and household goods. Some of these very articles of furniture, such as Governor Carver's armchair, old spinning wheels, odd-looking seats and chests, and the big iron kettles in which they boiled their dinners, and also Captain Miles Standish's sword, we can see at Plymouth to-day.

While the men were moving the goods, and until rude structures had been prepared for their shelter on shore, the women and children remained on the Mayflower. Of course the best houses that could be made were very rude affairs. In fact, rough though they were, it was a hard task to build them at all; for hardly one of the company was really fit for such work.

Many times the weary men were forced to wade in deep snow. When they ran their loaded boat on the sandy beach, they often had to leap into the cold water up to their waists to pull it ashore. More than once they were obliged to be out all day in a furious storm of rain and sleet, which froze on their clothes till every man wore a covering of ice.

56. Suffering, Sickness, and Death make Sad Havoc.—Thus it came about that the Pilgrims suffered severely from exhaustion and disease. There were soon only a few men well enough to chop down the trees for their houses. Without beasts of burden, the tired workers themselves had to drag the logs as best they could, and then with slow and painful toil hew them to the right size and shape and put them in their proper places.

SAMOSET'S FIRST VISIT TO THE PILGRIMS.

Through that long and tiresome winter nearly all sickened, and many died. Before spring one-half of those who had landed from the Mayflower were gone. That the Indians might not know how terribly the numbers had been diminished by death, the bodies were buried secretly; and the graves were marked by no mounds nor stones, but were made level with the surrounding soil.

The wonder is that these Pilgrims, ill, hungry, and cold, did not become discouraged, give up their enterprise, and go back to England in the Mayflower. Splendidly courageous indeed they were to pursue their purpose so bravely. Weeks and months they worked and suffered, but they never flinched. They were content and even happy in the consciousness of freedom gained and duty done. They had come to stay—and they stayed.

At last the dreary winter wore away. Spring came, bringing the soft south winds and the songs of birds. Busy hands were soon planting and cultivating. The hearts of the Pilgrims were filled with hope.

57. A Kindly Visit from the Indians.—One day in early spring they were surprised at seeing an Indian march boldly into their settlement, saying, "Welcome, English! Welcome, English!" His name was Samoset. He had learned a little English from fishermen on the coast of Maine. The settlers received him very kindly. After several hours he went away.

In a few days he came back with another Indian named Squanto, who had once lived in Plymouth but had been kidnapped and carried to England. Squanto said that Massasoit, the chief of the tribes in the neighborhood, was near by, and that with sixty of his men he would shortly pay a visit to the Pilgrims. The Indian chief soon appeared and was cordially received. He promised to be a good friend to the English, and in return the settlers agreed to treat the Indians kindly. For over fifty years this promise was sacredly kept.

Squanto made himself very useful to the Pilgrims. He showed them how to plant maize by first manuring the ground with fish, then putting the kernels and the alewives together in the hill. The grain now first received the name of Indian corn. He also taught the settlers how to catch eels by treading them out of the mud with their feet. Shortly afterwards Squanto came to live with the Pilgrims, and proved himself their firm friend.

Sometimes other Indians were hostile. Once a chief named Canonicus, who was an enemy of Massasoit and did not like the Pilgrims, sent to Governor Bradford a bundle of arrows wrapped in the skin of a rattlesnake. He meant this to be a threat of war. The resolute governor threw the arrows on the ground, filled the snake's skin with powder and bullets, and sent it back to the chief! Canonicus was quick-witted enough to take the hint, and thereafter he let the Pilgrims alone.

58. First Houses built in the New Home.—The first building the Pilgrims put up was a log house twenty feet square, in which they stowed away their scanty provisions, furniture, guns, and powder. They slept there till houses were built for separate families. This storehouse also served as a kind of fort till they had put up a better one on top of the high hill, now known as "Burial Hill," close by. As they had no shingles nor boards, they used for a covering of the roof long grass and seaweed. The chimneys they made mainly of big stones; the upper part, however, consisted of large sticks plastered over with clay.

The dirt floor was soon trodden hard and smooth. The large cracks between the logs of the walls were filled with a kind of mortar made of mud and grass. In those days glass was very costly, and so for windows oiled paper was used.

After the storehouse was sufficiently advanced, the settlers began to work on other houses. They laid out a street which they called Leyden Street, and built their houses on each side of it. The same street with the same name is in Plymouth to-day. The whole colony was divided into family groups, each unmarried young man choosing a family to live with, and each group having its own dwelling.

59. Perils and Mishaps of the First Winter.—Even before the houses were finished, the men built a high picket fence around the whole settlement, with a stout gate on each side; for they were in constant fear of the Indians. In fact, they had to keep a sharp lookout every day, and a guard watched every night to give the alarm in case of danger. So watchful were they that, whether chopping wood, eating dinner, or at meeting on Sunday, every man had his gun close at hand, ready for instant use.

One day, soon after the storehouse was finished, it happened that Governor Carver and William Bradford were both within, sick in bed. Suddenly the dry thatch caught fire from the chimney sparks, and the whole roof went up in a blaze. The sick men were lifted out safely. No serious damage was done to anything but the roof, and that was soon replaced by a new one.

60. How the First Log Houses were built.—If we could have made a visit to one of the rough log houses of the Pilgrims after they had brought in their scanty furniture from the vessel, and when affairs had become a little settled, many things would have seemed strange to us.

There is no front entry to the house, for there is only one rough door, and that opens directly into the house; no parlor, no bedroom, no kitchen, but all in one, with perhaps a loft overhead. The inside walls are like the outside, rough, but plastered between the logs. The roof is made of timbers, for there is no sawmill for sawing logs into boards. The timbers do not fit closely, and although there is a covering of thatch, the snow blows in quite freely.

A SETTLER'S LOG CABIN.

61. A Peep into a Pilgrim's House.—Let us take a glimpse into one of these Pilgrim houses. The huge fireplace, made of rough stones laid in clay, fills nearly one whole side of the house. The men bring in great logs of wood for the fire. Even when the logs are on the fire there is room for a person to sit on a stool at each end of the logs, and yet be inside of the fireplace. This is the children's favorite seat.

The chimney has a big throat, as large as a hogs-head. One can sit at the end of the logs and look up and see the sky. The sides of the chimney are roughly laid, and the big stones project so far into the room that the children use them as a staircase in climbing up to their bed in the loft.

In those days nobody had ever heard of a stove. All the cooking of the family was done over a huge fire or in front of it. They used the iron pots and skillets they had brought from England, some of which are still preserved at Plymouth. If they had the good luck to shoot a wild goose or turkey, they thrust a long iron rod through it and roasted it above or before the fire, giving it a turn now and then; or else they hung it very near the fire with a stout string, turning it around at times. The wintry winds often dashed in strong gusts down the big chimney, making it freezing cold all through the house.

62. The Scant Furnishings of their Homes.—There were few or no chairs, but here and there a stool, or some solid blocks cut from the trees. In one corner, on a rude shelf resting upon two wooden pins driven into the log, were a few books,—always a Bible, a hymn book, the Psalms, and possibly a few others.

Hanging from a beam was a little iron cup, in which there was some fish oil, with a twisted rag or a bit of wick; this contrivance served for a lamp when needed. But the big fire usually answered for an evening lamp.

On one side of the room was a rough cupboard or case of shelves for their few dishes. They had no nice glass or china with which to make a display. The glass they had was coarse and of a brownish tint. The early settlers often used leather bottles, leather cups, and rough plates called trenchers, chipped from blocks of wood. Often two persons ate out of one trencher. At this time forks were not in general use. The Pilgrims cut their food with knives and then managed it with their fingers.

Their few pewter dishes they were very proud of, and they kept them in sight in the cupboard, bright with frequent scouring; for the Pilgrim women were excellent housewives, and everything about the house was scrupulously neat and clean.

PILGRIMS GOING TO CHURCH.

63. Other Articles of Household Furniture.—Around the log cabin were two or three big chests, in which each family brought over its goods. These were used to keep their better clothing in, if they had any, and for seats. In the corner was a spinning wheel to spin the wool for their clothing. On these large wheels the mothers and daughters used to spin great piles of wool and flax. Two or three of the houses had large looms—machines on which the thread they spun was woven into stout cloth for the family.

We should have seen no timepiece in their living rooms. There was neither clock nor watch in the whole settlement. On sunny days the women knew when to have dinner ready by the noon mark, as it was called—a notch cut on some beam near the window, showing just where the line betwixt sunshine and shadow came at twelve o'clock.

In the corner of the log house was the gun, close to the door, where it would be ready for use at any moment.

Although the family slept in the one big room, we should not have seen any bed in the daytime. It was turned up against the wall, and fastened to the side of the cabin. At night it was turned down and nearly filled the room. None of the beds were very soft, for they were filled with hay or leaves. By and by, after they had shot enough wild fowl, they had feather beds.

64. Around the Dinner Table.—When the little family gathered around the table for dinner, there was before them neither an abundance nor a variety of food. There was no milk, butter, nor cheese; for there was no cow in the colony. It was four years before a cow was brought over from England. They had no eggs, no beef nor pork nor lamb, and of course no vegetables yet, nor any nice white bread. The provisions they brought in the ship were partly spoiled, and were nearly used up. So they had to get food as best they could.

Now and then the colonists killed some game, but they had to be careful and not waste their powder and shot. One day they shot and cooked an eagle; but, as Bradford wrote in his journal, it was "woefully tough." They could not often shoot a bear or a deer. They obtained some corn of the Indians by trading such trifles as they could best spare. The records tell us that once a Pilgrim bartered a little dog for a peck of corn.

65. The Daily Fare becomes scant; Hardships increased by Hunger.—By and by all the other food failed, so that their main article of diet was corn. This they made into meal by pounding it on smooth stones. But even this supply from the Indians was often scanty and uncertain, so that at times they were without it until, after a year or two, they raised their own crops.

The rest of their provisions they obtained from the ocean—clams, lobsters, and various kinds of fish. But their fishing boat was so frail and their hooks and nets were so poor that this source many times disappointed them.

Thus, the two articles on which they chiefly depended being Indian corn and sea-food, they were sometimes entirely destitute, unable to obtain either.

What a condition! "I have seen men," wrote one of the Pilgrims, "stagger by reason of faintness for want of food; they knew not at night where to have a bit in the morning." They were so badly off that if it were possible for a friend to visit them, the best they could offer him would be a piece of fish and some water!

PILGRIMS WATCHING THE RETURN OF THE MAYFLOWER.

Such was the daily living of the first Pilgrim settlers in this country. Such were a few of the hardships they bravely and patiently endured. And yet, strange to say, when the Mayflower sailed for home in the early spring, as we have before stated, not one of these stout-hearted men and women returned in her to England.

CHAPTER VI.
THE INDIANS AND HOW THEY LIVED.

66. How the Indians looked; the Clothes they wore.—Let us now learn a few things about the Indians as they were before their habits and mode of life had been changed by contact with white men.

The heads of the Indians were always bare. It was customary for them to allow one tuft of hair to grow longer than the rest. This was called the "scalp lock." When a fight had been finished, this lock served as a convenience to the victor. It enabled him to remove handily the scalp from the head of a dead enemy, and to carry it easily away as a trophy of triumph.

The Indians had the curious custom of smearing their faces and their bodies with red paint. On great occasions, such as the holding of a tribal council or a war dance, they painted themselves a more brilliant red. The bright color was believed to give a formidable aspect. They decked themselves with queer ornaments of many sorts. Around their necks they wore strings of shining stones, bits of mica, baubles made of copper, and animals' teeth highly polished. Feathers were held in great esteem. Success in war entitled the victor to wear eagles' feathers as a mark of the greatest distinction. In this love of finery the men were fully as vain as the women.

LONG HOUSE OF THE IROQUOIS INDIANS.

The clothing of the Indians was, for the most part, fashioned out of the dried skins of animals, such as the deer and the beaver, whose flesh had been used for food. Unlike that of civilized people, this clothing was seldom or never changed, but was worn till it was worn out. If not unwashable, it was rarely washed. The "noble red man" was not a model of cleanliness. He had never heard of soap.

67. What the Indians had to eat.—The food of the Indians varied with the place and the season, but game and fish were the principal articles. Their game was chiefly deer, bears, moose, raccoons, foxes, wild geese, and wild turkeys. Having no salt nor spices, no bread nor potatoes, neither milk, butter, nor cheese, their living must have lacked such relish as we give to ours.

In the settled villages the Indians cultivated rude gardens. In these they raised corn, beans, squashes, and tobacco; but, considering the crudeness of their tools, we must suppose that the crops were scanty. The squaws used to cook corn and beans together, making succotash. Both the dish and the name have come to us from the Indians. Green corn they used to roast in hot ashes, very much as we sometimes do now at clambakes or other outings. Meat they commonly cooked by thrusting a stick through it and holding it over the fire; but they sometimes boiled it in rude earthen pots. Fish they broiled on a frame of sticks.

68. The Indian's Struggle for a Living.—The principal work of the Indians was to get food enough. They did not hunt or fish merely for sport, as men and boys of our time are apt to do. To the Indian, hunting was the serious task of providing for his family and himself. At times the supply became very slight. It was especially so in the winter. Then they really suffered from hunger, and were forced to eat ground-nuts and acorns—anything to keep alive. But when they had had good hunting they would eat enormously. At times, when game was scarce, different tribes would have savage fights for the best hunting ground.

Their only drink was water. After the white man came they learned the use of rum and whiskey, and would pay a great price for what they called "fire water." On the other hand, the white man learned from the Indian the use of tobacco. It was a bad bargain both ways.

69. Hardships of the Indian Women.—The Indian warriors occupied themselves with war and the chase. They looked upon ordinary labor as degrading, and fit only for women. These they treated very much as slaves. The squaw did all the everyday work—building the wigwam, raising the crops, making the clothes, and weaving bark mats for the beds. On journeys the women carried their infants, or papooses, on their backs.

With some tribes woman held a higher place. She had a considerable degree of influence in public matters, and often decided the question of peace or war. She could even drive away her husband if he failed to bring home game or fish enough for the family.

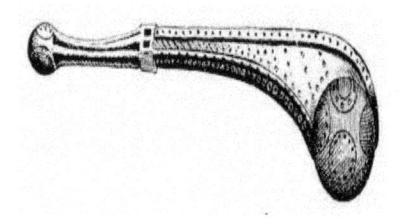

INDIAN WAR CLUB.

70. The Indians' Weapons.—Indian wars were conducted in a manner entirely different from that of civilized nations. The weapons were the bow and arrow, the hatchet of sharp stone, and the war club. The bowstring was made of Indian hemp or the sinews of the deer. The arrowhead was of sharp flint or bone; its point was often made of an eagle's claw or the spur of a wild turkey. The stone hatchet, called "tomahawk," had a long handle and was a powerful weapon.

After the Indians had seen the white man's guns, hatchets, and knives, and could obtain such things for themselves, the use of their own rude weapons was abandoned.

Gunpowder was for a long time a mystery to the Indians. At first they thought that it grew from the ground, like the tobacco plant. It is said they once sowed some of it in the spring, expecting to see it take root and grow. They supposed every white person knew how to make it; and so, once upon a time, when they had captured two young girls, they tried to force them to make a supply of it.

INDIAN STONE HATCHET.

71. How the Indians fought.—In battle, Indians did not come out in fair and open fight, as is the custom of white men; but their skill consisted in surprises, shooting from behind rocks and trees, skulking around at night, and killing the enemy asleep. Captives in war were frequently tortured in the most barbarous ways; sometimes they were tied to trees and were slowly burned to death or were shot. But it was a high standard of Indian valor to bear the sharpest pain without flinching, with never a groan or any sign of suffering.

INDIAN CALUMET OR PIPE OF PEACE.

The Indians, believing as they did that all animals were protecting or unfriendly spirits, often addressed them as if they were human beings. The story is told of an Indian who shot at a large bear and wounded him. The bear fell and lay whining and groaning. The Indian went up to him and said: "Bear, you are a coward, and no warrior. You know that your tribe and mine are at war, and that yours began it. If you had wounded me, I would not have uttered a sound; and yet you sit here and cry and disgrace your tribe."

72. The Use made of Wampum, or Indian Money.—Indians had little use for gold or silver, but they had something in its place, which they called "wampum." This was made of bits of seashells like beads. The pieces had a hole in the center, so that they could be strung in long strips or made into belts.

Wampum was used for a long time as regular money or the medium of exchange between the Indians and the whites, and even between one white and another. Strings of it were passed around for purposes of trade, as we now use coins of silver and gold. But after a while, as seashells became plentiful, wampum became almost worthless, and then the Indians were glad enough to take the white man's silver money.

TREATY-BELT MADE OF WAMPUM.

Among some of the tribes, bands of wampum were woven into ornamental belts, and these were decorated with colored beads combined into striking figures and designs. The wampum belts were often given as a pledge that the giver would faithfully live up to certain terms of a treaty.

73. Indian Tools and Snowshoes.—As the Indians had so little to work with—no iron for knives, nor tools of any kind except flinty stones made sharp and called "hatchets"—it is wonderful how ingenious they were in supplying their personal wants. They kneaded in oil and softened with heat the furry skins of animals, and from these they made excellent garments for winter. From dried deerskins they fashioned a sort of soft serviceable shoe called the "moccasin." This was wrought from a single piece of the leather. It fitted snugly to the foot and was tied with strips of buckskin at the ankle.

The danger of starving in the winter when the snow was deep led the Indians to invent the snowshoe. This was made of a light framework of ash, filled with meshes of rawhide, thus presenting a broad surface to the snow. By this contrivance the Indians could travel in winter as easily as in summer.

It is said that an Indian upon snowshoes could easily travel forty miles a day. Strangely enough, all the cunning of the white man has never availed to make anything better for such a purpose.

74. Indians as Hunters.—The Indian contrived ingenious traps for catching bears, moose, and other sorts of game. One of these devices consisted of a long and heavy log, carefully balanced upon a post placed upright in the ground, with a log attached to one end of it. The roving animal would approach, and by jumping attempt to get the bait that was so attractive. The movement would cause the log to fall, and thus, perhaps, the creature would be killed.

Fish were killed by shooting them with the arrow as they swam; or they were caught with hooks of bone, or taken in rivers by means of a weir, or brush fence, fixed across the stream. Sometimes they were taken in nets woven from the bark of the elm, and in traps of wickerwork not unlike the lobster pots now in use.

The Indians had a remarkable faculty, resembling that of the ventriloquist, whereby they could imitate the voices of woodland creatures—the hoot of the owl, the cry of the wild turkey, the howl of the wolf. By this means they could readily attract animals of various species to a spot where they might easily kill them. Even hostile Indians out searching for game were in this manner sometimes allured to the place of danger.

75. Story illustrating the Indian's Keen Observation.—It is marvelous what quick eyes the Indian had to see almost instantly things that other persons would never see at all. The story is often told of an Indian who returned one day to his wigwam and found that a large piece of venison had been stolen. He looked carefully around, and then started off for the thief. He asked the first man he met if he had seen a little old white man with a short gun and a small dog with a short tail. Afterwards he explained how he learned all these points. He said he knew the thief was little, for he had to pile up some stones to reach the venison; old, by his short steps;

white, by the toes of his tracks turning out; that he had a short gun, for when it fell to the ground from where it leaned against the tree, it made a short mark in the dirt. He knew by the dog's track that the dog was small; he knew that the dog had a short tail, because a short groove had been "wiggled" in the dust where the dog had sat while his master was stealing the meat!

AN INDIAN CAMP OF TO-DAY IN THE FAR WEST.

76. The Indians were Cruel, Cunning, and Revengeful.—As to character, the Indian had, like all the rest of us, a good and a bad side. Though usually silent and moody in the presence of white men, travelers tell us that the Indians had lively games when by themselves, and enjoyed fun and frolic and story-telling like other people. They were crafty and treacherous, as well they might be from their constant warfare.

INDIAN ATTACK ON A SETTLER'S HOUSE.

They were cruel and remorseless in their revenge, and they never forgot a wrong. Full of cunning, they took pride in ingenious tricks. They would wear snowshoes with the toes turned backwards, that the enemy might think they had gone the other way! In their homes they were filthy, lazy, and improvident. They were passionately fond of gambling, after they had learned it of the whites!

On the other hand, they were patient of hunger, cold, and fatigue, and were wonderfully brave. They were hospitable to an acquaintance in need, even sharing the last of their food with him. They were grateful for benefits, and never forgot a kindness. Their promise was almost sacred, and the pledge of their chief was rarely broken.

When the early settlers in this country treated the Indians kindly, they usually received kindness in return, as we shall see later in reading William Penn's dealings with the Indians in Pennsylvania. But now and then some rude white man was cruel or dishonest in dealing with them, and then he learned that the red man knew what revenge means.

If any serious offense was given to the Indians they brooded over it, and then, eager to inflict more harm than they had suffered, instead of punishing the offender alone, they spent their revenge upon all they could reach of the white race. So they sprang suddenly upon peaceful villages and cruelly killed innocent men, women, and children.

77. Anecdote of Tecumseh.—The true Indian warrior had a certain proud dignity that challenged respect. At a great council of the government with the Indians, the famous Indian chief, Tecumseh, after he had made a speech, turned to take a seat, when it was found that by accident no chair had been placed for him. General Harrison instantly called for one. It was brought by the interpreter, who said, "The Great Father wishes you to take a chair." "My father!" he said with dignity, as he wrapped his blanket about him to seat himself in Indian style upon the ground; "the Sun is my father, the Earth is my mother, and on her bosom will I repose."

78. Care and Training of the Indian Children.—The care and training of Indian children were peculiar. When the little papoose was very young, it was not fondled nor much attended to. Quite early it was placed in a small trough of bark and strapped in with a mat or skin in front, the little bed being padded with soft moss. This bit of a cradle was handy to carry around, to lean against a log, or to hang up in a tree.

INDIAN PAPOOSE.

As they grew up, they were as happy as other children. Their parents made toys for them, and their older mates taught them songs and games. As soon as they were large enough, each had his share of work to do. The girls had to help their mothers to dress skins for clothing, to bring wood and water, and to work in the rude garden.

79. The Indian Boy's Early Training.—The Indian boy was early trained for hunting and war. His first lessons were to manage his bow and arrows, and then he was taken into the woods to shoot. He was taught to set traps for small game, and his father often slyly put some animal in the snare to encourage the young hunter.

So the boy was taught, not arithmetic and grammar, but all about birds—their colors, their different whistles and cries, and what each note means; their food and habits, where they nest, how they fly, and the best way to shoot them. His lessons included the study of rabbits and squirrels, of beavers and foxes, and of all such game.

BOY WARNING SETTLERS OF AN INDIAN ATTACK.

By the time the Indian boy had seen twelve or fourteen snows, as the Indian would say, he could make his own bows and arrows and could help make canoes. He had received many lessons about shaping tomahawks and war clubs, and how to use them. Playing ball was a favorite game with Indian youth. Catlin, the celebrated authority on Indian life, tells us that he used to ride thirty miles to see a ball game, and would sit on his horse all day to see a match played by six to eight hundred or even a thousand young Indians.

80. How the Indians buried their Dead.—For the most part the Indians buried their dead in mounds or in shallow graves, sometimes prostrate, but often in a sitting posture facing the east. But some tribes placed the body on a high scaffold raised on long poles out of the reach of wild beasts. Beside the body were carefully placed the weapons of the dead, paints, any favorite trinkets he used to wear, and food to sustain him on his journey to the far-off Happy Hunting Grounds.

CHAPTER VII.
THE DUTCH IN NEW YORK; THE QUAKERS IN PENNSYLVANIA.

81. The Search for a Shorter Route to India.—We must not forget that during all these years the European nations in their desire for riches were often searching for a shorter route to China and the East Indies. They hoped to succeed in this either by sailing to the north of Europe or America, or by finding some opening across the newly discovered continent. For more than a hundred years after the time of Columbus many a daring navigator came forward to undertake this business.

82. Sir Henry Hudson, the Bold and Skillful Mariner.—Several years before the Pilgrims landed at Plymouth, a bold and skillful mariner named Henry Hudson, a friend of Captain John Smith, was hired by some London merchants to search for the imaginary northern passage. For this purpose he made two perilous voyages. Once he sailed along the eastern coast of Greenland until the ice stopped him. After three months he returned to England. The next year he tried it again, and sailed farther north, but as before was turned back by the ice.

Hudson tells us that on one of these voyages two of his sailors saw a mermaid swimming close to the ship's side. The upper parts of her body were those of a woman, but below she was a fish, and as big as a halibut! Probably the creature was a seal, an animal with which English sailors were not at that time familiar.

83. Hudson enters the Dutch Service.—At last, in 1609, Hudson, who had now become famous, entered the service of the Dutch East India Company and sailed from Amsterdam to find the long-sought route. Living near the ocean, the Dutch at this time were great sailors and traders. They owned more ships than all Europe besides. Their sails whitened every ocean. They were glad to hire "the bold Englishman, the expert pilot, and the famous navigator," as they called Hudson, to brave the perils of the Arctic seas.

Again this intrepid sailor, "the Nansen of the year 1608," went too far north, and again he found himself caught in the ice of the desolate Arctic regions. He now made up his mind to go farther west. He coasted along Greenland, passed southward to Newfoundland, sighted Cape Cod, and then sailed as far south as Virginia. Finding the English settlers there ahead of him, he turned about and steered north again, keeping close to the wild and unknown coast.

84. Hudson sails up the Hudson River in the Little "Half Moon."—
In September, 1609, Sir Henry found himself not far from the mouth of a broad river, and dropped anchor near what is now Sandy Hook. The Indians here were kind to their strange visitors, and came on board the vessel to trade. They brought grapes, furs, and pumpkins, and traded them for beads, knives, and hatchets.

THE "HALF MOON" ON THE HUDSON.

After a few days the anchor of the little "Half Moon" was raised, the sails were spread, and Hudson was slowly wafted past the Palisades and far up the noble river which still bears his name. Because for many miles the water at high tide was salt, he thought that he had surely found the long-wished-for passage to India.
No white man had ever before sailed up this, perhaps the most beautiful of American streams. With what wonder and hope must the captain and his men have gazed on the lovely scenery, rich in the gorgeous hues of autumnal foliage! In fact Hudson, in the story of his voyage, says that the lands on both sides were "pleasant with grass and flowers and goodly trees,—as beautiful a land as one can tread upon."

85. Kindly received by the Indians.—The Indians, filled with curiosity, flocked from far and near to the banks of the river to see the "great white bird," a name they gave the "Half Moon" on account of its white spreading canvas wings. As they peeped out from the rocks and woods along the shore, they had the same feelings of curiosity and awe as did the natives that gazed in wonder upon the vessels of Columbus more than a hundred years before.
Hudson sailed north until he reached a point near where Albany now stands. As the river now became narrower and its water fresh, he was convinced at last that he could never find his way to India by this route.

86. Hudson returns Home; his Sad Fate.—After a time, disappointed at his failure to reach India, Hudson sailed out of the river and across the ocean to England, and afterwards to Holland. The stout-hearted mariner never saw his "great river" again. On his next and last voyage he sailed farther north and entered the immense land-locked bay that now bears his name. He thought that he had this time surely discovered the long-sought opening to the Pacific. Imagine his dismay when, after coasting around its sides for nearly three months, he was forced at last to believe that this inland sea had no western outlet!

The long Arctic winter came. Hudson's men were nearly starved. They had endured so many hardships that in a frenzy of despair and wrath they at last bound their captain hand and foot, thrust him on board a small boat with his son and some sick sailors, and set them adrift. This was the last ever seen or heard of Hudson.

Probably, like De Soto, the bold navigator found his grave in the vast waters that he was the first to discover.

87. The Dutch claim the Territory; Manhattan Island bought of the Indians.—The Dutch now laid claim to all the territory along the Hudson River, and in 1614 they took possession of it under the name of New Netherland. In a few years they began to establish trading posts, where they might buy of the Indians the skins of bears, beavers, and otters.

After a time the Indians sold the Dutch the island of Manhattan for the sum of twenty-four dollars. This settlement, then called "New Amsterdam," was the beginning of what is now one of the largest and richest cities in the world—Greater New York.

88. The Dutch Settlers prosper.—For the first few years the settlers in New Amsterdam were poor; but after a time richer and more influential men made homes for themselves in this colony. They secured from the Dutch East India Company the right to own by purchase from the Indians a tract of land sixteen miles in length and extending an unlimited distance into the interior, and to establish there a colony of fifty people. The rich landholders were called "patroons," and their great estates laid the foundation of the wealth of many of the leading families of the Empire State.

DUTCH WINDMILL.

89. How the Dutch People lived.—As the Dutch prospered, they built better houses. These were of wood. Each house had on its roof one weathercock, and often many of them. The gable ends were built of various-colored bricks brought over from Holland.

A DUTCHMAN OF NEW AMSTERDAM.

The Dutch women were excellent housekeepers. We owe to them the doughnut, the cruller, cookies, and many other delicious articles of skillful cookery. Many a pleasant custom had its origin with these genial Dutch settlers, such as the Christmas visit of Santa Claus, the display of colored eggs at Easter, and the friendly visiting on New Year's day. The floors in these thrifty homes were covered with white sand, on which quaint figures were sketched with a broom. There were huge fireplaces with Dutch tiles of different colors, on which were represented scenes from the Bible. The Dutch men were fond of good food and of their pipes. They used to have in front of their houses a porch or "stoop," sometimes called a "bowerie," on which they could sit and smoke and tell stories and take their ease generally. The men wore several pairs of knee breeches at once, one over another, with long stockings, and with huge buckles at the knees and on the shoes. Their coats, too, were adorned with great buckles of silver or brass.

The women were neatly dressed, usually wearing several short petticoats of many colors. Their stockings were of their own knitting, and had as many hues as the rainbow. Their shoes had very high heels.

90. Peter Stuyvesant, the Last Dutch Governor; New York surrenders to the English.—The last Dutch governor was Peter Stuyvesant, brave and honest, but a very stubborn man. He was so obstinate that he was nicknamed "Headstrong Peter." He was also known as "Old Silverleg," because, having lost a leg in war, he used a wooden one adorned with strips of silver. He was a tyrant in his way, and at length his people would not endure his tyranny, especially as the English settlers in the same region enjoyed more liberty and had increased more rapidly in numbers and riches than they.

PETER STUYVESANT.

And so it happened that when an English fleet sailed into the harbor in 1664, the people did not come to the help of "Headstrong Peter," but gladly surrendered the town to the English in spite of "Old Silverleg's" wrath! The name of the colony was changed to New York in honor of the Duke of York, the brother of King Charles II.

91. How the Quakers were persecuted.—About forty years after the Pilgrims had built their homes in Plymouth, the members of a peculiar religious sect, the Society of Friends, were bitterly persecuted in England. In spite of their ill-treatment, which lasted for many years, they greatly increased in numbers. A few men and women of wealth and of high social position joined them.

These Friends, or Quakers as they were commonly called, were singularly blunt in speech and plain in dress. But they were an honest, sober, God-fearing people. They wished to treat all men as friends, brothers, and equals. They did not approve of war and would not serve as soldiers. As they believed all men equal, they recognized no superiors: they would not doff their hats to any one, not even to the king, for they thought "the Lord forbade it." They said they would acknowledge no master, king, or lord, save only Him who was their "Master in heaven," the "King of Kings and Lord of Lords."

Naturally enough, in those days of bigotry and intolerance the doctrines and behavior of the Quakers made the king and his great men very angry. They threw hundreds of them into prison. Consequently, many of the Quakers left their homes, came to this country, and settled in Massachusetts. But the stern sons of the Old Pilgrim Fathers would not endure them. They drove them away or put them in prison. The Boston Puritans even hanged four Quakers who had repeatedly come back after having been several times punished and driven into exile.

WILLIAM PENN.

92. William Penn becomes a Quaker.—About the time King Charles II was restored to the throne of England (1660) there lived in that country a handsome young man of noble birth and talents of the highest order. William Penn was his name. There is a portrait of him in the dress of an English cavalier, with flowing curls over his shoulders, and a face of manly tenderness and beauty. This man, the founder of Pennsylvania, was the only son of a brave English admiral who had won signal victories for his country during the Dutch war, and was held in high favor by the king and the royal family. While Penn was a boy and in college, his heart was stirred within him by listening to the Quaker preachers. He believed they were right. He was convinced that he ought to join them, and did so in spite of the ridicule of his rich and titled friends.

93. Young Penn falls into Disgrace with his Family and is sent from Home.—Young Penn was expelled from college and sent home. The old admiral, in his anger because his only son would disgrace his family by uniting with the despised Quakers, drove him from his door. The mother, however, interceded, and the stubborn youth was allowed to travel for a time on the Continent to divert his mind from what they called his foolishness.

Alas for the old admiral's ambitious plans for his gifted son! William was out-and-out a Quaker; and no title, honors, or favor could induce him to give up his faith. He pleaded with the king to allow the English people freedom of conscience, so that they might worship God as they deemed best. He tried in vain to procure the release of the Quakers from the prisons where hundreds of them were then confined. For a time Penn was himself shut up in the Tower of London, the prison of offenders of high rank. While there he wrote his best known work, No Cross, no Crown. The king's brother, the Duke of York, however, soon brought about his release.

94. Penn inherits Wealth; secures a Grant of Land from the King.—Penn's father was after all a generous man and regretted his treatment of his son. On his death, in 1670, he left him all his estate. Penn made a good use of his wealth. He devoted his time, money, and talents to secure legal protection in England for the persecuted Quakers. The task was almost hopeless.

In his despair Penn longed to build a quiet home for his people in the wilderness of America. He had heard of the happiness and prosperity of the Pilgrim settlements, and he now planned to lead his brethren across the Atlantic. The gallant admiral at his death had a claim against the government of about eighty thousand dollars. Now King Charles was a spendthrift and always in debt. Penn told the king that he would accept lands in America instead of money in payment of this claim. The easy-going monarch was only too glad to take up with this offer, for he had plenty of land in America but very little silver and gold.

On condition that he should be paid two beaver-skins every year, the king granted Penn a large tract of land on the western bank of the Delaware river, and named it Pennsylvania, or "Penn's Woodland."

A Prosperous Quaker.

95. A Colony of Quakers established in Pennsylvania.—Penn now planned to send his Quaker colony to the new home in America. He came over in person in the fall of 1682, and landed at New Castle, Delaware. Penn sailed in an open boat up the broad and beautiful Delaware River until he came to the place on which his chief city or capital was soon to be laid out. The "Quaker King," for thus he was called, was received with great joy by the people. They knew that he would keep his promise to secure full freedom of conscience and speech for all. He called it a "free colony for all mankind."

No person was compelled, as were the Pilgrims of New England, to attend any church or practise any form of religious worship. Only murder and treason were punished with death. Before this Penn had written to the colonists, saying, "You shall be governed by laws of your own making; I shall not usurp the right of any, or oppress his person."

96. Penn selects a Location for his Capital; Philadelphia, "the City of Brotherly Love."—On a neck of land between the Schuylkill and the Delaware, Penn selected a site for his "faire and greene country towne"—a city of refuge and a home of free speech and conscience. And he generously bought the land from some Swedes, who had bought it from the Indians.

Penn now laid out his city and gave it the Bible name of Philadelphia, which means "brotherly love." As he stood with his friends on the high ground and beheld the country in its autumn foliage, the good man said: "I have seen the finest cities of Europe, but I never saw so beautiful a place for a city as this."

97. His Kind Treatment of the Indians.—Penn knew how cruelly some of the other colonies had treated the Indians. This should not be done in Pennsylvania. The Indians must be fairly dealt with. Their lands were not to be taken away by force, but must be openly bought and honestly paid for. If a settler wronged an Indian, he was to be punished. In short, in this Quaker colony they were all to live together as brothers.

That everything might be done in a business-like way, Penn sent word to various tribes of Indians that he would meet them on a certain day to make a treaty. He wanted them to hear what he had to say. He sent word to them that he was a man of peace, and no firearms would be brought to the meeting. The Indians gladly accepted Penn's invitation.

98. The Celebrated Treaty with the Indians.—On the chosen day they came from far and near. They met under the branches of a great elm tree a little north of Philadelphia. This giant son of the forest, called ever afterward "The Treaty Tree," became an object of deep interest. It was protected with extreme care. During the Revolutionary war, even the British officers posted guards around it to prevent its branches from being used for firewood. The venerable tree blew down some ninety years ago. Its rings proved it to be two hundred and eighty-three years of age. A monument with a suitable inscription now marks the spot where Penn and the Indians met to pledge in "unbroken faith."

PENN'S MEETING WITH THE INDIANS.

First, there was a feast of good things to eat, and numerous presents were given to the delighted red men. The chiefs then seated themselves on the ground and the council began. Penn carried no arms, wore no uniform, and had no soldiers. He was at this time thirty-eight years old, graceful and fine-looking, was dressed in a suit of drab-colored clothes, had a blue sash around his waist, and wore a broad-brim hat, which he did not take off for the sake of fashion or ceremony.

The Indians, seated around their chiefs, listened attentively while the "Quaker King" spoke. He told them that the English and the Indians were to obey the same laws, and both were to be equally protected in their rights. No advantage should be taken on either side, but all should be openness and love; that the great God above was the Father of both white and red men, and that all were brothers and should live together in peace. His words, so full of kindness, good will, and justice, won the hearts of the dusky natives.

"We will live in peace with William Penn and his children," said the Indians, "as long as the sun and moon endure." This treaty was never broken.

99. The Indians take Penn at his Word, and live afterwards at Peace with the Quakers.—After this talk was over, the pipe of peace was lighted and passed round, and each took a whiff.

The Indians took Penn at his word. They believed in him and they kept their part of the compact. It is said that not a drop of Quaker blood was ever shed by an Indian, so much did the red men love and honor the name of William Penn.

The good Quaker often visited the Indians at their councils, or at their "powwows," as their festive gatherings were called. He went in and out among them, visited them in their wigwams, and ate roasted corn and hominy with them. He had frolics with the Indian children, joined in the outdoor games of the warriors, and talked to them about their faith in God, whom they called the Great Spirit.

100. The Quakers prosper; Trials of Penn in his Old Age.—We are not surprised that the Quaker settlers prospered. In two years there were six hundred houses; also schools and a printing press. Philadelphia had grown more in three years than New York City in half a century. After a few years the founder of the colony went back to England. He continued to watch over his far-away colony, sending out emigrants and in every way promoting its interest.

After some time Penn returned to this country, but remained only two years. In his old age he met with sore trials. His son disgraced him by his riotous living, his trusted agent proved dishonest, and at length the good Quaker was financially ruined and was flung into prison for debt. Not long after his release he died at the age of seventy-eight.

101. Subsequent Prosperity of the Quaker Colony.—When it once became known that in Penn's colony a man could worship God as he pleased, enjoy personal rights; that poor men could own their farms, and that there was no dread of the Indians, we are not surprised that colonists quickly flocked to Pennsylvania. This settlement surpassed all others in America in rapid growth, and was for many years more prosperous and comfortable than any other. About one-third of the inhabitants were Quakers, and these were always a thrifty and peaceful people.

At the close of the Revolutionary war Philadelphia was larger than either Boston or New York. Among the thirteen colonies Pennsylvania ranked third in influence and population, being surpassed by none but Virginia and Massachusetts.

CHAPTER VIII.
THE FRENCH AND INDIAN WARS.

102. Prosperity of the Early Colonists.—For fifty years or more after the colonists had established their homes in the wilderness of the New World, they were growing rich and strong. They cleared away forests, planted fields, traded with the Indians, and built for themselves more comfortable houses.

Especially was this the case during the years when Cromwell and his party were in power in England, and until after Charles II was restored to the English throne. The settlers boldly pressed further and further on, crossing great rivers, climbing steep mountains, and building log cabins in far distant regions.

The colonists in Pennsylvania and Virginia pushed westward into the valley of the Ohio, while the English settlers in New York made their way through the forest toward the Great Lakes.

103. The French in North America.—More than seventy years before Jamestown was settled, a French explorer by the name of Cartier had entered the Gulf of St. Lawrence, sailed up the river of the same name, and taken possession of the country in the name of France. This same region became afterwards the great French stronghold in America.

A Frenchman by the name of Champlain sailed up the beautiful river St. Lawrence, and was so charmed with the scenery of the country that in 1608, the year after Jamestown was settled, he began to plant a colony on the site of what is now Quebec. The settlement soon became a city and the capital of the French possessions in America.

The French were also the first explorers of the vast interior regions of our country. Their fur traders and trappers kept on good terms with the Indians, and slowly pushed along the shores of the Great Lakes until they had established a chain of trading-posts from the St. Lawrence to Lake Superior. About the time of King Philip's War in New England Father Marquette discovered the upper Mississippi, and floated down this great river nearly as far as the mouth of the Arkansas.

104. La Salle floats down the Mighty Mississippi.—The bravest and ablest of all the French explorers was a fur-trader by the name of La Salle. This daring man, whose life was filled with romantic adventures and hardships, bravely undergone, gave France the right to claim as her own the vast domain of the Mississippi valley.

On Lake Erie, La Salle built a small vessel, in which he sailed to the westward over the Great Lakes. In the year 1682, with a few companions, he floated down the mighty Mississippi until he reached the Gulf of Mexico.

LA SALLE AT THE MOUTH OF THE MISSISSIPPI.

With solemn ceremonies he claimed for France all the country drained by this great river and its branches. This enormous territory, extending from the Alleghanies to the Rocky Mountains, he named Louisiana in honor of his king, Louis XIV. The narrow strip of land held by the English along the Atlantic seaboard seemed a feeble possession compared with the vast untrodden wilderness known as "New France."

Hand in hand with the French explorers and fur-traders, and often in advance of them, went the Jesuit missionaries. In their efforts to carry their religion to the Indians and convert them to their faith, these zealous men boldly struck out into the unbroken wilderness of the great West. They often became brave and intelligent explorers. All hardships and all dangers, and even torture by the Indians, they endured without a murmur.

105. Beginning of the Contests between the French and English Colonists.—At the time the French and English were making settlements on this continent, and for many long and weary years, with very short intervals of rest, Europe was cursed with war. Whether these cruel strifes between the nations arose from political ambition, greed for gain, or common jealousy, there was always intermingled the same old undercurrent of religious hatred. The French settlers in this country were Roman Catholics, while the English were almost all Protestants. Hence it is not strange that these bitter religious controversies were not confined to the Old World, but stained with blood the soil of the New.

The English colonists dearly loved their mother country; her wrongs were their wrongs. Hence when war was declared between France and England, the English colonists readily took up arms against the French.

106. The French and Indian Wars.—In the seventy-four years from 1689 to 1763 the American colonies were involved in four wars, occupying in all twenty-seven years. These were called by different names; but the last and most important is known as the "French and Indian War," which began in 1755 and lasted about eight years.

These long contests really made one continuous series of hostile operations, with only a breathing-spell now and then. It was one long-drawn-out and stubborn battle to decide whether the French or the English should be masters of North America. Jealous of the rich and prosperous English colonies on the seaboard, and having determined that England should not control the whole of this vast continent, the French built a chain of more than sixty forts stretching from Montreal to New Orleans.

The French had always treated the Indians with more consideration than had their rivals. The Jesuit missionaries had converted many of the red men to their religious belief. Sometimes the French took Indian women for wives, and often they adopted the red man's ways of living.

107. The Indians ally themselves with the French.—When these sons of the forest found the English slowly but surely crowding them out of their haunts and homes, and saw that their hunting grounds were getting reduced to mere strips of territory here and there, it was not strange that they felt bitter towards the ever-encroaching new-comers. The tribes had steadily diminished, and they were unable to cope single-handed with the English. Hence they naturally looked to the French for help, and the French readily induced the Indians to join them against the English and their American descendants.

It was a fierce struggle. English and American blood flowed like water before it was ended. The Indians never fought in open field, but always after their own fashion. They trusted to sudden attacks, especially at night, and to rapid raids, doing their savage work suddenly and retreating swiftly into the forest.

Lonely families and small settlements suffered most. Like lightning out of the clear sky came the horror of an Indian night attack. The war-whoop waked the midnight sleepers and the glare of burning cabins lighted up the darkness.

The massacre of defenseless women and children crimsoned the earth in scores of settlements during these cruel wars.

INDIANS ATTACKING A SETTLER'S CABIN.

108. The Indian Attack on Deerfield in the Massachusetts Colony.—
One bitter cold night in February, 1704, the French and Indians attacked the town of Deerfield in the western part of Massachusetts. For this purpose they had walked all the way from Canada on snowshoes. The people had been warned of their danger, but the watchmen fell asleep, and the villagers were awakened by the war-whoop of their savage foes. About fifty men, women, and children were killed, and nearly a hundred half-clad captives were marched off through the deep snows. Those who could not keep up were killed with the tomahawk.

The minister of the village, Rev. John Williams, his wife and six children, were among those captured and carried to Canada. The wife lagged behind and was killed. Strange to say, however, the minister and all his children, though they suffered all manner of hardships, and were sold as captives, after a time reached home in safety. The good man lived to write an account of his adventures.

One little girl seven years old was treated kindly by her captors and was brought up as one of their tribe. She married an Indian chief and long afterwards visited her people in Deerfield. She wore the Indian dress and had come to love the wild life. Her former friends and neighbors begged her to stay with them, but "she returned to the fires of her own wigwam, and to the love of her Mohawk children."

109. Hannah Dustin's Famous Adventure with the Indians.—The story of Hannah Dustin, of Haverhill, Mass., has often been told. One day in 1697 the Indians attacked the village. Mr. Dustin saved all his family except his wife and her nurse, who were captured. They marched these women and an English boy many long days to their camp on an island far up the Merrimac River. As Mrs. Dustin's babe prevented her keeping up well on the journey, an Indian cruelly killed it.

The boy, who understood the Indian language, heard the savages tell of the horrible tortures they intended to inflict upon their captives. When Mrs. Dustin heard of this she laid her plans. She made the lad slyly learn from the Indians how to swing a tomahawk and where to strike.

One night, when the savages lay around the camp-fire sound asleep, the three captives arose softly, each killed with one blow the Indian nearest, then three more, and so on till ten were finished. One young boy and one squaw escaped. It was an awful thing for Mrs. Dustin to do, but the memory of her murdered child made her brave and strong. They seized an Indian canoe, and the three paddled swiftly down the river, and half dead with hunger and fatigue reached home. Their friends could hardly believe their eyes. The heroic woman brought home ten Indian scalps as proof of what she had done.

110. How the Colonial Boys learned to shoot.—We can now well understand that the settlement of a new country amid hostile Indians demanded from our colonial fathers eternal vigilance, and developed in them remarkable skill with firearms.

Even the colonial boy, we are told, as soon as he was big enough to level a musket, was given powder and ball to shoot squirrels. After a little practice he was required to bring in as many squirrels as he was given charges for the gun, under penalty of a severe lecture, or even of having his "jacket tanned"!

At the age of twelve the boy became a block-house soldier, with a loophole assigned him from which to shoot when the settlement was attacked by the Indians.

Growing older, he became a hunter of deer, bears, and other wild animals, and had at any moment, day or night, to be in readiness to pit his life against those of hostile Indians.

111. Capture of Louisburg.—During the third French and Indian war, which began when George Washington was a boy of fourteen and which lasted four years, the New England colonists determined to strike a hard blow against France. They fitted out an army of about four thousand fishermen and farmers, put their expedition under the command of General William Pepperell, and sailed from Boston to capture Louisburg on the island of Cape Breton.

With its walls of masonry thirty feet high this was the strongest fortress on the continent except Quebec, and was known as the "Gibraltar of America." It commanded the entrance to the Gulf and the mouth of the St. Lawrence. With the aid of a British fleet the colonists laid siege to the great fortress.

After a lively contest of about six weeks, Louisburg was taken (1745). The colonial army returned to Boston and was received with shouts of joy. But at the close of the war Louisburg was restored to the French. Great was the wrath of the colonists, who spoke of the day of surrender as "a black day, to be forever blotted out of New England calendars."

112. The Struggle beyond the Alleghanies.—For a long time the Alleghany Mountains served as a natural boundary between the English settlements in the East and the French trading-posts and forts in the West.

Meanwhile the English settlers were steadily pushing westward over the mountains and beginning to trade with the Indians on the other side. The French merchants often met their hated rivals in the woods and quarreled with them. From the first, England claimed all this country as her own, and looked upon the building of French forts as an invasion of her territory. The French stirred up the Indians to drive the English away, and would not even allow them to make so much as a survey of land in the rich Ohio valley.

113. Young George Washington selected for an Arduous Undertaking.—This action of the French aroused the wrath of the prosperous Virginia colony and of its energetic governor. He decided to send a letter to the French commander warning him to leave the country. Governor Dinwiddie selected for this task a land surveyor only twenty-one years of age. His name was George Washington. He was even then known for his courage, his sound judgment, and his knowledge of the Indians.

It was a journey of more than a thousand miles there and back, through an unbroken wilderness. With seven companions young Washington set out on his perilous trip in the fall of 1753. They climbed mountains, swam streams, and threaded their way through mountain ravines, following Indian trails which no white man had ever seen before.

After many hardships they reached the French posts. The French commander read the letter that Washington had brought from the governor of Virginia. He replied that he was there by command of his superior officers, and that he meant to drive every Englishman out of the Ohio valley! There was nothing for Washington to do but to start for home. Winter had now set in and it was soon severely cold. The homeward journey became a serious matter. The pack-horses gave out. The brave young leader and his guide pressed ahead on foot. Often as they lay down at night their wet clothing froze fast upon them. They secured an Indian as a guide, but he proved a scamp. One evening at dusk he raised his gun and fired at Washington, but missed his aim. The guide seized the savage, flung him to the ground, and would have killed him, but Washington spared his life. After many hardships and dangers the two men reached home in safety.

114. The Beginning of the Final Struggle.—The final struggle was now impending between England and France to determine which should control America. The contest began in earnest in Virginia. Washington had taken advantage of his perilous errand to the French commander to select a place for an English fort. It was at the point where the Alleghany and Monongahela rivers unite to form the Ohio. This is the spot where the city of Pittsburgh now stands. It was the main entrance to the valley of the Ohio. For many years it was called the "Gateway of the West." The English built a fort on this spot, but the French easily captured it and held it under the name of Fort Du Quesne.

115. Braddock's Ill-Fated Expedition.—Affairs now became so serious that General Braddock was sent out from England with two regiments of regulars. Early in the year 1755 he began his march through the Virginia forests to recapture the French stronghold. He selected Washington as a member of his staff. "I want you," said the British general, "to take your Virginia riflemen and go with me and my veterans to drive the French from Ohio." Washington consented. He joined Braddock's army with three companies of Virginia riflemen.

WASHINGTON ATTEMPTING TO RALLY BRADDOCK'S REGULARS.

The English general and his regulars were brave, but they knew nothing about fighting Indians. Never did an army seem better prepared. They felt sure of victory. Soon they plunged into the forest. There were no roads there. After a hard march of four weeks they came within a few miles of the French fort. Washington warned the proud British general of his peril. "The Indians," said he, "may attack us in yonder deep pass. Let me go ahead with my riflemen and skirmish for the savages."

Braddock was an old soldier, and he thought he knew more than his young staff-officer who had learned from experience how to fight Indians. The general laughed at the well-meant advice. Next day, as they were marching through a deep ravine, suddenly came the yells of savages and the crack of rifles. The British veterans were eager to fight, but they could see no foe. The men were shot down like sheep.

The young Virginian and his riflemen leaped behind trees and rocks and fought the Indians in their own way. All was confusion. Braddock acted bravely. He had five horses killed under him. He did all that a valiant man in such a situation could do; but it was in vain.

116. Washington saves Braddock's Army from Destruction.— Washington and his Virginia rangers saved Braddock's army from destruction. The French and the Indians knew well the tall figure of Washington, who was in the thickest of the fight, and they kept firing at him. Two horses were shot under him. Four bullets passed through his clothing, but he did not receive a scratch.

Many years afterwards an old Indian chief came to see Washington, and told him that he had fired from ambush on the dreadful day of Braddock's defeat, and both he and his young warriors had often aimed at him as he rode about delivering the general's orders; but as they could not hit him, they had concluded that he was under the protection of the Great Spirit and could not be slain in battle.

Braddock was at last hit. He sank to the ground mortally wounded. "What is to be done now?" he faintly asked. "We must retreat," replied Washington.

A retreat was ordered, and Washington and his riflemen defended the rear so well that what was left of the routed army at last reached a place of safety. More than seven hundred of them had fallen, including Braddock himself and three-fourths of his officers. What a penalty the proud British general paid for refusing to take good advice!

117. The Virginians fight desperately for their Homes.—The French were now left in full possession of all the region west of the Alleghanies. The Indians took advantage of the situation to make fresh attacks upon the Virginia colonists.

The Virginians fought with desperation for their homes. Washington was put in command of the forces. He wrote that "the supplicating tears of the women and the moving petitions of the men melted him into deadly sorrow." Three years after the Braddock calamity, Washington again marched his men through the woods against Fort Du Quesne and recaptured it.

The capture of this stronghold was an important event to the colonists, for a highway which was never afterwards closed was then opened to the great West. The name of the fort was changed to Pittsburgh, in honor of England's illustrious prime minister, William Pitt, who had planned the expedition.

It was just this experience in hard fighting against the French and Indians that providentially aided in fitting Washington to win success as commander-in-chief of the American forces in the fast approaching war of the Revolution.

118. Quebec, the carefully guarded Stronghold.—We must remember that there had been fighting for nearly two years in America before England really declared war against France in 1756. During this time the French had held the mastery, and the English had met with sad reverses. A new leader had now come into power in England, the great statesman, William Pitt.

The influence of this remarkable man changed the course of affairs as if by magic. He fully understood America's greatest needs. From this time the English were everywhere successful. Important forts were taken from the French, such as Niagara, Ticonderoga, and Crown Point.

There was only one great stronghold left to the French. This was Quebec on the St. Lawrence. It was not only one of the strongest fortresses in the world, but it was commanded by the Marquis de Montcalm, one of the ablest generals of his time.

WOLFE'S MEN CLIMBING TO THE PLAINS OF ABRAHAM.

119. How Quebec was taken.—A brave young officer, General Wolfe, was sent out from England to command the attack on Quebec. The outlook was enough to discourage any one, however experienced and skillful. The fort itself is on a high point of land overlooking the city. The English troops were on the river-bank, hundreds of feet below.

Every movement of the English was reported at once to the French. Wolfe was at first repulsed at every point. One day, as he was reconnoitering, he discovered a steep and narrow path which led up the precipitous bluff to a level spot known as the Plains of Abraham. He made up his mind to climb it with his men.

Soon afterwards the English troops were quietly rowed down the river, under the cover of darkness, to a little bay since known as Wolfe's Cove. As the young English general glided along in his boat, he quoted extracts from Gray's "Elegy in a Country Churchyard." As he repeated the stanza beginning, "The boast of heraldry, the pomp of power," he said that he would rather have written that poem than take Quebec. The little pathway was reached. Wolfe leaped first on shore. Under his leadership the English soldiers climbed the steep.

At sunrise on the morning of Sept. 13, 1759, the British army, five thousand strong, stood on the Plains of Abraham. Great was the amazement of the French general, for he thought it impossible for any one to scale the cliffs. Montcalm chose to come out of the fortress and fight the English on the open ground. This was a fatal mistake, for after a fierce struggle the French were defeated.

In the hour of victory Wolfe was fatally wounded. While dying he heard the cry, "They run! they run!" Rousing himself he asked, "Who run?" Upon being told it was the French he exclaimed: "Now God be praised; I will die in peace!" Montcalm was also fatally wounded. When told he could not live, the gallant Frenchman cried out, "So much the better; I shall not live to see the surrender of Quebec!"

The French retired within their fortifications, but in a few days Quebec was surrendered into the hands of the English. The fate of Canada was decided by the fall of this city.

120. The End of the War and the Result.—Although the victory at Quebec practically ended the French and Indian War, it was not until 1763 that peace was declared. By the treaty France gave up to England the whole of Canada, together with all the territory between the Alleghanies and the Mississippi, except the city of New Orleans. She retained a few barren islands near Newfoundland as a shelter for her fishermen. The vast region spreading westward from the Mississippi towards the Pacific, under the name Louisiana, together with the city of New Orleans, was made over to Spain.

CHAPTER IX.
EVERYDAY LIFE IN COLONIAL TIMES.

121. Severe and Curious Punishments.—In the early colonial times the laws were for the most part rigid and the punishments severe. Criminals were occasionally branded with a hot iron. If a man shot a fowl on Sunday, he was often publicly whipped. Small offenses were punished in a way which would not be tolerated in our times. A woman who had been complained of as a scold was placed in front of her house with a stick tied in her mouth. Sometimes a common scold was fastened to what was known as a "ducking stool" at one end of a seesaw plank, and ducked in a pond or river!

Some crimes were punished by making the offender stand up on a stool in some public place, while fastened to his breast was a large placard on which his crime was printed in coarse letters, as LIAR or THIEF. There were in some colonies public whipping-posts for the special benefit of hardened offenders. In other cases the stocks were used, the culprit being seated on a bench in a public place, his feet projecting through holes in a plank; or the pillory, where he had to stand up with his neck and wrists painfully confined in a similar way. These last two modes of punishment were a source of no small amusement to the throng that gathered around, whose jeers and scorn must have been hard to bear. Once a couple of men in Plymouth county had a brisk little quarrel, and they were punished by being bound together for twenty-four hours, head to head and foot to foot.

CULPRITS IN THE PILLORY AND STOCKS.

122. How Sunday was kept.—Sunday was rigidly observed in New England. In olden times, and almost to our own day, the Lord's Day was made to begin at sunset on Saturday evening. Sunday schools were not then known. But every person was compelled to attend religious service or be punished. If a man stayed away from church for a month without a good excuse, he might be put in the stocks or into a wooden cage. No word could be spoken with impunity against the church or the rulers. He who used his tongue too freely was placed in the pillory or stocks, or was fined, and in some extreme cases he lost his ears.

The minister was the great man of the village. He was looked up to and consulted about nearly everything, and he generally decided what punishment should be inflicted on evil-doers. In earliest times the people were called to meeting by drumbeat or by the blowing of a horn. The log meeting-house had oiled paper windows, or, if of glass, small diamond-shaped panes set in leaden frames made in England.

Inside there was no fire and there were no cushions. Families did not sit together as now; but old men, young men, and women all sat by themselves. Boys occupied the pulpit steps or the gallery. On a bench just below the preacher sat the row of deacons, facing the congregation. If aged, they wore bright-colored flannel caps to protect their heads from numerous drafts. It was the business of the deacons to "line off" the Psalms as the people sang them. Books being very scarce, most of the congregation did not have any: accordingly the deacon would read aloud two lines, and when these were sung, read the next two, and so on. Every one sang. There was no choir, no organ, no instrumental music of any kind, and no hymns such as we have now. They sang the Psalms, which were arranged in metre for convenience in singing.

123. The Discomforts of attending Church in Colonial Days.—As the meeting-house was bitter cold in midwinter, women often carried foot-stoves, small sheet-iron boxes containing a few hot coals, which were a source of great comfort. The sermons were tedious, lasting two hours or even more; for those patient people valued a sermon very much according to its length. On the pulpit stood an hour-glass, which a deacon would reverse when the sands of the hour had fallen through.

Since the seats were hard, and the sermons long, and the men and women had worked early and late through the week, it was no wonder that some of the hearers were sleepy. It was, however, a serious offense to sleep in meeting. The watchful tithing-man, as he was called, was always on the lookout for drowsy people. It was his duty to see that the Lord's Day was respected by every person. He was armed with a long rod, one end tipped with a hare's foot and the other with a hare's tail. If the slumberer was a woman, he used to touch, possibly to tickle, her face with the soft fur. But if a youngster nodded, his head got a sharp rap from the rabbit's foot.

People in those days had to be thrifty. To save wear and tear, boys and girls walked barefoot to church in summer, with their shoes and stockings under their arms. They put them on as they entered the meeting-house, taking them off again as they started for home.

NEW ENGLAND FIRESIDE IN COLONIAL TIMES.

124. The Food in Olden Times; what it was, and how it was served.— In old colonial times our wheat bread was comparatively unknown. Loaves were made of mixed Indian meal and rye, not unlike the brown bread of our time. Baked pumpkin with milk was a favorite dish. Bean porridge was always a common article of food, and in some parts of the country it is still popular. It was made by boiling beans with the liquor in which corned beef had been cooked. It was very convenient for wood-choppers in winter to carry a frozen piece of porridge in their pockets and thaw it out for dinner in the woods. The longer it was kept, the better it tasted. Hence the common rhyme, "Bean porridge hot, bean porridge cold; bean porridge in the pot; nine days old."

In well-to-do families the cupboard or dresser shone with well-scoured pewter plates, platters, and porringers. Square wooden plates were often used; but with some poorer families there was one common dish used, from which the whole family helped themselves with their fingers.

Instead of forks, which were not known, they had thick and clumsy pewter spoons. These were easily broken, and they often had to be melted up and run over again into moulds by men who traveled from house to house for this purpose. In fact shoemakers, tailors, dressmakers, butchers, and other highly useful artisans traveled about from one family to another in pursuit of work.

125. Schools in Olden Times; the Schoolmaster; Schoolhouses and how they were furnished.—In most of the colonies the settlers were hardly located in their new homes before they began to provide schools for their children. In 1635 the town of Boston "voted to entreat brother Philemon Pormont to become schoolmaster," and, in 1647, the law was passed which is the foundation of the splendid educational system of Massachusetts.

Only six years after Boston was founded, the sum of two thousand dollars was set apart to found "a seminary at Cambridge," which has now become Harvard University. For years afterwards, every family gave annually one peck of corn, or one shilling in money, to support the young college.

Besides the usual branches, the early schools were required to teach religion and morals and the laws. They taught little enough of what we call school studies.

The schoolhouses were rough and crude. They usually had but one room. Within the room, the door and the big fireplace were on one side, while against the other three walls was a long, rough shelf, in front of which was a seat made of a split log with legs driven beneath. The pupils faced the wall with their backs to the teacher. In front was another lower bench filled by the younger pupils. The teacher sat near the middle of the room, and there the classes stood to recite. The sessions were long, seven or eight hours a day. The boys had to furnish the firewood, and if any unlucky fellow failed to bring in his share, he had to sit in a cold corner for that day. When the fire was brisk, the scholars were almost roasted on one side and nearly frozen on the other.

The teachers were often incompetent, either broken-down men or needy widows. The children brought each a few pennies a week for tuition. There were not many text-books, and the supplies were very scanty. The scholars often learned to write and "cast accounts" on pieces of white birchbark.

NIGHT WATCHMAN ANNOUNCING THE CAPTURE OF CORNWALLIS.

126. Newspapers, Traveling, and the Night Watchman.—The first printing press was set up at Cambridge in 1639. It was used chiefly to print sermons and small pamphlets. The first newspaper published in America was the Boston News-Letter in 1704. It was a weekly, a brown sheet hardly more than a foot square. News traveled slowly, for there was little communication between city and city. Travelers were few, and conveyances were slow. A stage-coach that made forty miles a day between New York and Philadelphia was called, on account of its great speed, the "flying machine."

In the cities, news was announced in the daytime by the public crier, who walked the streets ringing a large hand-bell, and pausing at the corners, where he recited his message of child lost, or reward offered, or the happening of any important event. In the night the town watchman, with rattle and lantern, paced the streets, stopping every person he met after nine o'clock to demand his name and business. He also called aloud the hours of the night in a sing-song tone: "Twelve-o'clock-and-all-'s-well."

Sometimes his night cry was intensely interesting. At Philadelphia in October, 1781, evening after evening every one went to bed anxious about our army at Yorktown, and hoping every hour to hear tidings of victory. One night the old watchman's cry was heard echoing along the lonely streets: "Two-o'clock-and-Cornwallis-'s-captured!" How the windows flew up! and how the hearty cheers burst along from house to house all through the city!

127. Other Details of Home Life in the Colonies.—The home life of the colonists improved as the years passed, but until the Revolution it was very crude. In the families of well-to-do people the earth floors of early days were replaced by boards, the proudest decoration of which was a sprinkling of white sand, which on great occasions was swept into ornamental waves with a broom. The door latch was for a long time of wood, lifted by pulling a string hanging outside. Hence the hospitable invitation used to be: "Come over and see us! We keep the latchstring out." At night the string was drawn in, and that locked the door.

As there were no friction matches, fire was started by striking a spark with flint and steel, which was caught on a bit of half-burned rag, and then brought to a blaze with a splinter of wood tipped with sulphur. On a cold morning, if one's fire was out and these tools were not at hand, the resort was to send a boy to a neighbor for a brand!

128. How our Forefathers clothed themselves.—The clothing worn by men, women, and children was nearly all home-made from the wool of their own sheep. It was a matter of pride with a good housewife to supply all the nice warm clothes needed by her family, and the daughters were brought up to card and spin and weave clothing, bedding, and table linen. After a time very fine linen was made, especially by the Scotch-Irish settlers who were skillful in raising flax and in weaving linen. We may safely infer that the women of those days were obliged to work early and late to provide warm clothing for themselves and oftentimes for large families. In fact it was for many years regarded as almost a disgrace to purchase clothing which might have been made at home.

HOSPITALITY IN A SOUTHERN MANSION.

But some were disposed to shine in apparel more showy than their purses could afford or their rank allow. All such victims of personal vanity were liable to be ordered to appear before the court; for any person whose estate was less than a thousand dollars was "forbidden to wear gold or silver lace, or any lace above two shillings a yard." Once a "goodwife" by the name of Alice Flynt was required to show that she was worth money enough to be able to wear a silk hood. But the woman proved that she was, and she was allowed to wear her finery in triumph. In like manner, "goodman" Jonas Fairbanks was arrested for wearing "great boots," meaning boots with high tops that turned over showy red. He too escaped punishment and continued to sport his extravagance.

129. How the Wealthier People lived.—But after a while in the cities, the really wealthy, of whom there were not a few, often dressed in fine style. Gentlemen when fully equipped wore three-cornered cocked hats, long velvet coats, embroidered silk waistcoats with flaps weighted with lead, breeches coming only to the knees, long silk stockings, and pointed shoes adorned with large silver buckles. Stately men wore their hair powdered, a long queue hanging down the back, where it was tied with a black ribbon. The clothing was often enriched with gold and silver lace, and glittering buttons. A mass of lace ruffles adorned the wrists and flowed over the hands. The street cloak glistened with gold lace, while a gold-headed cane and a gold snuff-box confirmed the wearer's title to rank as a gentleman.

Ladies of wealth in the city wore rich heavy silk over stiff hoops, and towering hats adorned with tall feathers, with hair massed and powdered as if with snowflakes. All the fashions of high life were very exacting and precise. The wealth and style of the cities were displayed in the fine houses, the heavy, rich furniture imported from England, the massive silver plate of the tables, the luxurious living, and the choice wines.

The forms of address, too, showed the social rank. The terms "lady" and "gentleman" were applied only to persons of recognized standing. Our everyday title of "Mr." was conferred only upon ministers and the officers of the law, and upon their sons if college bred. The title "Mrs." was limited to the wives of prominent men. But if Mr. John Smith was proved guilty of any offense, as theft or lying, he was always afterwards known only as John Smith. For ordinary people above the grade of servants the title of "Goody" was in common use, meaning either "Goodman" or "Goodwife."

CHAPTER X.
THE BEGINNING OF THE REVOLUTION.

130. Our Forefathers, Men of Rare Ability and Sterling Character.—Many of our forefathers who had been driven from England to this country by persecution were men of rare ability and sterling character. Some had served their nation with credit in the army; others had won social and political honors. Independent in their way of thinking, fearless in speech and action, they were sternly opposed to governmental oppression. They believed that royal power should be held within well-defined limits. They would not tamely submit, as many did, to abuses from a bad government and tyrannical kings.

131. The Story of their Wrongs told to their Children.—Now we may safely believe that the early settlers told their children all about the persecutions in England. The young folks learned well the sad tale of how their fathers had been punished, and some of their neighbors hanged or burned alive for worshiping God in what they thought the right way, and how, for this reason, they had sought a shelter in the New World.

As the years passed, these children grew up to be men, and in their turn they told it all to their sons. Again, when the new generation came upon the stage of action, the fathers repeated it to their boys, and these, when they attained manly strength, became the very heroes that fought so bravely at Bunker Hill and King's Mountain and on many another battlefield!

132. A Feeling of Brotherhood among the Colonies.—Then there was a sense of freedom, an inspiration to liberty, in this open, unsubdued, apparently boundless land. The free ocean, the immense forests, the eternal mountains, all seemed to teach that here man was to be his own master; that in this wide, new country, the people were destined to rule themselves, and not bound to obey some stupid and obstinate king three thousand miles away.

The colonies along the coast, having the same language, with similar laws and customs, and having shared like sufferings from hunger and cold and the Indians, were naturally drawn together by a feeling of brotherhood.

133. Cruel and Short-Sighted Policy of the Royal Governors.—Before long there came up real grievances. One fact that diminished the affection of our forefathers for the mother country was the harsh treatment they received from many of the governors sent over by the king. For the colonies were not allowed to elect their own governors, nor could they choose even the governor's council of advisers. These were appointed by the monarch far away, who cared little for the Americans except to extort money from them.

Indeed, the English king seemed to think almost anybody would do for governor who contrived to wring money enough out of his distant subjects. Many of the royal governors were self-conceited, arrogant, and tyrannical. Consequently in some of the colonies there was almost incessant quarreling between the governors and the people. By and by the colonies came to be treated, not as a part of the home country, but as a sort of foreign district to furnish a royal revenue.

134. The Colonies begin to prosper.—Notwithstanding all their hardships, the colonies prospered. The people were wonderfully enterprising. They built ships and made a great deal of money by trading with the West Indies, France, Spain, and other countries. The New Englanders alone had over five hundred vessels engaged in domestic and foreign commerce and in profitable fisheries.

The early colonists were ingenious. They built and ran a sawmill a hundred years before one was erected in England. They exported great quantities of excellent lumber. They began very early to manufacture farmer's tools, leather, boots and shoes, woolen cloth, hats, glass, paper, salt, and gunpowder. The sale of these goods and of many other things produced by them made a profitable trade. In return the colonists bought in distant lands a great amount and variety of other merchandise.

135. The British Government begins its Tyrannical Policy.—But the English rulers, seeing all this prosperity, became jealous and said: "This will never do! We must stop it! Those distant colonists across the ocean are driving a great trade; the foreign nations they deal with get their money. We must have it; we must compel them to do all their trading with us." And that is what the English government tried to do. By 1750 not less than twenty-nine Acts of Parliament had been passed with the intent to have all of the loss in trade fall on the colonies and all the gain come to England.

In 1761 it was decided to enforce the so-called Navigation Acts, forbidding the colonies to have any foreign commerce except in British ships. Our colonial merchants were not allowed to export goods, nor to import any except from England or her colonies. They must not import any sugar or molasses without paying on it a heavy duty, which went to the king. Under these unjust laws the British traders could fix low prices on all they bought, and high prices on all they sold, and thus by this double-edged method could shape their profits to suit themselves.

136. Other Absurd and Tyrannical Laws.—Still more odious than these navigation laws were other absurd and tyrannical regulations made to cripple the industries and manufactures of the colonies. The fact was, the English Parliament meant that England's workshops should do all the manufacturing, her merchants all the trading, and her ships all the carrying for the colonies, that they might keep in England all the immense profits of the colonial trade.

To bring this about, laws were passed forbidding the manufacture of all such goods as English shops could produce. For instance, iron must not be made from the abundant mines of our country. We must buy all our hardware from England. It was a crime to use the wool from our own sheep in making woolen goods, and we were forbidden to sell these articles from one colony to another. For example, a Boston hatter could be punished if he sold his hats in New York. Men were forbidden to cut down trees on their own lands for staves and barrels. For wooden ware, as chairs, tables, wheels, wagons, the raw material must be sent to England to be worked up, and the finished goods brought back to this country.

137. A Bitter Feeling aroused against the Home Government.—Now all these laws seemed very harsh and unjust. And, indeed, they were well-nigh intolerable. They crippled and almost ruined the business of the colonies, and violated what our forefathers regarded as their natural right to make what they pleased and sell where they pleased.

These laws were so unjust that our forefathers thought there was not much wrong in evading them. They smuggled goods and carried them home. British officers went around and searched houses from cellar to attic, often with rudeness and insults. This conduct created much bitterness of feeling. Pine trees of twelve inches or more in diameter were marked with the "king's arrow," which showed that they were to be saved for use in the navy. It was a criminal offense to cut down any such. However much a settler might need them to build his house, he was forbidden to touch them. In fact, before he cleared his land, he had to pay an officer to come and make the arrow mark on the king's trees!

These unjust and absurd statutes produced a vast deal of ill-will toward England. If they had been strictly enforced, no doubt the Revolution would have come several years before it did. And yet there was also much friendly feeling for the mother country. The friends and relatives of the colonists still lived there, letters were constantly exchanged, and hundreds of people coming and going every year kept up an affection between the two countries. Our people in those times always called England "home."

BRITISH STAMP.

138. The Obnoxious Stamp Act.—There came at last one event which, of all the troubles, hastened the Revolution. The French and Indian War had cost both England and the colonies a great deal of money. King George wanted to compel the colonies to pay part of this expense, and accordingly Parliament passed in 1765 the "Stamp Act," the most unpopular measure ever tried with the colonists. This law required that stamped paper should be used for all bills, bonds, notes, wills, and deeds, and even for all pamphlets, almanacs, and newspapers.

Stamps for this purpose had to be bought of stamp officers appointed by the king. They were for the most part not unlike our revenue stamps. One kind was a red-ink seal, made with a hand stamp; the other a seal on blue paper, to be fastened on the article. The cost varied from one cent to fifty dollars each. No document was legal unless stamped.

Our people at once saw that if England could levy taxes in this way, she could in many other ways, and there would be no end to such high-handed and tyrannical laws. Besides, there were no American representatives in Parliament, and Americans had no voice at all in the matter. They felt that the tax thus laid upon them was wrong. They did not object to paying the cost of a trifling tax. They felt bound to resist the rank injustice of the demand. It was not the amount but the principle at stake.

139. The Indignation of the People.—The people were aroused. A storm of indignation swept over the land. Violent opposition broke out along the entire length of the colonies. They pledged themselves to stand by each other. The cry passed through the land: "No taxation without representation!" This became the watchword of the country. They did not wish to avoid paying a fair assessment in a fair way; but they insisted that, as always before, their own legislatures and not Parliament should levy the contribution. Our forefathers declared over and over again that they would not be taxed by a governing body three thousand miles away, whose members had never seen America.

140. Patrick Henry and his Bold Speech.—One day the Virginia Assembly was in session. Washington was there in his seat, and Jefferson, then a young law student, stood listening at the door. Patrick Henry stoutly argued that Virginia was not bound to obey any law which was plainly a menace to the common freedom of Englishmen.

"Cæsar had his Brutus," said the bold and eloquent orator; "Charles the First his Cromwell, and George the Third"——

"Treason!" shouted the Speaker of the Assembly, and the cry, "Treason, treason!" rang through the room.

PATRICK HENRY'S BOLD SPEECH.

The intrepid patriot finished his sentence: "may profit by their example. If that be treason, make the most of it!"

141. The People combine to resist the Hated Law.—The people combined to resist, and a stamp-tax congress was held in New York. Lovers of liberty would not deal in stamped goods. They refused to buy a single stamp. Riots occurred at the stamp offices. Packages of stamps were seized, and some were publicly burned in the streets. Boxes of stamped paper arriving in vessels were seized and thrown overboard. Publishers of newspapers decorated their headlines with skull and cross-bones instead of stamps. Stamp officers were dragged out and compelled to swear they would not sell any stamps.

PATRICK HENRY.

On the day for the law to take effect, funeral bells were tolled, flags were at half-mast, and shops were closed. New England, New York, Virginia, and the Carolinas all felt alike and acted alike. William Pitt, also called the Earl of Chatham, one of the greatest of Englishmen, took his stand on the side of the colonies in a speech of surpassing eloquence and power. The hated law was repealed in just one year from its passage.

This happy news was received both in England and in America with bonfires, ringing of bells, and universal rejoicings. But the joy was short-lived. King George, "industrious as a beaver and obstinate as a mule," and his followers in Parliament were not slow to pick a fresh quarrel with the Americans.

The next year the English Parliament made a law requiring duties to be paid on paper, glass, paints, and tea. Again the liberty-loving Americans were a unit in opposing any kind of taxation that seemed to them illegal. Some of the legislatures protested to Parliament, and King George answered by breaking up the legislatures. The people indignantly refused to buy any goods at all from England while these taxes were demanded. English traders found their business going to ruin. Ships came loaded with British goods, and had to carry them back.

142. Bitter Hatred of the British Soldiers.—So bitter was the opposition in Boston that a regiment of British troops was sent there to force the people to submit even at the point of the bayonet. But a brave people, determined to be free, is not so easily forced.

The citizens of Boston were ordered to furnish lodging and food for the soldiers. They would not do it—not they! Their hatred of the soldiers grew more bitter. Brawls often occurred on the streets. The soldiers on their part began to be insulting.

143. Boston Boys stand up for their Rights.—Even the children took part in the quarrels, as an incident will show. During the winter the boys used to build snow-slides on Boston Common and slide down upon them to the frog pond. The English soldiers destroyed these slides, merely to provoke the boys. The young Americans complained of the injury and set about repairing it. However, when they returned from school, they found the snow-slides destroyed again.

THE BOSTON BOYS MAKE THEIR PROTEST TO GENERAL GAGE.

Several of the boys now waited upon one of the under-officers, and told him of the conduct of his soldiers; but he would have nothing to say to them; and the soldiers were more impudent than ever. At last the boys called a meeting and sent a committee of the largest of their number to General Gage, the commander-in-chief. He asked why so many boys had called upon him.
"We came, sir," said the tallest, "to demand satisfaction."
"What!" said the general; "have your fathers been teaching you rebellion, and sent you to show it here?"
"Nobody sent us, sir," he answered, while his cheek reddened and his eye flashed. "We have never injured nor insulted your troops; but they have trodden down our snow-slides and broken the ice on the pond. We complained and they called us young rebels and told us to help ourselves if we could. We told one of your officers of this, and he laughed at us. Yesterday our slides were destroyed for the third time; and, sir, we will bear it no longer."
General Gage was a kind-hearted and courteous gentleman. He looked at them with admiration, and said to an officer at his side: "The very children draw in a love of liberty with the air they breathe. You may go, my brave boys; and be assured, if my soldiers trouble you again, they shall be punished."

144. The Boston Massacre.—One night in March (1770) some soldiers stationed in Boston got into a quarrel, and the noise increased until the guard was called out. As the platoon of regulars drew up in line, most of the crowd fell back.

A few remained and reviled the red-coat soldiers, shouting, "Lobster-backs! Fire if you dare, you cowards! You don't dare to fire!"

Captain Preston, the officer in command, gave the word, "Fire!" The regulars fired.

Five men were killed and several wounded. There was now intense excitement in Boston. The Old South Church was crowded with an angry town-meeting. Thousands filled the streets near by. The people demanded that the troops be removed. The governor promised to remove one regiment. "Both regiments or none," was the watchword.

Samuel Adams waited upon the governor, and stretching forth his long right arm, and pointing his finger at him, he sternly demanded, in the name of three thousand freemen, that the royal governor remove every British soldier from Boston.

"I observed his knees to tremble," said the stern patriot in after years; "I saw his face grow pale—and I enjoyed the sight."

Before sunset of the same day the British troops were removed from the city and sent to a fort in the harbor. Not until then did the meeting in the Old South break up.

This unfortunate affair was the so-called "Boston Massacre." It did more to mould public opinion than weeks of vigorous protest and fine argument could have done. It was one step, and an important one too, toward the final appeal to the sword and the bayonet.

145. The Famous Boston Tea Party.—In view of all these troubles, England took off the taxes from everything but tea. King George said he must have one tax to maintain the principle of the right of taxation. But the colonists refused to drink tea imported from China! The women were patriotic and made their tea of raspberry leaves, sage, and other plants, rather than use the hated foreign article.

But the government of England was determined we should buy tea, and the merchants sent shiploads of it to our large cities. The Americans were firm. They vowed that not an ounce of it should land. There was only a few cents' tax on each pound. What our people disputed was the right of the king to tax. When the tea reached New York and Philadelphia, none dared to receive it, lest their houses should be pulled down about their heads. In Charleston, S. C., some was taken ashore, but as no one would buy it or pay the duty, it was hid in damp cellars, where it soon spoiled. In Annapolis it was burned.

At Boston warning was several times given to the masters of the ships to sail out of the harbor. On the last day before the tea must be landed or be prevented by force from landing, a town-meeting was held in the Old South Church. The crowd in the church, and in the streets about it, numbered more than seven thousand people. "It was to be," says John Fiske, "one of the most momentous days in the history of the world." The discussion continued until dark, and candles were brought in. It was decided that the tea should not be landed.

"Who knows," shouted one in the audience, "how tea will mix with salt water?"

The church fairly shook with cheers.

Then up rose Samuel Adams and quickly said: "This meeting can do nothing more to save the country."

This was the signal. A war-whoop was heard outside the door, and forty or fifty men, disguised as Indians, went quietly aboard the three vessels, and before the nine-o'clock bell rang three hundred and forty-two chests of tea had been cut open and their contents emptied into Boston Harbor. This was the famous "Boston Tea Party" we have so often heard of, and it took place in the middle of December in 1773. A large crowd of the friends of these men stood on shore until the deed was done, and then, without doing any other injury to property, all separated and went home in the clear, frosty moonlight.

The next morning there was not a chest of taxed tea in Boston, on shipboard or on shore, and Paul Revere was riding post haste to Philadelphia to let the good people of that city know that Boston had at last thrown down the gauntlet.

One of the "Indians" found a handful of tea in his shoe the next morning. He carefully saved it and sealed it in a bottle. It is still shown as a souvenir of this informal "tea party" in Boston harbor.

One rash fellow, probably thinking that his family would like a good drink of real tea, cut open the lining of his coat and waistcoat, and, watching his chance, filled them with tea; but he was caught in the act and handled pretty roughly.

146. Attempts to punish Boston.—"Boston shall be punished," said King George when he heard of the "tea party." Parliament passed the "Boston Port Bill." By this act the port of Boston was closed. No vessel could go in or out except under the most rigid conditions. The object of course was to frighten or force the Boston people into yielding to the royal power.

Near-by towns and the other colonies came to their help by sending food and other needed articles. The southern colonies sent flour and rice, the middle furnished corn and money, and many towns sent sheep and cattle. One town in Connecticut sent a flock of two hundred and fifty sheep. Marblehead sent fish, and other towns grain.

Warm sympathy came from Virginia. "If need be," said Washington, "I will raise a thousand men, subsist them at my own expense, and march myself at their head for the relief of Boston." In fact all the colonies took up the cause of Boston as their own. Of course the blockade made great hardship for the poor. There was much suffering from the scarcity of fuel and food. Still the people, as resolute as their leaders, made little complaint and caused no disorder.

Dr. Joseph Warren overheard some British officers boast that if a patriot ever addressed the people again in the Old South Church, he would surely lose his life. This was enough. Warren begged the honor. The church was so crowded that he had to get a ladder and climb in through a window at the back of the pulpit. Many British officers were present who annoyed the speaker with groans and hisses. The fearless patriot, however, made a stirring speech "on the baneful influence of standing armies in time of peace."

147. The Home Government adopts Stringent Measures.—The charter of Massachusetts was annulled, and its free government taken away. General Gage, the commander of the British army in America, was ordered to Boston with several regiments and was appointed military governor with despotic power. Cannon were mounted on the heights, tents pitched on the Common, and companies of red-coats were marching to and fro in the streets.

The effect was exactly what the wisest men in Parliament had predicted. They had said that the colonies would unite more firmly, and that the American people would be driven into open rebellion. King George was obstinate and used all his influence to push the most obnoxious Acts through Parliament.

148. The First Continental Congress.—The first Continental Congress held its first meeting at Philadelphia in September, 1774. The ablest men of the colonies were sent as delegates. They forwarded to the king a candid statement of their grievances. It did no good. Massachusetts was declared in a state of rebellion. In truth, it looked like it.

Such a condition of affairs could not last long. The feeling was intense against the king and his all-powerful friends. Arguments were useless. The royal authority was boldly and stubbornly defied. The sword and the bayonet must now decide whether king or people were to rule in America.

"The contest may be severe, but the end will be glorious," said the martyr-patriot Warren, who soon after fell at Bunker Hill.

CHAPTER XI.
LEXINGTON AND CONCORD.

149. The Patriots prepare for War.—When General Gage began to increase slowly the number of troops in Boston, and especially when he began to fortify Boston Neck, it was plain enough that this meant war. The people on their part began to prepare anxiously for the coming struggle. Every one felt that desperate times were near at hand. The patriots quickly collected arms and ammunition and, having packed them in loads of hay and similar disguises to deceive the British spies, sent them for safe keeping to Concord, about sixteen miles northwest of Boston.

150. Gage forms Plans to capture Military Stores.—General Gage soon learned this, and made secret preparations to capture these supplies. Inasmuch as in previous expeditions of this kind he had met with failure, the advantage of a surprise was this time to be increased by the presence of a large force. The Americans, however, were quite as keen of sight and hearing as their enemies, and had even more reason to keep a sharp lookout.

About midnight on the 18th of April, 1775, Gage quietly sent out from Boston nearly eight hundred soldiers. He had two objects in view; to seize the military stores at Concord, and to arrest Samuel Adams and "his ready and willing tool," that "terrible desperado," John Hancock.

Gage thought the start of his midnight soldiers was quite unknown to the Americans. He never suspected that Warren and other vigilant patriots had been watching every movement, and were determined to thwart his plans. At about ten or eleven o'clock, two hours before the British soldiers embarked, a signal lantern hung out of the belfry of the Old North Church in Boston, and in a few minutes another by its side—"One, if by land, and two, if by sea"—flashed the tidings of the coming expedition.

151. The Country about Boston aroused.—An hour or two before the British troops began to cross in boats to Charlestown, two horsemen, who had been watching for the lantern lights in the steeple, dashed out on swift steeds by different roads towards Lexington and Concord: William Dawes went like an arrow over Boston Neck, and then through Roxbury and Watertown, while Paul Revere across the water sped as if on wings from Charlestown. Their swift horses' hoofs clattered sharply in the quiet of this beautiful night, striking fire from the stones in the darkness. But at almost every house they paused a moment to arouse the sleepers. "Wake up!" they shouted. Windows flew open.

"What's the matter?"—"What's the mat-ter?"

"Matter enough, you'll find, by daylight!" was the hurried reply. "The British are coming!"

152. The Night March to Concord.—Meanwhile the British soldiers were marching along rapidly through the cool April night. They made no noise. There was no drumbeat; the officers gave their commands almost in whispers. Only the clatter of the horses' hoofs and the steady tramp of the marching men broke the silence. When day dawned they approached the village of Lexington, ten miles from Boston and about two-thirds of the way to Concord. They were not entirely surprised to find, even so early, a squad of armed minute-men awaiting them, for they had heard church bells ringing and had seen, all along their march, lights moving to and fro in the farm houses.

153. The Patriots make a stand at Lexington.—The British arrived at Lexington about half-past four. Ready to meet them were some sixty or seventy men drawn up on the village green close beside the meeting-house, with loaded guns. As they stood there, silent and fearless, on that sweet spring morning, April 19, 1775, their leader, Captain John Parker, who fifteen years before had climbed the Heights of Abraham by the side of Wolfe, addressed them briefly.

"Stand your ground. Don't fire unless fired upon," said Parker; "but if they mean to have a war, let it begin here!" Seventy men against eight hundred! War it was, and it did begin there.

PAUL REVERE'S RIDE.

Major Pitcairn, who soon afterwards fell at Bunker Hill, rode up and cried out:—

"Disperse, you villains! Throw down your arms, you rebels, and go home!"

He then discharged his pistol and, turning to his soldiers, cried, "Fire!" Instantly flashed out the first volley of the Revolutionary War, and eight of the farmer minute-men fell dead!

The number of the Americans was so small in proportion to that of the British that the only sensible course was to retreat. They retired with a few parting shots at the enemy. Then the red-coats, giving three cheers, marched on towards Concord, six miles farther.

The patriots at Concord had the day before received some hint of the proposed capture, and had removed most of the military stores to the woods. The British found two cannon, which they spiked, and some cannon balls and gunpowder, which they threw into the river. Then they destroyed a quantity of flour, cut down the liberty-pole, and set fire to the courthouse.

154. The Fight at Concord Bridge.—While they were busy doing this, fresh minute-men, about four hundred in number, were coming in from all the adjoining towns. They gathered near the old North Bridge to drive away some regulars who had begun to take up the planks. As the militia approached, the British soldiers fired and killed several. Among the dead was Captain Isaac Davis. Long after life was extinct, the fingers of this brave patriot, as if still true to his purpose, held firm grasp on his gun.

Major Buttrick, a leader among the soldier-farmers, shouted, "Fire, fellow-soldiers! Fire!" Obedient to this order, the Americans in return "fired the shot heard round the world!" The regulars fell back in confusion. The minute-men held the bridge, and the enemy began a hasty retreat.

THE MINUTE-MEN ATTACKING THE BRITISH REGULARS ON THE RETREAT.

Our men were too few in number to join in a square pitched battle with the trained British soldiers; but as soon as these began to withdraw, the patriots followed them closely and kept up a brisk discharge of musketry. The previous volleys and the bell-ringing had aroused the whole adjacent country, and fresh men came pouring in from every side. Most of them were without their coats; but they had guns in their hands and they knew how to use them.

155. The British begin their Retreat.—Occasionally the retreating soldiers would stop and shoot back, and then hurry on and even run, to escape the deadly bullets. Soon the minute-men, leaping over the stone walls, ran on ahead, or, cutting across at some bend of the road, got a long

distance in advance. Then as the column came on, the Americans, from behind barns, trees, rocks, and walls, would pour a storm of shot into the staggering ranks. So from right and left, behind and before, came in showers the fatal balls of the minute-men. A British officer afterwards said, "It seemed as if men dropped from the clouds."
You remember Longfellow's description:—

How the British regulars fired and fled,How the farmers gave them ball for ball,From behind each fence and farm-yard wall,Chasing the red-coats down the lane,Then crossing the fields to emerge again,Under the trees at the turn of the road,And pausing only to fire and load.

The British suffered fearfully in this six-mile march. The weather was as sultry as in midsummer, and the dust was suffocating. They had been on the road without food or water from midnight to noon. They were worn and exhausted, and the ceaseless shot of the Americans, who were all trained to the use of the rifle, brought down some of the regulars at almost every step. To go on was perilous, to pause long was fatal. Dead and wounded men and horses lay all along the road.

Thus beset, the British pushed on, hurrying back over the dreadful distance till they reached Lexington. Here they were rejoiced to find a thousand soldiers sent out from Boston under Lord Percy to meet them. These had marched out of Boston to the tune of Yankee Doodle! They were formed in a hollow square, and into this shelter rushed the runaway red-coats, falling upon the green grass from pure exhaustion, "with their tongues hanging out of their mouths, like dogs after a chase." Lord Percy allowed a rest of only about half an hour, knowing very well that the longer he delayed the greater would be the increasing swarm of armed men gathering around him.

156. The Panic-Stricken British Regulars at last reach the Shelter of the Men-of-War.—The British commander had now in all nearly eighteen hundred men, and he made straight for Charlestown, the nearest point of safety. But in spite of this large force, the minute-men with their unerring aim kept on his flanks, picking off the regulars, especially the officers, all along the road. In vain the officers threatened; the men ran like sheep. At sunset the British reached Charlestown and found themselves safe under the shelter of their men-of-war.

If Percy's reinforcements had not come up, all the British soldiers that started back from Concord would have been killed or taken prisoners. The king's regulars had been driven in rout and almost panic before the stout-hearted minute-men. Well might General Gage feel keenly the disgrace.

The loss on both sides at Lexington and Concord was small. Most of the fighting took place on the retreat, where the loss of the Americans was about fifty killed and forty-three wounded, while the British lost in all two hundred and seventy-three men.

157. What the Eventful Day showed.—Thus began and ended one of the most eventful days in the history of our country. It witnessed the opening conflict of the American Revolution.

When that sturdy patriot, Samuel Adams, heard the crackle of the musketry, he exclaimed, "What a glorious morning is this!" He knew that the time had come when the people must draw the sword.

The Americans had now shown that they could fight. They saw the promptness with which they could assemble, and they felt that, if need were, they could defend themselves. The British also learned that the American farmers could fight, and that, too, on the spur of the moment. They found that the colonies were not to be frightened into submission. It became plain to each side that very serious work was near at hand. The grim figure of WAR cast its long black shadow into the future.

The shots of these resolute farmers echoed far and wide. They told the whole world that a people stood ready to give their lives in defense of their rights; that they fought after their own fashion, and they fought hard.

THE FIGHT AT CONCORD BRIDGE.

158. The Minute-Men; the Work they did, and how they did it.—The minute-men were bands of enrolled patriots pledged to start at a minute's notice to a call for their services. They had few good weapons, mostly shotguns for hunting birds and squirrels. They were short of powder and ball. In many of the families the women melted or pounded up their pewter spoons and dishes into bullets and slugs.

The minute-men were numerous in every town, and when the alarm was given, they would leave plow or shop, hurry home, take down the gun from its hooks over the fireplace, bid good-by to wife and children, and be off to help their country in its peril.

Israel Putnam, in leather frock and apron, was at work in a field on his farm in Connecticut when he heard of Lexington. Leaving the plow in the furrow, he jumped on his horse and rode the hundred or more miles to Cambridge in eighteen hours. John Stark was at work in his sawmill in New Hampshire when the news of Lexington came. He stopped the mill, hurried home, took down his rifle, and rode on horseback to Cambridge. In his haste he even forgot to put on his coat!

Every town had a company or two of minute-men and of militia soldiers, who regularly met and drilled. The soldiers and the officers of these companies were usually the best citizens of the towns. Thirty-one towns were represented among the patriots who hastened to the fight on the nineteenth of April.

159. Tablets now shown along this Historic Road.—If some day we should take a ride over this very road, we should notice along the way numerous landmarks of that famous contest—carved monuments, houses with bullet holes carefully preserved, bronze tablets on houses, marking some spot of special interest. At Fiske's Hill, in Lexington, an inscription records that at a well near by two soldiers met to drink. The British grenadier raised his gun and said to James Hayward, "You are a dead man!" "And so are you!" replied the minute-man. Both fired; one was instantly killed, and the other mortally wounded.

On Lexington Common we should see a stately monument with a long inscription reciting the event.

At Concord Bridge would be seen a noble statue of the Minute-Man, beneath which on the pedestal are Emerson's famous verses:—

Here once the embattled farmers stood,And fired the shot heard round the world.

CHAPTER XII.
THE BATTLE OF BUNKER HILL.

160. More Regulars sent to Boston.—The battle of Lexington, fought as we have read, on the nineteenth of April, 1775, was a most momentous event, since it showed for the first time the resolute purpose of the Americans to draw the sword and defend themselves from British oppression. The news reached England near the end of May. Those Lexington muskets said plainer than words that the colonies would not submit to unjust taxation.

Fully aware that the situation was becoming serious, the British government sent a large number of fresh troops to reinforce the garrison in Boston. These came under the command of Generals Howe, Clinton, and Burgoyne, and made in all an army of about ten thousand men.

161. A Patriot Army is gathered around Boston.—The patriots, too, were gathering in large numbers around Boston. They came by hundreds from all directions. Quite a large body was from Connecticut under Colonel (afterwards General) Israel Putnam. General Ward was commander of these forces until Washington arrived at Cambridge on July 3, 1775, and first took command of the American army under the old elm.

On the twelfth of June, General Gage issued a proclamation declaring all those in arms to be rebels and traitors, but offering pardon to all who would lay down their weapons and obey the British governor. Two, John Hancock and Samuel Adams, were excepted. Their patriotism had been too intense and outspoken to be forgiven.

WASHINGTON TAKING COMMAND OF THE PATRIOT ARMY.

The American army, now nearly twenty thousand strong, formed a line of encampments in a great semicircle of sixteen miles, halfway around the city from Roxbury Neck to the Mystic River. They soon learned that Gage intended to break through the American lines into the country for a supply of provisions.

162. Plans to checkmate the British.—General Ward, having discovered that the British were planning to sally forth through Charlestown, determined to strike first and so defeat their project. It was decided to seize and fortify some suitable hill in Charlestown. Colonel William Prescott, a well-tried soldier of the French-Indian wars, and grandfather of Prescott, the famous historian, was ordered, on the sixteenth of June, to march that night with nearly a thousand men to Bunker Hill and throw up breastworks.

Soon after sunset the soldiers were formed in a hollow square on Cambridge Common, and President Langdon of Harvard College offered prayer. The good man then gave them his blessing and bade them "Godspeed." At nine o'clock they started on their silent march. At Charlestown Neck they met General Putnam with more soldiers and wagon-loads of picks and shovels.

163. Entrenched on Bunker Hill.—Prescott led them to the top of Bunker Hill. After consultation with his officers, he moved on through the darkness to Breed's Hill, which had a better command of the city and the shipping. The lines were soon staked out, and at midnight the farmer soldiers began their entrenchments. So rapidly did they work that the dim morning twilight disclosed a large square of fresh trenches crowning the hill, with long wings stretching right and left. They had made a fort in a single night.

How surprised the British were at the sight, as the sun rose on a beautiful summer morning! They could scarcely believe their eyes. It seemed like a work of magic. A thousand men had shoveled as they never shoveled before, and not a British sentry had heard the click of their spades. They saw at once that the Americans, if they only had time enough to plant a battery of cannon there, could very soon drive them out of Boston. So the only thing for them to do was to drive the Americans from that hill, and that too without delay. Accordingly, the British men-of-war, Lively and Falcon, and then the forts on Copp's Hill in Boston immediately opened fire.

Meanwhile some hundreds of fresh soldiers arrived to help the Americans, hungry and weary with their hard night's work. The shot and shell from ships and fort dropped around and among them, but they worked bravely on in the hot sunshine till nearly noon. At the left, on the northern slope of the hill, they moved some rail fences so as to build long double lines close together, and stuffed the space between with new-mown hay, making an excellent breastwork.

164. The British prepare to storm the Entrenchments.—Things are now looking serious. The Americans can see and hear the British in Boston preparing for an attack. Prescott sends hurrying messengers to General Ward at the Cambridge headquarters for more soldiers. During the forenoon General Stark arrives with five hundred fresh New Hampshire troops, who were posted behind the rail fence on the extreme left. Next General Warren comes, and, laying aside his rank, takes a place of danger among the troops. The combat hastens, and every minute throbs with emotion.

Soon after one o'clock twenty-eight large boats are seen crossing over from Boston, loaded with soldiers and artillery. The Americans are now exchanging shovels for muskets and preparing for the foe. Now the red-coats are landing at the foot of the hill! See! they are forming in two columns, their bright cannon and muskets glistening in the hot sun. It is now about three o'clock in the afternoon. They begin to march up the hill!

General Howe's column is on our left, to break through the grass wall and push his way behind our forces. Their other column, under General Pigot, is marching up the hill to attack our redoubt in front. They are coming slowly in the hot sun of a bright June afternoon. The artillery booms and crashes incessantly with a deafening roar.

General Gage has ordered that Charlestown be set on fire, and the flames and smoke of five hundred burning buildings make a terrible scene. All the surrounding heights, house-tops, and spires are crowded with thousands of anxious spectators breathlessly watching the thrilling sight.

"Here were sister, wife, and mother, looking wild upon each other,And their lips were white with terror as they said, 'THE HOUR HAS COME!'"

165. The Battle begins.—Behind those hasty breastworks fifteen hundred patriots lie silently awaiting the steady march of over three thousand trained British soldiers. Still on and up they toil, burdened with their heavy knapsacks, pausing to fire as they march.

"Don't fire until I give the word," said Prescott; "then fire low! Pick off the officers."

Putnam shouted to his men: "Powder is scarce, boys, don't waste it; wait till you see the whites of their eyes."

When the red-coats came within about a hundred and fifty feet of the breastworks, suddenly came Prescott's sharp order:—"Fire!" Instantly a flash of flame blazed along our entire line, and down fell the whole front of the advancing ranks. Under the ceaseless rain of bullets the British veterans gave way and retreated down the hillside in disorder.

Then burst forth from our side a strong shout, the first ringing cry on this continent for national independence. But it was a sad sight—the long rows of dead and dying soldiers, mowed down as if by a sudden sweep of a giant scythe.

"Oh, the sight our eyes discover as the blue-black smoke blows over! The red-coats stretched in windrows as a mower rakes his hay."

Inside the breastworks some were killed and many wounded. Prescott, Putnam, and Warren were passing up and down the line, cheering and encouraging the patriots.

166. The British beat a Hasty Retreat to their Boats.—The British officers rallied their troops as best they could. Death and wounds had thinned their number by hundreds, and the survivors were far from willing to make a second charge against that wall of fire. But the threats of the officers and even blows with their swords finally compelled them to it.

Up they marched again, firing as they came, their ranks moving slowly, stepping over the bodies of their fallen comrades.

"Wait, boys!" shouted Warren. "Don't fire yet! Wait."

On they came as before, nearer and nearer, until the distance was less than thirty yards to our silent but fatal line, when instantly there burst forth another long blaze of fire, even deadlier than before.

BATTLE OF BUNKER HILL.

The Americans were by practice good marksmen, and the bright red coats and shining belts of the enemy made excellent targets. The British returned the fire, and a brisk discharge of musketry was kept up for a few minutes. But it was useless. Hundreds of their number fell dead on the fatal slope, and in spite of their officers, the broken ranks staggered and retreated, flying in a panic to the shore.

167. The British advance to the Third Attack.—Now all was fright and confusion among the British. They were dismayed at the deadly reception our untrained soldiers had given them. General Clinton, who had been watching the battle from Copp's Hill and saw the day going against them, instantly hurried over with fresh troops. Once more the British regulars formed at the foot of the hill.

We may imagine with what mingled feelings the Americans, gazing down through the rifts of smoke from burning Charlestown, watched the movements of the reinforced foe. Putnam and Warren again went around cheering our men.

Prescott shouted, "Let's drive them back once more, and they cannot rally again."

But alas! the stock of powder was giving out! The patriots had only three or four rounds left, and as for close fighting, there were only about fifty bayonets to all their guns. Orders were passed along to use their powder carefully, to hold fire until the enemy came within twenty yards, and to make every shot tell.

Meantime the enemy's cannon from the ships had got a better range, and were pouring in a galling fire. The prospect on our side was beginning to look desperate. Short of powder; without bayonets; confronted by brave enemies always twice our number, and now with fresh troops; tired out with marching or digging all night and shoveling or fighting all day; for the most part without food and water,—our men still defiantly held the fort.

At five o'clock the British formed for the third attack, advancing now in three columns to charge us on three sides. This time their knapsacks were laid aside, and they marched in light order. Up they came as before, only slower; for they realized that they had a dangerous enemy before them. They reserved their fire. When they reached that same deadly range, once more our ramparts poured forth the deadly volleys.

The British wavered, but then rallied and rushed forward to the breastworks with fixed bayonets.

"Make every shot tell!" shouted Prescott to his men.

As the British began to climb over our earthworks, our soldiers spent their last shots upon those who mounted first. Among those who fell dead at the redoubt was Major Pitcairn, who at Lexington had cried out, "Disperse, ye rebels!"

168. The Patriots forced to retreat from Lack of Ammunition.—Their powder all gone, what could the patriots do but retreat? This they did in good order for raw soldiers, many staying to smite the enemy with the butts of their muskets, then with the barrels after the butts were broken off, and some even with stones. The British were now closing in upon them on all sides, and at last Prescott, to avoid being completely shut in, gave the word to retreat. He was one of the last to leave, defending himself with his sword from the bayonets of the enemy.

Alas! one shot of the last volley from the British killed our beloved Warren! When General Howe heard of this he said, "Warren's death is equal to the loss of five hundred men to the Americans."

Stark and Knowlton held the grass fence till the troops had left the top of the hill, and then retreated with them in good order to Charlestown Neck.

On their way back they met at Bunker Hill General Putnam, who had collected fresh soldiers and wanted to occupy the trenches he had formed there, and make a fresh stand against the enemy. But the British ships on both sides could rake this position, and it was decided to move back to Prospect Hill, which our forces fortified. It was about six o'clock when the retreat began.

169. Bunker Hill and the Lesson it taught.—In less than three hours, and with only one hour of actual fighting, all these fearful scenes were enacted. The Americans, with about fifteen hundred men, lost four hundred and fifty killed and wounded. But the British, with over three thousand, had lost one thousand and fifty-four, of whom one hundred and fifty-seven were officers!

Although in form the result of the battle was a defeat, as our army lost their ground, yet its effect upon the Americans was that of a victory. It taught them that they were a match for the British troops in a fair fight. This knowledge nerved them to further resistance against royal oppression. Thus this battle, the first clear bugle-call of the Revolution, proving beyond all doubt that the British troops were not invincible, was worth just at this time many decided victories to the Americans. To the patriots of every colony it gave strength and heart, and the belief that their cause would succeed. In the march of events and of ideas Bunker Hill was of momentous importance. It gave the shock that made the patriots conscious of their might; it cleared their vision and roused them to action.

When Washington first heard of the battle he was riding on horseback to take command of the army at Cambridge. "Did our men stand fire?" he asked of the messenger. Being told that they did, and that they waited till the enemy was only eight rods off, he said, "The liberties of the country are safe!"

But if the Americans learned that they could fight, the British learned it too! General Gage wrote home: "The trials we have had prove the rebels are not the despicable rabble too many have supposed them to be."

"If they call that a victory," said a French general, "two or three more such would extinguish the British army."

"I wish," said General Greene, "that we could sell the British another hill at the same price."

After Gage had made his formal report of the battle to his superior officers in England, he was called back in disgrace, and was never entrusted with another military service. Generals Howe and Clinton learned a costly lesson, and never again through the war that followed did they lead their men in an open field against entrenched American soldiers.

Such, briefly told, is the story of Bunker Hill. The truth is, the whole movement was on the part of the Americans an audacious act. There was more heroism in it than military prudence. General Ward had at Cambridge only a few barrels of powder for his entire army; and to send a thousand men to entrench before a well prepared enemy, in front of batteries and warships, though it needed to be done, was yet, from a military point of view, a very rash act. On the other hand, General Gage made a very unwise military movement. No wonder he was censured for the reckless sacrifice of his soldiers at Bunker Hill.

170. Bunker Hill Monument.—On the crown of the hill and in the center of the old redoubt stands the splendid monument that tells of this famous struggle. The square shaft is of Quincy granite, thirty-one feet on each side at the base, fifteen feet at the top, two hundred and twenty-one feet in height. Inside, a stairway of two hundred and ninety-four stone steps leads to a room at the top, whose four windows command a view of wonderful extent and beauty. Just by the base of the monument we can see to-day a little grassy ridge, the slight remains of the breastworks of 1775.

The corner-stone was laid by Lafayette in 1825, exactly fifty years after the battle, and on that occasion Daniel Webster delivered one of his greatest orations. In front of him sat forty venerable survivors of the conflict. The finished structure was dedicated in 1842. On this occasion Webster again delivered a magnificent oration.

CHAPTER XIII.
THE DECLARATION OF INDEPENDENCE.

171. The Colonists still regard themselves as English Subjects.—It seems to us now very remarkable that all through the year 1775, notwithstanding the conflicts at Lexington and Concord, and even after the battle of Bunker Hill, our forefathers still considered themselves loyal British subjects. Although they were violently opposing the despotism of the king of England, they never for a moment hesitated to acknowledge him as their rightful ruler. They regarded all the unjust acts of the king and the Parliament as so many encroachments upon their rights as Englishmen, just as much as if they were living in their old home in England instead of in a British colony. They insisted that, although they were three thousand miles away, distance did not diminish their just claims as free subjects of King George. They had fought as Englishmen, not against England.

Therefore, even for months after Bunker Hill, the colonists had no intention of separating from the mother country. Very few had much faith in such a scheme, and still fewer had seriously urged it. A large number of the people, probably a majority, thought the quarrel might even at that time be settled, and the colonies might resume their former friendly relations with England. All they had asked and all they had fought for was simply their rights as Britons.

Washington, when he took command of the army soon after the battle of Bunker Hill, said that he abhorred the idea of our separating from the mother country, and becoming an independent nation. Franklin declared that he had traveled all over the country and talked with all classes of people, but had never heard independence mentioned.

172. Slow Growth of the Idea of Independence.—We must not fail to remember that the idea of independence took form very slowly. The first "Stamp Act," so offensive to the colonists, became a law in 1764, more than ten years before actual hostilities broke out. During all those years our ancestors were gradually losing their friendly feeling for England. They were slowly drifting towards an open conflict, in fact, the Revolution.

This hostility to England grew to be a serious matter after the battle of Bunker Hill. It was deepened and embittered early in 1776 by a number of events that still more sharply estranged America from her unkind mother. After the battle the British continued to occupy Boston with many hostile demonstrations, just as if it were an enemy's country, until at the end of a long siege they were driven out by Washington. This weary investment caused a great deal of bitterness. Everything took on the sombre shadow of war, and this of course meant permanent hostility to England.

Another step that greatly angered the Americans, and very justly too, was a British proclamation, the design and effect of which was to destroy all the commerce of the colonies by forfeiting their ships. This was itself equal to a declaration of war by England.

Then three petitions to the king, George III, by three different congresses, were treated with indifference or even with insolent contempt. The only obvious effect of the petitions was to goad England to greater severities. To a proposal at one time to exchange prisoners, it was answered that England "received no applications from rebels, unless they came to implore the king's mercy." This stinging and insolent reply necessarily implied that all American patriots were rebels; that they were guilty of treason; that, but for the king's mercy, they must expect the penalty of treason, which is death!

173. Active Measures taken by the British.—Meanwhile obstinate King George, humored by his prime minister, Lord North, was busily making enormous preparations for pushing the war upon a large scale. Already twenty-five thousand British soldiers had been sent to America, or had been enlisted for immediate service. But so large a party in England was opposed to the war against their own countrymen in the colonies, that the king could not raise at home all the troops he needed. So he made a bargain with a German state, Hesse, hiring twenty thousand foreign soldiers to cross the ocean and fight his rebellious subjects.

"INDEPENDENCE HALL," PHILADELPHIA, AS IT APPEARED IN 1776.

When our forefathers heard of this, it angered them more than anything else that had been done. But even worse still, it was learned that the British government was taking steps, by means of secret agents, to employ the Indians to fight on the British side, and use their tomahawks against British colonists!

Finally, to all petitions and appeals the English government replied that it would not abate any of its demands, and that it would accept from us nothing short of entire submission and obedience.

174. Independence slowly but surely becomes a Stern Necessity.— Now, if we recall all the wrongs as to taxation that we have read of in a previous chapter, and add to them this list of subsequent outrages, the preparations for a long war, the hiring of Hessians, and the incitement of Indians to fight us, we must see that our forefathers were compelled to regard England as their determined enemy. Such were the successive steps by which the old feeling of loyalty to the mother country gradually vanished, and bitter hostility took its place.

What should the colonies do to protect themselves? This was the all-important question. The people had been tending toward the conviction that the only remedy was to break off all connection with England and to be independent.

But it was a long while before this feeling became general. It was a steady and natural but slow growth. The public indignation, constantly strengthened by repeated British outrages, at last culminated in mature conviction—a conviction that the only course left us was to be wholly free, and to stand by ourselves among the nations of the earth.

As this conviction became stronger and stronger among the good people all along the narrow coast line from Boston to Charleston, it soon found expression in many ways. The few newspapers spoke out; public meetings were called to discuss it, and conventions dared to announce it.

THOMAS JEFFERSON.

People learned at last that their chief enemy was the king. They saw that the controversy which began merely as a colonial struggle for their rights as British subjects had grown broader and deeper, till it became a contest for our rights as MEN and for the freedom of our entire country from British control. A pamphlet entitled "Common Sense," written by Thomas Paine, an Englishman who had recently arrived in America, had an enormous sale and exerted a powerful influence. It abounded in ready wit, sharp reasoning, and rough eloquence. It stimulated the longing for independence and the determination to be free or die. In May, 1775, the people of Mecklenburg County in North Carolina were the first to pass resolutions advocating independence. They sent them to their delegates in Congress; but these at that early day did not dare present them.

In May, 1776, Congress, then in Philadelphia, following the trend of public opinion, advised the colonies to consider themselves as no longer holding any powers under the authority of Great Britain. That was about the same as a declaration of independence. Many colonies accordingly set up state governments of their own without asking the king's consent.

175. Steps taken for a Formal Declaration of Independence.—The second Continental Congress met at Philadelphia, May 10, 1775. Early in June, 1776, one of the delegates, Richard Henry Lee, of Virginia, offered a resolution that "these United Colonies are and of right ought to be free and independent states." John Adams, of Massachusetts, seconded it in a powerful speech. Three weeks of delay, to enable some of the colonies to send in their approval, occurred before its adoption. Then a committee of five, consisting of Benjamin Franklin, Thomas Jefferson, John Adams, Roger Sherman, and Robert R. Livingston, who had been appointed to draw up a formal statement, presented the Declaration of Independence.

176. The Declaration of Independence; what it said to the World.— The simple and yet luminous words of this Declaration were written by Jefferson. His draft was prepared in his lodgings, on a little writing desk which still exists. Jefferson, in after years, delighted to tell how the final vote was hastened by the extremely hot weather and by the fact that there was a stable near by, and swarms of flies came in through the open windows and added much to the discomfort of the patriots already worn out with the debate and the heat.

JEFFERSON READING THE DECLARATION OF INDEPENDENCE TO FRANKLIN.

Jefferson read his "fair copy" of the Declaration to his friend Benjamin Franklin. The old philosopher was delighted with the terse style and the vigorous sentences.

"That's good; that's right to the point," said he; "that will make King George wince. I wish I had written it myself."

One of Franklin's biographers declares that it is fortunate that Franklin did not compose the Declaration, for he would surely have put a joke into the immortal document!

Every line and sentence of the Declaration of Independence stirred the hearts of the people then, and it does even now, after the lapse of more than one hundred and twenty-four years. It embodies in a noble and enduring form the hopes, feelings, convictions, and aspirations of every true American. When first proclaimed, it said in thunder tones to all the world that here was a people in far-away America willing to give their fortunes and their lives for what they believed to be right.

177. Independence declared.—On the second of July, 1776, the sub-committee of five patriots submitted to Congress the important document. There was deep silence as the solemn and earnest words were slowly read. Hearts beat faster and eyes flashed at the recital of the tyranny of the king and the sufferings of the people.

A three days' discussion followed. Jefferson remained silent under the sharp criticism, but the genial old philosopher, Franklin, sat next to him and soothed his feelings by telling him stories that fitted the case.

At last the great Declaration of Independence, in its final form, was adopted, July 4, 1776.

During the discussion there was intense excitement in and around the old State House in Philadelphia, where Congress was in session. Thousands thronged about the building, watching the barred doors and closed window shutters with feverish anxiety. The faces of the crowd are turned upward to the steeple, for there hangs a bell brought from London nearly a quarter of a century before, bearing the prophetic and singularly appropriate words of Scripture, "Proclaim liberty throughout the land unto all the inhabitants thereof."

LIBERTY BELL, INDEPENDENCE HALL, PHILADELPHIA.

It had been arranged by some one that the bell should be rung the moment the Declaration of Independence was adopted. The old bell-ringer placed a small boy at the hall door to await the signal of the doorkeeper. When at last the vote for independence was declared, the doorkeeper gave the signal, and the boy ran out shouting, "Ring, ring, ring!"
And the old bell-ringer did ring as he never rang before!

THE PEOPLE WAITING FOR THE FINAL VOTE ON THE DECLARATION.

178. How the Declaration was received by the People.—After it had passed Congress, the Declaration was sent to be read to the people throughout the thirteen colonies. It was received everywhere with the greatest joy. Bells were rung, cannon were fired, fireworks were burned, and flags were flung to the breeze. The bands played martial music, and even the smallest towns and villages were in a blaze of excitement. Washington ordered the Declaration to be read to all the brigades of the patriot army in and around New York City. The occasion was celebrated the same night by pulling down the leaden statue of George III on Bowling Green, and casting it into bullets.
The magic word was INDEPENDENCE.

John Adams truthfully predicted that these demonstrations of joy would be reflected in many a year to come by the people of our free country.

The eloquent words of the Declaration of Independence had been pronounced, but it was left for Washington and his little army to make it good.

England at this time was the most powerful nation in the world. Her navy was large, and her army was fully equipped and well drilled. Her resources were vast, and she had now made up her mind to crush the "rebels" in America. To men in foreign lands it seemed madness for the feeble colonies in America to resist the royal power of England.

The Declaration of Independence after a time was signed by fifty-six delegates from all the colonies.

179. Incidents connected with the Great Event.—If we look at a facsimile of the signatures to the Declaration, we notice that the name of Stephen Hopkins, of Rhode Island, was written with a tremulous hand. This was due to a partial paralysis. After he had signed, he smiled at his irregular penmanship and said, "You see my hand trembles, but my heart doesn't!"

John Hancock's signature is noted for its big, bold letters.

"There," said he, "John Bull can read that without 'specs'!"

As they gathered round to sign their names to the document, "pledging their lives, their fortune, and their sacred honor" to maintain and defend their action, every one of them understood very well that, if this revolution failed and, he should be captured, he was liable to be hanged as a traitor.

John Hancock said to a group of the signers, "We must stand by each other; no pulling different ways—we must all hang together in this matter."

"Yes," said Franklin, "we must indeed, or we shall all hang separately!"

The Fourth day of July, marked by the momentous event popularly known as the adoption of the "Declaration of Independence," has properly become our National Holiday. The day has been celebrated, just as our forefathers said it would be, with the firing of cannon, the ringing of bells, parades, and bonfires. From that day to the present, the immortal document has been listened to with reverence by our people.

180. What the Declaration of Independence should mean to us.— Thus we have traced the growth of the passion for liberty which finally reached its loftiest expression in this noble Declaration. Read it and let it grow into your memory. Do not forget that lovers of liberty, the world over, regard it as the sublimest state paper ever produced by man, marking the grandest advance in political progress ever made by the human race.

To us of the present day its chief charm lies in its noble beginning and its no less noble end. We care little now about the faults and the follies of King George, but the bold assertions of great truths in the opening sentences of the Declaration appeal as warmly to us to-day as they did to those for whom they were first written.

It is interesting to know that it was signed by men of lofty purpose and exalted character, every one of whom held to his last day a reputation never dishonored. These were the chosen men, worthy to be leaders with Washington of the young nation.

For good or evil this most momentous step was now taken. There was no choice left the colonies but to win by hard fighting or to be crushed by their enemy.

CHAPTER XIV.
THE BURGOYNE CAMPAIGN.

181. First Campaign for the Control of the Hudson fails.—It did not require much intelligence on the part of the British government to perceive that it would be wise policy to separate if possible one group of its revolting colonies from the rest. This was practicable only along the line of the Hudson. The two long lakes, Champlain and George, with the navigable river, almost made a great water highway from Canada on the north to the sea on the south.

The plan to cut off New England from the other colonies was acted upon in the summer of 1776. Carleton, a most efficient British general, came down from Canada, captured Crown Point, and got as far as Ticonderoga, when, having heard nothing of Howe, who was to come up from the south, he was forced by the lateness of the season to return. Howe had been delayed and baffled by Washington until it was too late to march north to meet Carleton. Thus the first campaign for the control of the Hudson proved a failure.

182. The Plan for the Second Campaign.—The British ministry at once planned for another attempt during the next summer. This time the invasion was to be carried out by three separate armies working towards a common point. The main attack was to be made from the north. The army in Canada was to march south, capture Ticonderoga, and go down the Hudson to Albany. This part of the campaign was entrusted to General Burgoyne.

Meanwhile Sir William Howe was to go up the Hudson and join his forces with those of Burgoyne at Albany. Now, as there were many Tories in central New York, and also powerful Indian tribes friendly to the British cause, a small force under the command of Colonel St. Leger was to sail up the St. Lawrence to Lake Ontario, land at Oswego, and then march down the Mohawk valley to join Burgoyne on the Hudson.

The English government built great hopes upon Burgoyne's expedition. No expense or effort was spared to make it a success. Money and supplies were furnished without stint.

183. Burgoyne begins Operations with a Great Army and Much Show.—When Burgoyne opened his campaign in the early summer of 1777, he had command of the best army that had yet taken the field in America. There were about four thousand English veterans, three thousand Germans, or Hessians as they were called, nearly five hundred Indian warriors, and a small force of Canadians. Most of the soldiers, as well as the officers, were veterans. Forty cannon, well served and equipped, made up the artillery train.

It was a splendid and imposing sight when this army in the middle of June sailed into Lake Champlain in a large flotilla with bands playing and banners flying. Burgoyne was a clever, agreeable, and well-bred man, and a brave soldier; but he was vain, headstrong, and self-confident.

The British general served a great feast to his Indian allies on the shore of the lake near Crown Point. He was dressed in showy uniform, and so were all of his chief officers. He made a pompous speech to his savage guests, who were adorned with war paint on their faces and eagles' feathers in their hair. He told them not to scalp the wounded, nor murder aged men, helpless women, or children. These "wild hyenas," as Burke called them in one of his great speeches before the English Parliament, promised to obey their "great white father."

The sturdy settlers knew what an Indian promise meant, and they speedily packed their goods and sent their families across the Green Mountains to the Connecticut Valley. Burgoyne had written poetry, and many poor plays, and so now he wrote in his high-flown style an address to the American people. All were warned against driving off their cattle, hiding their corn, and breaking down the bridges in his way. He threatened to let loose his savages upon them if they disobeyed. He also made a stirring address to his soldiers, in which he gave out the famous watchword, "This army must not retreat."

184. The Capture of Ticonderoga and what followed.—Every one supposed that Fort Ticonderoga would be a barrier to Burgoyne. Unfortunately the commander, St. Clair, had failed to secure a neighboring position which commanded the fortress. No one thought it possible to drag cannon up the steep and rugged sides of this mountain; but the British general worked night and day in hewing out a path, and with oxen dragged up his cannon and placed them in position to pour a plunging fire into the fort.

The next morning the top of the crag, now named Mount Defiance, was swarming with British troops. St. Clair saw with amazement the trap in which he was caught. The next night the far-famed fortress was abandoned, and the Continental army retreated southward. At daybreak the British and the Hessians sprang to arms, ready to follow sharply both by land and water the retreating army. So hot was the pursuit that the Americans were forced to destroy their boats. All the wagon-loads of arms, stores, and baggage fell into British hands.

There was a sharp fight a few days afterwards in the woods at a place called Hubbardton, where the rear guard of the Americans, under Warner, was surprised early in the morning, while the men were cooking breakfast. They made a gallant and stubborn resistance against the picked veterans of

Burgoyne's army. Warner was outnumbered and defeated, but the pursuit was so checked that St. Clair was able to bring what was left of his army safely to Fort Edward, where he joined Schuyler.

185. Burgoyne, elated by Success, begins to make Blunders.—The curtain now falls upon the first act of this great war drama. Burgoyne had been highly favored. Ticonderoga had fallen in a night. Everybody was astounded. The news fell like a sound of doom over the land. Washington wrote to Schuyler: "The evacuation of Ticonderoga is an event of chagrin and surprise not apprehended, nor within the compass of my reasoning."

Burgoyne now began to boast that victory would certainly crown his future movements, and even predicted the speedy end of the war and the submission of the colonies. He hurried off a special messenger to King George, telling the king that everything was going just as he wished it. The king rushed into the queen's apartments, says Walpole, clapping his hands and shouting, "I have beat them! I have beat all the Americans."

In reality, Burgoyne's troubles were just beginning.

In his haste to crush the Americans before they could combine against him, Burgoyne began to make serious blunders. For instance, it was a fatal mistake when he decided on marching to Fort Edward through the wilderness, instead of going back to Ticonderoga and proceeding thence up Lake George and on to Fort Edward and the Hudson. Time, that all-important factor in military campaigns, was lost sight of by this over-confident British general. Again, Burgoyne made another serious mistake in underestimating the fighting qualities of his enemy.

186. General Schuyler carries out a Masterly Policy.—Fortunately for the Americans, Schuyler was an able and experienced general, and Washington knew it. He had less than five thousand poorly armed men, but he faced the situation bravely. He knew that if he could delay the British invaders for a time, men enough would rally for the defense of their homes to meet his foe in open battle. He did at once the best thing possible. He put every obstacle in Burgoyne's way that ingenuity could devise or experience suggest. He made the axe and the crowbar help him.

Hundreds of trees were felled across the road. All the cattle were driven out of reach. The country was stripped of all provisions. The bridges were burnt, the creeks choked with stumps and stones, and the wood-roads were destroyed. The aspect of things began to change. Schuyler did his work well. He abandoned Fort Edward and fell back to Stillwater, where he entrenched himself and waited.

It is only about twenty-six miles from Skenesboro to Fort Edward, but it took Burgoyne twenty-four days to march this distance, and even then he had to wait two weeks longer for the arrival of his artillery. New roads had to be made, forty bridges built, and supplies and heavy ammunition carried through an almost impassable wilderness.

187. The Sturdy Pioneers of the North rise in Defense of their Homes.—Meanwhile, what were the stout-hearted pioneers of the north doing? The time for prompt action had come. The frontiersmen rose nobly to the demands of the situation. Burgoyne's Indians, ever since they left the Canadian border, had been ravaging and scalping. Never was a British general more mistaken than when he thought such bloody work would frighten the American people. It aroused the fierce spirit of revenge in them as no other act could have done.

188. The Murder of Jane McCrea.—The sad story of Jane McCrea has been read and re-read ever since this beautiful girl was tomahawked and scalped by Burgoyne's savages. It is not certain just how it happened. It is true that a party of Indians seized and carried away Miss McCrea, and a Mrs. McNeil with whom she was visiting in the latter's home near Fort Edward.

It is also known that Jane was betrothed to one of Burgoyne's officers, and as her own home was in New Jersey, it is probable that the unfortunate girl was planning to meet her lover.

Some say that the Indians quarreled over a barrel of rum that was to be given them as a reward on her safe arrival; others claim that a band of American militia fired into the party. At all events, Mrs. McNeil came alone to the English camp.

The next day the body of the murdered girl was found near a spring, pierced with three bullets. An Indian came into camp with a scalp, which

Mrs. McNeil recognized as that of her friend by its black, silky hair, more than a yard long.

There was nothing unusual about the murder, for it was only one of many such. The deed has, however, been woven into song and story, which have been repeated with endless variations in detail for more than six-score years. The name "Jenny McCrea" became a watchword to the stout and resolute farmers who were hastening from far and near to the scene of action.

189. Burgoyne gets his First Hard Blow; Desperate Fighting in the Mohawk Valley.—The first hard blow Burgoyne received came from the west. Colonel St. Leger, as we remember, was marching with seventeen hundred men down the Mohawk Valley. He came to a stronghold called Fort Stanwix, and ordered its commander, Colonel Gansevoort, to surrender. The demand met with a pointed refusal, and the British began a regular siege.

HERKIMER DIRECTING THE BATTLE.

Everywhere through this beautiful valley was great excitement. General Herkimer, a militia officer over sixty years of age, a thorough master of Indian warfare, was a man of might in this section. Eight hundred hardy pioneers of this frontier region rallied at the veteran's call and marched with him to the relief of the fort. The younger officers would not listen to the old general's advice to move with caution.

"You," said the old patriot, stung by their taunts, "you, who want to fight so badly now, will be the first to run when you smell burnt powder."

There was not a proper advance guard, and the men fell into an ambush of the Tories and their Indian allies on the steep slope of a ravine, near a place called Oriskany. A desperate fight began hand to hand and from tree to tree. The worst thunderstorm of the season put an end to the battle for about an hour.

Herkimer was shot in the leg in the early part of the encounter. He was lifted from his fallen horse and placed, at his own request, upon his saddle, propped against a beech tree. The old soldier lighted his pipe, and though the bullets were whistling about him, and men were falling thick and fast within a few yards, he coolly continued to direct the battle, giving his orders calmly, as if on a parade ground. Through the leafy depths of the forest rang the clashing of steel, the crack of rifle, and, above all, the hideous yells of the savages. Suddenly the Indians raised the retreating cry of "Oonah!" and in an instant they were gone! The desperate fighting was too much for the Tories, and they too fled, leaving the patriots in possession of the hard-earned field.

Thus was fought one of the most hotly contested and, for the numbers engaged, one of the deadliest of the Revolutionary battles. No quarter was given on either side. Of the eight hundred men under Herkimer that fought on that sultry August day, only about a third ever saw their homes again.

The brave old Dutchman was carried to his home, where, propped up in bed with pillows, he calmly smoked his pipe, read his Bible, and waited serenely for the end. He died a few days later. He had fought what was perhaps the most desperate battle of the Revolution, and he was victor.

190. Gallant Defense of Fort Stanwix; First American Flag raised.—In the mean time St. Leger, in spite of this heavy check, moved up to within one hundred and fifty yards of the fort and again demanded its surrender. The gallant Gansevoort made a flag from portions of an old blue coat, a white shirt, and some strips from a red flannel petticoat, and raised it above five captured British flags and defied his foes to take the fort. We should remember the date, August 6, 1777; for it is claimed that this was the first American flag with stars and stripes that was ever flung to the breeze.

RAISING "OLD GLORY" FOR THE FIRST TIME.

While the siege was in full progress, the besiegers suddenly broke up their camps and retreated toward Canada in great confusion, leaving behind them their cannon, supplies, and even their tents. What was the matter? Arnold had been sent north by Washington immediately after the fall of Ticonderoga, and had arrived at Schuyler's headquarters three weeks before. Restless and impatient, he was despatched by Schuyler to relieve the brave garrison. On his way he captured and was going to hang as a spy a half-witted but ugly young Tory. The boy's mother begged his life.

Arnold granted the mother's request on condition that the young fellow should take some friendly Indians with him and hasten to the British camp and so alarm St. Leger as to induce him to raise the siege and retreat! The frightened Tory set out on his perilous errand, his brother being held by Arnold as a hostage, and reached the British camp just as the Indians were holding a "pow-wow" over the dubious enterprise in which they were engaged.

As the savages saw the Tory's coat full of bullet holes, and listened to his wonderful story of his own narrow escape, and heard that Arnold was close on their heels with two thousand regulars, the savages said, "The pow-wow said we must go"; and go they did in utmost haste. In vain the British officers stormed and swore. The troops were seized with a panic. St. Leger and all his army retreated in disorder, broken and beaten, to Oswego, and afterwards to Montreal. The valley of the Mohawk was safe. St. Leger's defeat dealt a severe blow to the plans and prospects of Burgoyne. Arnold was now able to rejoin Schuyler.

191. Burgoyne plans a Raid into the Country to secure Supplies.—All this time Burgoyne was hard pushed for food. Every pound of bread and meat had to be brought from Canada. Nobody but Tories would sell him an ounce of beef or an ear of corn.

The British general was also anxious to strike a blow at the good people of New England. He knew that the supplies of the patriots were stored at Bennington. Supplies he must have. On August 11 he sent off Colonel Baum with about five hundred Hessians, Indians, and Tories on a plundering trip to this little village.

Four days later a second division of about six hundred men was sent under Colonel Breymann to help Baum, for it was evident that the situation was looking ugly. Instead of raiding the country, Baum, learning that the militia were gathering in all directions, entrenched himself on a hill about four miles from Bennington and waited for reinforcements.

192. The Men of New England rally to defend their Homes.—The men of New England, instead of waiting till their houses were burnt, their crops destroyed, and their wives and children scalped, were rapidly arriving from far and near to meet their hated foe. The instant the Hessians and Indians threatened to come over the line, the men of New England knew there was only one thing to do and it must be done at once. That was to kill as many of the enemy as they could and drive the rest back. They had already prepared for this.

Not every man was able to act as did staunch old John Langdon, who kept a store in Portsmouth. He said to the New Hampshire Assembly: "I have three thousand dollars in hard money. I will pledge my plate for as much more. I have seventy hogsheads of rum, which shall be sold. Our old friend John Stark, who defended the rail fence at Bunker Hill, will work like a beaver to stop Burgoyne."

Among the rugged hills of northern New England no other man had such a personal following as had John Stark—a man of dauntless courage, rough simplicity, and real Yankee shrewdness.

In appearance Stark was a man of medium size, well proportioned, and of great strength and endurance. It is remarkable that in all his years of hard service in the French and Indian wars, and in the many severe battles of the Revolution, he had never received a wound. He lived to be ninety-four years of age. He survived all the high officers that had taken part in the Revolution except Sumter, the famous southern general.

Messengers rode on fast horses over the hills with orders for the men to rally at once. Each man packed his knapsack, grasped his rifle, left the women to get in the crops, and started for Charlestown on the Connecticut River, where Stark had raised his standard. Old men of seventy and even boys of fifteen turned out. Some of the farmers brought clock weights, some their pewter spoons and porringers, to be melted into bullets. The metal was kept running into the bullet moulds night and day. An old rusty cannon was found; it was mounted on a pair of cart wheels and dragged over the Green Mountains.

The story is told of one mother whose boy of only fifteen was ready to start, but had no coat. The patriot mother took a meal bag, made a hole for the head, two more for the arms, cut off the feet of a pair of her long stockings which she sewed on for sleeves,—and hurried him away to Stark's camp!

193. How John Stark whipped the British at Bennington.—Stark was now ready to march against Baum. On August 14 he was within a mile of the British camp. The next day it rained heavily. Fighting in such pouring torrents was out of the question. The Hessians worked hard on the entrenchments all day, and Stark sheltered his men in brush huts and under the lee of fences.

One hundred men from the Berkshire Hills arrived in the night. A minister who could fight as well as preach came with them in a sulky.

"General Stark," said he, "we have never had a chance to fight, and if you don't give us a chance now, we shall never turn out again."

"Do you want to fight now in the rain and at night?" said Stark.

"No," said the good man.

"Well, then," said Stark, "if the Lord gives us sunshine once more, and I don't give you fighting enough, you needn't turn out again."

Old soldiers who had fought behind the rail fence at Bunker Hill with Stark, and who had been in the front ranks with him at Trenton, knew that there would be no boy's play in the coming battle. The next morning, which was Saturday, August 16, broke clear and hot.

STARK ADDRESSING HIS MEN BEFORE THE BATTLE OF BENNINGTON.

The ever-active and energetic Stark determined to storm the hill before reinforcements could reach the enemy. This was a desperate undertaking for country militia armed only with muskets and fowling pieces, without bayonets or side arms. Baum was well entrenched on a hill behind breastworks defended by highly disciplined veterans.

About midday Stark, calling his men together in a large field, leaped to the topmost rail of a fence, steadied himself by a tall post, and addressed his troops in the historic words: "Now, my men, yonder are the Hessians. They are bought for seven pounds tenpence a man. Are you worth more? Prove it. To-night the American flag floats over yonder hill, or Molly Stark sleeps a widow!"

Foreseeing that there would be close work with the Tories, who were dressed in farmers' clothes, like most of his own men, Stark gave orders that a corn husk in the hatband should be the badge of his own men. Five hundred men were sent to form in the rear of Baum's entrenchment, and two hundred more were massed on the right as a flanking party.

It is now about three o'clock. With all his men in position Stark gives the word "Forward!" The battle begins in earnest. With wild shouts the farmer-soldiers press forward, using their rifles with deadly effect. The Indians, panic-stricken, yelling like demons, take to their heels, and make their escape into the forest. They have no intention of being caught in a trap. The Hessians stand their ground and fight bravely.

For two hours there is hot work, "one continuous roar," as Stark afterwards said. The old cannon on cart wheels fires stones, for there are no cannon balls! At last Stark leads his men in a fierce charge. Baum falls mortally wounded, and his men surrender. A wild hurrah goes up. The battle is won.

It was in the nick of time. Breymann arrived with fresh troops and began a lively attack. Stark rallied his men. A hundred and fifty "Green Mountain boys," hearing the roar of the battle, came up in the rear at just the right moment. They fell upon the Hessians like a thunderbolt, routed them, and would have captured them all if it had not been nearly dark. As it was, the enemy retreated in haste under cover of the darkness.

The pioneer settlers of New England had proved themselves more than a match for entrenched regulars. Stark had beaten two of Burgoyne's best officers in a pitched battle. The victory was won by the sheer hard fighting of men who were well led.

194. Mighty Efforts of the Patriots to crush Burgoyne.—The battle of Bennington was a severe blow for Burgoyne. His army never fully recovered from it. A thousand of his best men were lost, besides cannon, arms, and supplies of war. Even the savages began to leave in large numbers.

The effect of this brilliant victory on the country was magical. It began to be thought that the whole of Burgoyne's army might be captured. Militia came in increasing numbers even from points on the Atlantic coast.

Washington had some time before sent two of his best officers—Arnold, who as a fighter in pitched battles was unsurpassed, and Morgan, who came with five hundred sharpshooters, each man of whom, it was said, could hit a squirrel with his rifle at a distance of three hundred yards.

THE BATTLE MONUMENT AT BENNINGTON, VT.

Congress, misinformed, now set aside the noble General Schuyler and sent Gates, a schemer and intriguer, to supersede him. Schuyler's wise forethought and steadfast courage had already begun to show results. By a stupid blunder of the British government, orders for Sir William Howe to march north to aid Burgoyne had been delayed.

General Lincoln had moved with two thousand men to the rear of the British army. The outposts of Ticonderoga had been retaken, and the road to Canada was thus closed for help or retreat.

195. The Hard-fought Battle near Saratoga.—Burgoyne soon found that he must do something. About the middle of September he crossed to the west bank of the Hudson and came within two miles of the American camp at Bemis Heights. Here took place, on September 18, a hotly contested battle known as that of Freeman's Farm. If Gates had been an able general, probably the British army would have been crushed and the Burgoyne campaign ended then and there. As it was, the deadly fire of the riflemen inflicted a severe blow.

Gates did not follow up his advantage. The two armies glared at each other. There was no rest for either side. There was sharp skirmishing all along the lines. The nights were made hideous by the howls of large packs of wolves that were attracted by the partially buried bodies of those slain in the battle.

At last, on October 7, Burgoyne came out from his entrenched camp with fifteen hundred picked men and ten cannon. A bloody hand-to-hand battle was fought.

Gates had removed Arnold from his command. Angry and desperate, this impetuous but hard fighter placed himself at the head of a detachment of the Continental troops, and under a terrific fire led the men to battle. Mounted on a dark-brown horse, he rode at full gallop over the field. He was greeted with wild cheers. "Call that fellow back," said Gates, "or he will do something rash." With mad fury his men charged and drove the enemy at the point of the bayonet.

In the final retreat a wounded Hessian, lying on the ground, took aim and fired at Arnold. The bullet killed his horse and wounded the general in the same leg that had been hit by a musket ball nearly two years before, at the storming of Quebec. A thousand times better would it have been had the bullet gone through his heart!

As Arnold fell, one of his men rushed up and was just going to bayonet the soldier who had shot his beloved general; but Arnold cried, "In Heaven's name, don't kill him! He is a fine fellow!" This was the moment when the general whom Washington so much admired for his rash bravery should have died.

In less than an hour the British were driven back and retreated behind their entrenchments.

Some time afterward, when Arnold had turned traitor and captured an American officer, he asked him, "What will your people do with me if they catch me?"

"If my countrymen catch you," replied the fearless patriot, "they will first cut off your lame leg, which was wounded at Quebec and Saratoga, and bury it with the honors of war, and afterwards hang the rest of your body on a gallows."

Darkness alone stopped the battle. General Morgan, as he saw a brave Scottish officer riding everywhere along the line, said to one of his best marksmen: "That is General Fraser. I admire and honor him, but it is necessary that he should die. Take your station in yonder bushes and do your duty." Shortly afterwards, this splendid Scotchman, who said to an aid when warned of his peril, "My duty forbids me to fly from danger," fell mortally wounded.

196. Effect of the Great Victory at Saratoga.—Such was the battle of Bemis Heights, or Saratoga. It was really fought within a very few rods of the place where the battle of Freeman's Farm occurred.

The rest of the story is soon told. Burgoyne retreated through the storm to Saratoga. The attempt to escape was hopeless. He was hemmed in on every side. The "trap" which the best British officers had foreseen, had been sprung. There was only one thing to do, and that was to yield to the inevitable.

Burgoyne, with his army of about six thousand men, surrendered October 17, 1777.

The battle of Saratoga has justly been called "one of the decisive battles of history." It made a profound impression in Europe. It was the defeat of Burgoyne's army that convinced France that it was time to come to the help of the American colonies. It lifted the cloud of gloom which had settled upon the hearts of the American people, and which had wrung despondent words even from the hopeful Washington.

From the day of this memorable victory until liberty was fully realized, four years later, in the final surrender at Yorktown, no true American gave up the idea of final triumph.

CHAPTER XV.
WASHINGTON AND THE REVOLUTION.

197. Boyhood and Youth of George Washington.—During the infancy of our nation there were many staunch and noble patriots; but far above all stood, and stands to-day, the majestic figure of George Washington. He came upon the stage at just the right time to give the vigor of his manhood to the military service of his country, and the maturity of his judgment to the formation of the new government and later to the presidency. He was born in Virginia on February 22, 1732.

In those days the country was thinly settled, good schools were rare, and even the rich planters did not find it easy to have their children well disciplined in learning. The future president had only a plain education in reading, writing, and arithmetic. In his childhood he showed a martial spirit. While at school he was often the captain of a little military company with paper hats and wooden swords, and even in their marches and sham battles the boy exhibited somewhat of the soldierly bearing and honorable character that distinguished him later in life.

He took an interest in study and enjoyed reading good books. He wrote an excellent hand, and some productions in his superior penmanship have been kept to this day, showing remarkable neatness and accuracy. They comprise lessons in geometry, forms of business papers, and even some neatly written extracts in verse. He studied by himself book-keeping and mathematics, especially land surveying, which was much needed in that new country. These studies proved of great value to him in after years.

198. Boyhood's Sports.—Washington when a lad was robust, fond of athletic games, running, jumping, and wrestling. In these healthful sports he outdid his comrades. He could surpass them all in throwing a stone across the Rappahannock. The boys all liked him, for he was generous and open-hearted, and they used to make him a judge in their disputes.

He was especially given to horsemanship, and delighted to break in the dashing young colts, and even to train dangerous horses.

199. Washington's Love for his Mother.—When Washington was about eleven years old his father died, and the family was broken up. George's mother, like the mothers of most great men, had a strong, upright character and brought up her children exceedingly well. Like all worthy boys, he dearly loved his mother and was willing to be guided by her wishes.

When about fourteen, he had a great longing to go to sea. Ships of war sometimes anchored in the Potomac River, near his home. The officers used to visit his brother's estate at Mount Vernon, and the boy no doubt listened eagerly to their stories of naval battles and adventures.

He passionately desired to become a sailor. His mother at last gave an unwilling consent. His trunk was packed and all was ready. But when the hour for parting came, the quiet entreaty of his mother, "Don't go, George," with tears running down her cheeks, changed his purpose.

This good mother lived until 1789, when she died at the age of eighty-two. Her lot was a rare one. She lived to see her son the most illustrious of living men, with a spotless fame, and as much admired for the purity of his character as for the greatness of his deeds. It is said that she used to listen to praise of him in silence, and only answered: "Yes, George was always a good boy!"

200. His Faithful Work as a Surveyor in the Virginia Wilderness.—It seems strange now, as we look back on his early life, to see how Washington unconsciously prepared himself for his great future. He employed a trainer and took a severe course of lessons in skillful fencing and sword drill, and, besides, he made a careful study of military science and tactics.

GEORGE WASHINGTON.

He became prominent as a young man of superb vigor, fond of study and work, and full of promise of great achievements. So Lord Fairfax, an eccentric nobleman, who was a great fox hunter and who much admired his young friend's bold riding, selected him to survey the thousands of acres of forest land that the king had granted to him beyond the Blue Ridge. This was a pretty large undertaking for a boy of sixteen! But the youngster was enough of a man to do it. He and his assistant took each a horse, a gun, an axe, surveyor's tools, and camp outfit. They spent months in the vast forests and among the mountains; cutting their paths through woods, fording rivers, facing the drenching storms, surveying and measuring by day, and writing out the notes in the light of camp-fires by night; living on the game they shot,—wild turkeys, squirrels, rabbits, and deer; often meeting Indians.

All this was just the school to prepare him for coming duties and for the great career he never then dreamed of. Here he gained in a high degree the hardy virtues of courage, self-reliance, promptness in danger, quick and prudent foresight, and unflinching endurance under difficulties.

On his return, young Washington had done his work so well that the Governor appointed him public surveyor. It was a prominent office, and he filled it honorably. His surveys were so correct that it is said they are used even to this day.

Lord Fairfax lived many years after this. He was bitterly opposed to the war of the Revolution. One day he heard the people shouting and cheering near his home. He asked his old negro servant what it all meant, and he was told that Lord Cornwallis had surrendered to General Washington. At this the old man groaned, "Take me to bed, Joe; it is high time for me to die!"

201. His Work as an Army Officer.—Washington was twenty-three years old when he was appointed on the staff of General Braddock. We have read in Chapter VIII the story of this disastrous campaign. The choice proved the Governor's insight into Washington's remarkable character. His surprising bravery, his insensibility to fear amid the whistling of bullets, his coolness in danger, and his maturity of judgment, really saved the whole campaign and rescued Braddock's shattered forces from total ruin.

WASHINGTON CROSSING A RIVER ON A RAFT IN THE WILDERNESS DURING MID-WINTER.

Shortly afterwards Washington withdrew for a while from military life. In 1759, he married Mrs. Martha Custis, a young widow with two small children and a large fortune. A short time after their marriage Colonel and Mrs. Washington, or Lady Washington, as she was called, retired to Mount Vernon, a fine estate of eight thousand acres which he had inherited from his brother Lawrence. His many visitors who expected to see a heroic figure could not have been disappointed in his personal appearance.

Washington was a man of noble presence, six feet two in height, of dignified and courtly manners and a noble military air. With health and wealth, a happy home and all that makes life pleasant, he was enjoying his honors and the comforts of rural life.

202. Advancement in Political Honors.—So high was the trust reposed by all in Washington that he was now elected to the Virginia legislature, the House of Burgesses, a signal proof of popular confidence. He always studied the business of every day carefully, though he seldom made speeches. When he first entered and took his seat, in 1759, the Speaker of the House rose and in eloquent language returned thanks to him in the name of the colony for his services during the war.

Washington stood up to reply; blushed, stammered, trembled, and could not utter a word.

"Sit down, Mr. Washington," said the Speaker with a smile; "your modesty equals your valor, and that surpasses the power of any language I possess."

For the next sixteen years Washington's life passed quietly and contentedly. Then was heard the distant thunder of the coming Revolution.

We may be sure that Washington studiously watched the course of events, and often went back to Mount Vernon from the public meetings with an anxious mind.

203. Becomes Commander-in-Chief of the American Army.—Soon a problem presented itself before the Continental Congress of which Washington was a member. Who shall be chosen Commander-in-Chief of our armies? Who shall be singled out for this most difficult task?

There was one man to whom all turned. On a motion of John Adams of Massachusetts the choice was George Washington—"a gentleman from Virginia who is among us, and very well known to all of us." The choice was unanimous. It was a spontaneous tribute to his superior military experience and skill; to the strength and purity of his character, the ardor and unselfishness of his patriotism, and the perfect confidence which his whole career had inspired.

Washington, in the course of his brief and modest speech of acceptance, said his service would be freely given without salary, asking that only his expenses be paid, and of which he would keep a careful record. His expense-books, kept during the Revolution in his own neat handwriting, are still carefully preserved.

With the promptness which was a part of his self-training, he began at once his new duties. In a few days, as we have read in Chapter XII, he took command of the patriot army at Cambridge.

We know how Washington's well-planned siege shut up the British army in Boston all that summer and all the next winter until March, when his admirable strategy compelled the proud Howe to sail silently away. This achievement of the brave Virginia officer, and of his raw farmer-soldiers against the much larger force of British regulars, well deserved the gold medal given him by Congress.

204. Takes Command in New York; his Masterly Retreat.—Howe and Washington, after the evacuation of Boston, moved their armies to New York, each knowing the other would do so. The British plan was to take and hold the Hudson River and thus to separate the troublesome New England colonies from the others. The possession of New York was therefore of vast importance.

Washington arrived first, and as the Brooklyn Heights opposite New York controlled the latter city, he did well to occupy this position. But it would have been very unwise to place all his army there. He stationed about nine thousand men under General Putnam in Brooklyn. The rest he used across the river in the city, and to hold Fort Lee and Fort Washington.

Against Putnam's force the British brought an army of twenty thousand, stealing a night march, and with their greater number defeated our troops. This severe reverse, which could not have been prevented by him, Washington followed with a military success; for in the night, which fortunately happened to be very foggy, he silently and safely withdrew all our remaining troops across the East River from the overwhelming British force. The boats were managed by companies of Marblehead fishermen, who thus had an opportunity of doing a most signal service. When Howe the next morning moved his victorious regulars again to the attack, his enemy was gone!

This masterly retreat from the very sight and under the guns of the enemy gave Washington a great reputation. He managed and watched it personally, spending two days and two nights in his saddle, without rest or sleep!

205. Some of the Many Difficulties with which Washington had to struggle.—But now came the trouble that distressed Washington all through the war—the lack of soldiers. The British government sent over thousands of disciplined troops, and kept them well equipped.

The colonies were uncertain and irregular in furnishing soldiers. The colonial money used to pay them rapidly lost its value; so that Washington was continually distressed to procure and retain enough troops. Besides, the terms of enlistment were usually short—six months or even less—and thus his little army was constantly dwindling away. To add to his anxieties, the supply of cannon, guns, powder, clothing, food, and all needed equipments, was often painfully meager.

How then could Washington with his small and ill-furnished forces—his "ragged continentals"—oppose successfully the much larger and well-supplied troops of the enemy? To keep risking battles with an army much stronger than his own would invite defeat and ruin.

But there were some things he could do—watch the enemy sharply, harass and worry him by repeated small engagements, obstruct his plans, and whenever possible attack a small separate body and defeat or capture it.

This is exactly what Washington did, and often with consummate skill. He won his best moves because he first carefully fought over all his battles in his own brain, and then fought them out with the guns of his soldiers; for he had a faculty of inspiring his men with his own high purpose. They admired him as a hero, trusted him as a friend, and loved him as a father.

206. The Brilliant Victory at Trenton.—Washington had successfully withdrawn the troops from Brooklyn, but he knew perfectly well that with his scanty force of half-trained men he could not risk a battle with four times as many of the well-drilled enemy—it would be certain ruin to the patriot cause.Our army now had to retreat across New Jersey, the British following closely all the way! It was a distressing movement and it produced general gloom. The country was discouraged, Congress was discouraged, the army itself was becoming discouraged. The British said Washington did not dare to fight, and that the war was about over.In all this gloom there was only one ray of light: Washington never despaired! Sorely tried, he yet kept up his faith and hope. Sick at heart but ever resolute, he declared to his friends that if all others forsook him, he would retire to the backwoods of Virginia and there make a final stand against Great Britain.Reaching the Delaware, the great commander crossed into Pennsylvania. General Howe came up on the east side, and then spread out his army, placing a thousand Hessians at Trenton.

See what Washington did. On Christmas night, 1776, he crossed the Delaware to attack the Hessians. The river was so full of floating ice that the Marblehead soldiers found it very hard to manage the boats. After the crossing, the men marched nine miles through snow and hail, sometimes marking the whitened ground with blood from their shoeless feet.

THE NIGHT MARCH TO TRENTON.

As they drew near Trenton, Washington, who rode in front, asked a man chopping wood by the roadside:—

"Which way is the Hessian picket?"

"I do not know," was the surly answer.

"You may tell," said the officer at Washington's side, "for that is General Washington."

"God bless and prosper you!" cried the man instantly. "The picket is in that house, and the sentry stands near that tree."

The Hessians, who were celebrating Christmas with wild revelry, were surprised, and soon forced to surrender.

Washington was in great danger from the superior forces of the enemy close at hand, and was obliged immediately to recross the Delaware with his tired troops and his prisoners. The weather was so severe that two men were frozen to death that Christmas night. Notwithstanding Washington's haste, he found time to visit the dying Hessian Commander, Colonel Rahl, and speak kindly to him.

It was a battle of this kind that showed the courage and genius of a great general who, in the midst of the most unfavorable circumstances, could plan well, fight well, and outwit the enemy! It was such masterful watchfulness and bravery as this that saved the country. Mighty applause now rang all through the land! "Hurrah for Washington, and hurrah for his ragged but plucky little army!"

Well might the people shout, for this was the first real victory of the continental army. Lord Howe was very angry and said it would never do, and he sent Cornwallis to defeat this rebel general. Let us see what Cornwallis did. The British general marched from Princeton with about eight thousand men, and found Washington's army of some three thousand with its rear to the river. At about dusk he planted his own army in front, and then felt sure of his prey. "At last we have run down the old fox," said the over-confident British general as he went to bed in high spirits, "and we will bag him easily in the morning." The situation was indeed a dangerous one for the patriot army.

WASHINGTON BEFORE TRENTON.

207. How Washington surprised the British at Princeton.—During the night Washington left a front line of camp-fires burning, and a few soldiers noisily digging trenches and throwing up breastworks, while his entire army made a circuitous march around Cornwallis, got in his rear, attacked Princeton early, captured three regiments and a lot of supplies, and moved on to Morristown, a strong place where the British dared not attack him.

In this battle the commanding figure of Washington riding to and fro on his white horse made a notable object for the enemy's marksmen.

These two battles brought Washington great applause all over this country and through Europe. Frederick the Great, King of Prussia, said: "This young American general opens a fresh chapter in the art of war; England hasn't a man to match him."

208. How Washington helped to defeat Burgoyne.—During the next year, 1777, Washington was busy watching Lord Howe and keeping him confined closely in New York. Although he lacked the army with which to fight any great battle, yet he did the greatest service. The British planned this year, as we have just read <u>in the preceding chapter</u>, a second effort to occupy the Hudson and divide the colonies.

But, as we have seen, the plan was doomed to failure. Burgoyne was wrecked by Schuyler and Stark, and the Mohawk force was defeated by Arnold and Morgan. Then all depended on Howe's army which was to come up the Hudson. But Howe could not come! Washington was skillfully blocking his plans, so that the British general could spare no soldiers. And so resulted the great surrender at Saratoga—the most cheering victory during this period of the war.

Howe's army then went by sea to Philadelphia and wintered there.

209. Sufferings at Valley Forge.—Washington wintered at Valley Forge, not far away. The winter was very severe. The patriot army was ill-fed, ill-clothed, and unpaid. Hundreds of soldiers were barefoot, their bloody steps tracking the snow. Hungry, shivering, and bleeding, they keenly felt how much it cost to be a "ragged continental."

The money issued was almost worthless, fifty dollars of paper for one of specie. It took six months' pay to buy a pair of boots; for England counterfeited the continental money, brought over huge parcels of it, and put it into circulation. Congress seemed neglectful. Discouragement prevailed.

Washington seemed to have the care of the whole patriot cause on his shoulders alone. He had everything to do,—appealing perpetually to Congress for action; begging the Governors for aid; getting food, arms, ammunition, and clothing; recruiting and drilling the army; planning campaigns; and so working unceasingly in every direction.

210. Help from France; the Battle of Monmouth.—In the spring of 1778 help came. The French sent ships, soldiers, and officers, and again the sun began to shine. Their help was of vital importance. Perhaps we could never have got on without it.

Sir Henry Clinton, who had succeeded Lord Howe, fearing the approach of a French fleet, now made up his mind to leave Philadelphia and march across New Jersey to New York. Washington sent forward a division of his army under General Charles Lee to pursue the British and give them battle. The patriots, ready and eager to fight, came up with the enemy at Monmouth. Unfortunately, the mischief-making Lee, now known to have been little better than a traitor, ordered a retreat.

As Washington advanced with the main army, he was filled with surprise and anger to learn from stragglers of Lee's treacherous action. He set spurs to his horse and galloped to the front.

According to tradition, this was one of the very few times when Washington was thought to have lost his self-control. With a fierce oath he demanded of Lee what he meant by retreating. Washington's look, according to Lafayette, was terrible.

"What is the meaning of all this, sir?" he repeated.

There could be no good answer. Lee quailed before his angry commander.

Having sent the apparently treacherous officer to the rear, Washington showed at once his superb generalship. Like Sheridan at Cedar Creek, about which we shall hear later, he inspired his men with fresh courage and led them against the enemy. The continental army now showed the results of the long winter's drill at Valley Forge. The lines were re-formed, the main army was brought up, and the British were soon repulsed.

Clinton retreated during the same night. He reached New York and the protection of the fleet before the patriot army could overtake him.

Such was the battle of Monmouth, fought on a very hot and sultry Sunday in June, 1778. It was the last battle in the north, and practically closed the campaign for the control of the Middle States.

211. The Story of Mollie Pitcher.—The account of this battle would not be complete without the oft-told story of Mollie Pitcher. During the day a soldier having charge of a cannon was shot down at his post. His newly wedded wife, a young Irish woman, was at the time bringing water for the thirsty men from a neighboring spring. She saw her husband fall at the cannon he was serving, and heard his commander order the piece to be removed from the field. Instantly dropping her pail, Mollie seized the rammer and, stationing herself by the gun, performed her husband's duty with skill and courage all through the battle.

MOLLIE PITCHER TAKES HER HUSBAND'S PLACE AT MONMOUTH.

The soldiers gave her the nickname of Major Mollie, and being presented to General Washington the day after the battle, she received a sergeant's commission, and Congress gave her half-pay for life! Some of the French officers, it is said, were so delighted with her courage that they presented her with a hat full of gold pieces and christened her "La Capitaine"!

212. Washington plans the Yorktown Campaign.—In the spring of 1781, Washington was still hemming in Clinton at New York. In the south, where there had been severe fighting for two years, General Greene had driven Cornwallis from the Carolinas up to Virginia, and our generous friend, Lafayette, had helped push the British general to the point of land at Yorktown. Washington, learning this, arranged that the French fleet should sail there and prevent the escape of the enemy by sea.

Then Washington planned what has been regarded as the proudest achievement of the war. He decided to hurry his own army to Yorktown, and with it and the southern forces and the French fleet finish the seven years' struggle.

Yes; but if Clinton should hear of it, he would sail from New York and checkmate the plan. How could Washington do all this and keep Clinton in the dark? Everything turned on that. He kept up a lively show of activity around New York, and had decoy letters written to his distant generals to come and help him capture Clinton's army. Very strange, but those letters reached the British general!

When the right moment came, leaving a small force at New York for show, Washington by a swift and skillful movement moved his army of six thousand through New Jersey. The Commander-in-Chief was unsurpassed at keeping a secret. His own generals did not know where they were going. They marched to Elkton, at the head of the Chesapeake, and took ships for Yorktown.

The hour for the final success of the patriot cause had now come. Cornwallis was shut in by sea and land. Washington with his own hand fired the first cannon of the attack. This was on October 9, 1781.

By night and by day the sound of the heavy guns was incessantly heard. The shells of the besieged and besiegers crossed each other in the air.

At one time during the siege Washington, with many officers about him, was watching an assault with intense interest. Those who stood near him were afraid he would be hit by a chance shot, and one of his aids ventured to say that the situation was very much exposed.

"If you think so," replied he gravely, "you are at liberty to step back."

A little later a musket ball hit a cannon near the group and fell at Washington's feet. General Knox grasped his arm.

"My dear general," exclaimed he, "we can't spare you yet."

"It is a spent ball," answered the Commander-in-Chief quietly; "no harm is done."

When the redoubts were taken, he drew a long breath and said to Knox, "The work is done, and well done!" During the battle, a famous Virginia officer, Governor Nelson, who had raised troops and supplied money at his own risk, was asked what part of the town it would be best to fire upon. He pointed to a large, handsome building, which he thought was probably the enemy's headquarters. It was his own house!

213. The Superb Victory at Yorktown.—After a few days of fighting, Cornwallis found himself in so hopeless a condition that he made an unsuccessful attempt to escape. Shortly afterward he was forced to surrender with eleven thousand men, a hundred and sixty cannon, a huge amount of camp supplies, and ten thousand dollars in money. Five days after the surrender, General Clinton arrived with ships and heavy reinforcements. Too late, Sir Henry, too late!

When the news of the capture of Cornwallis reached London, Lord North, the British Prime Minister, walked up and down his room, wringing his hands and crying out, "O God! it is all over! It is all over!"

How unspeakably the great leader's heart must have rejoiced at this famous victory; the labors, anxieties, and sufferings of seven years ending at last in glorious triumph! The whole country gave way to transports of joy. Congress appointed a day of general thanksgiving and prayer, and voted special thanks to the distinguished generals and many other officers. It was felt that a death-blow had been given to England's efforts to crush the colonies.

The victory at Yorktown practically ended the war. It took several years for the country to recover from the wreck and ruin wrought, to frame the machinery of our new government, and to lay the solid foundations of this grand edifice of constitutional liberty. In all this work of nation-building Washington was a prominent actor, no less sagacious as a statesman than as a skilled warrior.

214. Washington, the First President of the United States.—When it came to the choice of a first president, all eyes turned to that one stately figure—to him who had saved his country in war, and who in peace could best carry its precious interests safely in his great brain and heart. He was unanimously elected—not a vote for any other person—an honor never paralleled. With his usual modesty he would have declined; but his sense of duty and his willingness to serve his country made him accept.

His journey to New York was one continued ovation. Bells were rung, cannon fired, and eloquent addresses made. All the vessels in New York harbor were gayly decked with flags. When the dignified President-elect landed, the salutes of cannon, the ringing of bells, and the shouts of the crowd were multiplied tenfold.

On April 30, 1789, Washington took the solemn oath to perform the duties of the President of the United States.

On this important occasion he was dressed in a suit of dark brown cloth of American manufacture. He wore white silk stockings, silver buckles and a steel-hilted sword. His hair was powdered and tied behind, according to the fashion of that time. The day was given up to rejoicings; and in the evening there were illuminations and fireworks.

Washington was reëlected, and served his country honorably for two terms of four years each. His administration was worthy in every way of his great ability, his statesmanship, and his exalted patriotism.

MARTHA WASHINGTON.

215. Washington retires to Private Life.—Beloved and honored by a whole people, but weary of public life, Washington at last retired to his beautiful and beloved Mount Vernon to enjoy a well-earned repose. He took up his former manner of living. He began to repair his buildings and to improve his estate. His good wife, Martha, said that she and the general when he left the presidency felt like children just released from school, and she spoke of her satisfaction in settling down again to the "duties of an old-fashioned Virginia housekeeper, steady as a clock, busy as a bee, and cheerful as a cricket."

Washington was a model farmer. He gave personal attention to every detail. He rode on horseback ten or fifteen miles every morning, looking after his estate and its servants. Two o'clock was the dinner hour; three o'clock if there were guests of importance. The general would not wait more than five minutes for any guest, however distinguished. So much time he allowed for the difference of watches. "My cook," said he, "does not ask whether the guests have arrived, but whether the hour has."

Washington's dress and appearance were very simple. "How shall I know him?" asked a gentleman who was about to ride off in search of him.

"You will meet, sir," replied his friend, "an old gentleman riding alone in plain drab clothes, a broad-brimmed white hat, a hickory switch in his hand, and an umbrella with a long staff attached to his saddle-bow. That person, sir, is General Washington."

A pleasant story is told by a gentleman who was a guest at Mount Vernon. It seems that he coughed much during the early part of the night. "After some time had elapsed," said the guest, "the door of my room was gently opened, and, on drawing my bed curtains, I saw Washington himself, standing at my bedside, with a bowl of hot tea in his hand."

No wish for power, or regret at being no longer before the eyes of the world, ever disturbed the happiness of Washington in his retirement. A little over two years now passed happily at the great mansion, with its generous living and its gracious hospitality.

216. Sickness and Death; Universal Sorrow.—One day in December, 1799, while taking his usual ride on horseback Washington was exposed to rain, hail, and snow, with a raw wind blowing. The next day his family noticed that he had a slight cold, but he paid no heed to such trifling ailments.

The next day he was much worse, breathed with difficulty, and could hardly speak. His mind was perfectly clear, and he believed he should not get well. He was never unprepared for death. The same night he passed away.

Mourning spread over the whole country. In foreign lands as well as at home the news was received with sincerest sorrow. The American people felt that they had indeed lost their protector, the Father of his Country.

To Americans his memory will always be precious. His birthday is celebrated every year throughout our broad land; and the bell of every steamer that glides along the quiet Potomac tolls as it slowly passes Mount Vernon, the last resting-place of George Washington!

MOUNT VERNON, THE HOME OF WASHINGTON.

CHAPTER XVI.
THE WAR OF THE REVOLUTION IN THE SOUTH.

217. Utter Failure thus far to subdue the Colonists.—Midway in the war of the Revolution there was a period of over two years when active fighting was for the most part suspended. After the surrender of Burgoyne at Saratoga, the English seemed to lose heart. A feeble effort was even made by the British government to secure peace. England would yield everything except the claim of the colonies to independence. This was the very thing that now, after three years of fighting, the colonies would not yield.

Each side seemed to be tired of bloodshed. The patriots were in a bad enough way, and England had her troubles with other nations.

Of all the territory the British had occupied during three years, the only spot they now held was New York, and even there Washington's superb generalship with his small but active army was giving them constant trouble.

218. The British now attempt to subdue the Southern Colonies.— Thus it became necessary for the British to contrive some plan that would offer better results. They now proposed to go south, subdue one colony after another, and so push their conquests northward.

The British had already tried their hand at the south, and with results not quite to their liking. In June, 1776, General Clinton came with a fleet to capture Charleston. But Colonel William Moultrie had built on an island in the harbor a low redoubt of palmetto logs and sand bags, from which his guns made sad havoc with the fleet, while the British shot could not pierce through the tough, spongy logs of the fort. After a disastrous fight, Clinton went back disheartened. The gallant defense of this fort had a most wholesome effect upon the patriot cause.

SERGEANT JASPER'S BOLD DEED.

One heroic deed of the battle is often told. The flag of the fort floated from a high mast, against which the enemy directed their fire until the top of the flagstaff was shot away and fell over the ramparts on the beach. A daring soldier by the name of William Jasper leaped over the wall of palmetto logs, walked the whole length of the fort in the face of the enemy's fire, tore away the flag, fastened it to the rammer of a cannon, and floated it on the ramparts.

219. Disasters to the Patriot Cause.—In December, 1778, a large British force, sent from New York, landed and captured Savannah with about five hundred prisoners. The enemy also captured Augusta, brought all Georgia under British control, and put the royal governor back into office.

In October, 1779, our General Lincoln and a French fleet made a combined attack on Savannah, hoping to recapture it, but they utterly failed. These two disasters in two years were very discouraging to all Americans.

The year 1780 brought still worse fortune, for early in the year Clinton came again from New York and made a second attack on Charleston. In May he captured the city and all Lincoln's army, with four hundred cannon. Clinton then returned to New York, leaving Cornwallis in command with five thousand men.

The British, possessing Savannah and Charleston with the river connections, held the key to the whole of Georgia and South Carolina. They could obtain all their supplies by water, and so did not need to rely upon the country for support.

220. The Bitter and Cruel Warfare in the South.—The patriots did not now have a body of soldiers in the south large enough to call an army. The entire region was open to British plunder.

Bands of soldiers roamed through the country, plundering, burning, and killing without restraint. No mercy was shown to patriots. A squad of soldier bandits once came to the home of Thomas Sumter, the famous patriot officer, turned his wife and children out of doors and burned the house.

Sumter was a bold and energetic fighter in the wild warfare of the south. He was a tall and powerful man and of a very stern make-up. He lived to be ninety-nine years of age—the last surviving general of the Revolution. "But for Sumter and Marion," said Cornwallis, "South Carolina would be at peace."

There now remained in South Carolina but one battalion of patriot soldiers. These were about four hundred in number under Colonel Buford, then in the northwestern part of the state. Clinton sent against him a force of seven hundred regulars and Tories under Colonel Tarleton, an active but base and cruel man.

Tarleton surrounded the patriots and demanded their surrender. While Buford was quietly discussing the matter, his soldiers resting at ease under the protection of a flag of truce, Tarleton treacherously arranged his men for an attack. Suddenly the flag of truce was taken down, and instantly the British cavalry rushed from all sides upon Buford's men and killed one hundred and thirteen and wounded one hundred and fifty.

Even the boys were nerved to deeds of valor. A schoolboy named Andrew Jackson, thirteen years old, who had seen the dead of the Buford massacre, and helped care for the wounded, and whose own brother had been killed by the British, was himself captured. While under guard, a pompous British officer came up to him and cried out:—

"Here, boy! clean my boots!"

"No, sir! clean your own boots. I am a prisoner of war and entitled to better treatment."

Down came the officer's sword, aiming at the boy's head. Warding off the blow with his arm, he received a wound, the marks of which he carried to his grave. This boy grew up to become the seventh president of the United States!

221. General Gates meets with Disaster.—When General Washington learned of the disasters in the south, the loss of Savannah and Charleston and of Lincoln's army, he was anxious to send down General Greene, his right-hand man. But Congress unwisely interfered, and sent General Gates, who had contrived to get the credit of Burgoyne's capture at Saratoga.

In August, Gates moved to Camden, S. C., to meet Cornwallis. A strange battle ensued. Each general had planned to surprise the other by a night attack; the armies met in the dark. Both waited till daylight, and then the battle began. It was a disastrous defeat for the patriots. Gates's army was destroyed. This was perhaps the worst catastrophe of the war.

Now the patriot prospect was wretched enough. Where could there be any hope? The Tories all through the state were delighted, and thronged to the British side.

222. Marion proves a Source of Terror to the British.—The patriots felt now that they must defend themselves singly or in small groups; there was no army to help them. So they assembled, a few dozen here and there, and used their utmost endeavors on every opportunity to cripple the enemy. The British had small stations through the state, from which murderous raids could be made. They would plunder, burn, slay, and then return to their posts. To attack these posts, or to do any military work successfully, the patriots needed a leader. One soon came, Francis Marion, who combined a few groups of patriots and did most effective work with them.

MARION'S TROOPERS ATTACKING A BRITISH CAMP.

This gallant and intrepid partisan chieftain was rather below the middle stature, lean, and swarthy. His forehead was large and high, and his eyes black and piercing. He was at this time about forty-eight years of age, with a body capable of enduring great fatigue and every privation. He never tarnished his fame with acts of cruelty.

"Never shall a house be burned by one of my men," said he; "to distress helpless women and children is what I detest."

Marion used to wear a close-fitting red jacket and a leather cap. His body was so slight that he never did personal deeds of valor. His sword was so rarely used that once he could not draw it from the scabbard on account of the rust.

Never was Napoleon's guard more attached to their general than were Marion's men to the partisan chief who so often led them to victory.

223. How the "Swamp Fox" did his Fighting.—Marion was familiar with the country, and in many of the numerous swamps he occupied, with his troopers, secret haunts approached by devious paths not easily followed. The British, smarting under his attacks, called him the "swamp fox"; but he proved to them rather a wolf or a tiger. These patriots who sprang to his side to defend their homes were patriots indeed. They had no pay, no uniforms, and but scanty clothing. They were a shabby-looking band of soldiers; but their arms were strong and their hearts were true.

Many had no guns, until they supplied themselves from the enemy. They melted their pewter dishes for bullets. They often made their breakfast on blackberries, dined on potatoes and green corn, and not infrequently supped on the memory of their dinner.

Much of the time Marion himself did not have even a blanket. One night his bed of brush caught fire, and it not only burnt his blanket but singed his hair and spoilt his leather cap!

Marion always kept his plans secret, even from his own officers, until the moment for action came. There was an air of mystery in what he undertook, and a bustle of hearty enterprise about his movements, which gave a charm to life in his famous brigade. Marion enjoyed fully the confidence of his men, shared all their privations, and braved more than his share of their dangers.

224. One of Marion's First Exploits.—One of Marion's first exploits was against a large force of Tories under Major Gainey. Marion and his men fell on his camp at daybreak as suddenly as if they had dropped from the clouds. Gainey fled on horseback, closely pursued by Major James, who followed so fast and so far that he suddenly found himself alone and getting surrounded by Tories. His quick wits saved him.

Turning in his saddle and waving his sword, he shouted back as if to a large body of followers, "Come on, boys! Here they are!" The Tories scattered and fled! In this little brush Marion did not lose a man.

Marion was always on the alert—quick, dash, fire, away!—that was his way of fighting. No wonder he carried terror to the enemy. And yet he never used exactly the same tactics twice. Once he planned to fall suddenly on a force twice as large as his own. It had a watchful leader who could not be caught napping. Dangerous business, we say. Yes, but see how the "swamp fox" did it! He carefully hid a body of his best sharpshooters in ambush along the road about a mile from the British.

Then he made a lively attack on the enemy and soon retreated along this road. Of course the enemy followed briskly, when up sprang Marion's troopers in ambush and soon defeated them. "All's fair in war," says the proverb.

These furious and almost incessant attacks kept the British in terror. They never knew when they were safe.

225. Some of Marion's Famous Exploits.—Many a story of this daring chieftain's exploits used to be told by the evening fireside. In October, 1780, Marion brought hope to the patriots by one of his brilliant attacks. Colonel Tynes was gathering a large body of Tories to assist the British, and he held stores of guns, ammunition, and clothing for their use. Marion's scouts learned all the facts. These were just the articles he wanted for his half-clothed, half-fed, and poorly armed men.

For him to resolve was to act. He came cautiously at midnight. The camp-fires were burning; some soldiers were singing, some playing cards, some eating stolen chickens; but nobody was on guard. Marion's troopers rushed in with a wild shout, and the attack went all one way. A large number were killed, twenty-three were taken prisoners, and the supplies of the Tory camp were enjoyed by Marion's men for a long time. Not one of his force was lost.Soon after Gates's defeat, Marion learned by his scouts that the British were not far off with a large body of American prisoners. He sent at midnight a squad to hold the road to their camp, and before dawn he approached it silently with his own force. Just at daylight he made a sudden attack upon them. The surprise and the assault were an amazing success. Twenty-four of the enemy were killed or captured, and one hundred and fifty captives were set free, while not one of his men was lost.

226. Marion invites a British Officer to Dinner.—One day a young British officer came to Marion under a flag of truce, to plan an exchange of some prisoners. The business finished, Marion asked the officer to dine with him. The dinner consisted entirely of baked sweet potatoes brought by a negro on a piece of bark for a plate, with a log for a table.

"But this can't be your usual fare?" asked the Britisher.

"Yes, indeed," said Marion, "and we are lucky to-day to have enough for company."This was no idle talk to affect the young officer, but it did impress him; for the story is that on returning to his own camp he said, "It's no use trying; I've seen Marion, and I tell you that men who work for no pay and live on potatoes while fighting for their liberties, are not going to be beaten, and I am not going to fight any longer against them. I shall resign to-day."

MARION INVITES A BRITISH OFFICER TO DINE WITH HIM.

227. A Great Victory at King's Mountain.—After the Camden disaster the deep gloom continued till October, when Colonel Ferguson was sent with a force of British and Tories to the northwest to subdue the patriots in that region. Instantly there was a general uprising of the hunters and farmers of this wild and romantic region to defend their homes from the brutal enemy. These hardy mountaineers, ready to move at a moment's warning, came from every direction to a common meeting-place.

At King's Mountain, in North Carolina, where the British were entrenched, these American riflemen charged up the steep sides, surrounded the enemy, and cut them down till about half were killed and the rest fled in dismay. It was a brilliant victory, won by sheer hard fighting, and it brought supreme joy to the long-suffering patriots; for it proved to be decisive. It turned the tide of British rule in the south.

228. General Greene takes Command in the South.—A new Continental army was now to be sent from the north, and this time Washington had his choice of commanders. He sent one of his best and most trusted officers, General Greene, who had been a Rhode Island blacksmith. He knew how to fight; for he had served under the eye of Washington in many battles, and so had been well trained in military matters.

It was in December, 1780, that Greene took command of the so-called "southern army" at Charlotte, a little town in North Carolina. He had in all about two thousand men, but only eight hundred were fit for duty.

On the day Greene took command there were not three days' provisions in camp. He had no money. The people would not touch the Continental paper money. Ably, patiently, and brilliantly, this sagacious general at once set to work to effect his great purpose of driving the British armies from the south.

With Greene came another famous officer, General Daniel Morgan, the man who had marched with Arnold to Canada, and who commanded the infantry at Stillwater and Saratoga.

GENERAL GREENE TAKING COMMAND OF THE SOUTHERN ARMY.

This was the man who, when he heard of Lexington, led his riflemen six hundred miles in twenty-one days, from Virginia, to join Washington in Cambridge.

Morgan was of gigantic stature, vast physical strength, and wonderful powers of endurance. In his youth he was a teamster. One day by order of a tyrannical British officer he was given five hundred lashes for some slight offense. He walked away saucy and defiant as before.

Of a gentle and unselfish nature, resolute, fearless in battle, a born fighter, Morgan was the ideal leader of the riflemen of the frontier. His force was smaller than Greene's, who had detached him to occupy a post in South Carolina.

229. How General Morgan defeated the British at Cowpens.—Cornwallis in January, 1781, sent Tarleton with eleven hundred troops to meet Morgan and dispose of him. They met at Cowpens, but Morgan, with a smaller army, reversed the order and disposed of Tarleton! He killed a large number, ten officers and more than one hundred men, took over five hundred prisoners, with all the artillery and stores.

It was at Cowpens that Colonel Washington, a distant relative of the Commander-in-Chief, wounded Tarleton in a hand-to-hand combat. Shortly afterwards this hated British officer said to a lady:—

"You seem to think very highly of Colonel Washington; and yet I have been told that he is so ignorant a fellow that he can hardly write his name."

"It may be so," quickly replied the lady; "but no man can testify better than yourself that he knows how to 'make his mark.'"

At another time the haughty Tarleton, boasting of his own deeds and speaking with disdain of the continental cavalry, said to a lady:—

"I have a very earnest desire to see your far-famed hero, Colonel Washington."

"Your wish, colonel, might have been gratified," she promptly replied, "had you dared to look behind you at the battle of Cowpens!"

230. Greene's Masterly Retreat.—How angry Cornwallis was at the ruin of his best army at Cowpens! He started to pursue Morgan and punish him. But the patriot general foresaw this, and not having soldiers enough, he got well ahead, and one day at dusk crossed the Catawba River. The advanced detachment of Cornwallis's army came up two hours later, and waited for morning. That night a heavy rain swelled the stream and checked the British advance. Morgan pushed on to the Yadkin and crossed, meeting Greene's army.

Determined that his little band should not be destroyed, since the fate of the war in the south depended upon it, and not being strong enough to meet Cornwallis with his well-equipped regiments in open battle, Greene now planned a retreat with as much method and care as he would have exercised in preparing for a battle.

The river Roanoke for a long distance runs near the boundary between Virginia and North Carolina. The upper portion of this stream is called the Dan. Greene now started for the fords of this river, seventy miles away, with Cornwallis close at his heels. The roads were deep with mud and almost impassable. The patriot soldiers, wretchedly clothed and nearly barefoot, struggled along, marking the road, as Greene wrote to Washington, with blood-stained tracks.

"How you must suffer from the cold!" said the general to a barefooted sentry.

"I do not complain," replied the soldier; "I know I should fare well if our general could procure supplies; and if, as you say, we fight in a few days, I shall take care to get some shoes."

It was a most masterly and gallant retreat. The men were kept in hand, and a serious encounter with the enemy was avoided.

One morning during the retreat, when everything seemed dark, Greene rode up to the door of a tavern. The host, a true friend, met him.

"What! alive, my dear general?"

"Yes; tired, hungry, alone, and penniless."

The hostess, Mrs. Elizabeth Steele, was of the stuff of which patriots are made. She gave the weary general a good breakfast, and while he was eating she put in his hands a bag filled with bright silver dollars, saying, "You need them, and I can do without them."

As the story goes, the gallant Greene, admiring the devotion of the noble woman, stepped to the mantel, over which hung a portrait of King George, turned it to the wall, and wrote upon the back, "Hide thy face, King George, and blush!"

THE PATRIOTIC AND GENEROUS LANDLADY.

Cornwallis pressed the patriots hard through forests and over streams, but he was baffled at every move. Reaching the river Dan, the American army was safely carried over by the boats which its sagacious commander had arranged for many days before.

Cornwallis came up in hot haste only to find that the deep and rapid river flowed between him and his foe. It would have been madness for him to cross the river. He sullenly withdrew his army to a point farther south.

231. Greene now begins to fight and shows Rare Generalship.— Having recruited and rested his men, Greene moved his army south of the Dan and began active operations. He followed sharply after Cornwallis, and in March brought him to battle at Guilford. The fight was severe, and the British general, though he gained the advantage, was so roughly handled that he retired towards Wilmington, the nearest point on the coast.

Greene now made a bold and hazardous move. Instead of preventing Cornwallis from advancing to the north, he left the British general to do as he pleased, faced about suddenly and boldly marched to South Carolina. His plan was to thrust himself between the main British army and its southern division and then attack the latter and their fortified posts.

Like a skillful general, having decided upon this daring change, Greene acted quickly. He marched with all speed for Camden, one hundred and sixty miles distant. His object was to break the British hold upon South Carolina.

A brighter day was now dawning, and the sunshine of hope was soon to appear. The adroit activities of Marion, Sumter, and Pickens, and the skill and vigor of Greene and Morgan were now bringing their harvest, and they gave the patriots new life and cheer.

At Hobkirks Hill, near Camden, Greene attacked the British. He was defeated, but it was a fruitless victory.

"We fight, get beat, rise, and fight again," wrote Greene to a friend.

One by one the strong posts of the enemy in South Carolina fell into our hands. The British hold on both the Carolinas was slowly but surely broken. The enemy wisely kept near the coast. The last battle of the long and stubborn struggle was fought at Eutaw Springs, S. C., in September, 1781. The contest was desperate on both sides; but the British, badly crippled, retreated in the night to Charleston.

232. Greene's Brilliant Campaign in the South.—Greene had with the scantiest of means done a great work in his southern campaign. He had driven Cornwallis to Virginia, to meet his fate at Yorktown. He had cleared both Carolinas of the British and restored them to the patriots.

In few if any campaigns carried on with small armies was ever so effective and brilliant work done as did General Greene with his little force of patriots. Most mortifying was it to the haughty British commanders to know that they had been out-generaled, out-marched, and in the long run, out-fought by a Yankee blacksmith.

The war in the south was now soon over. Savannah was captured in July, 1782; in December, 1783, the British left Charleston. It was a proud day for Greene and Morgan and Marion when they followed with their army on the heels of the departing foe. As the patriots marched in, happy thousands cheered, and floral wreaths flew from crowded windows.

The noble Greene lived only a few years after he had carried the Revolution to a triumph in the south. He died in 1786 from the effects of a sunstroke.

Among the great generals of the American Revolution, it is generally admitted that Greene ranked, in military genius, second only to Washington.

General Anthony Wayne, called "Mad Anthony" on account of his daring, who had fought by the side of Greene, and who watched by the death-bed of his comrade, wrote to a friend: "He was great as a soldier, great as a citizen, immaculate as a friend. The honors—the greatest honors of war—are due his remains. I have seen a great and good man die."

CHAPTER XVII.
THE STORY OF ARNOLD'S TREASON.

233. A Gloomy Outlook for the Patriot Cause in 1780.—During the long war of the Revolution from Lexington in 1775 to Yorktown in 1781, there were many times when it seemed as if it were really of no use for the Americans to fight for independence. Of these years probably 1780 was the darkest.

We have just read of the sad disasters in the south during this year. If "hope long deferred maketh the heart sick," surely our forefathers had at this time ample cause for discouragement. It seemed to many, no doubt, that the policy of the British Parliament of "tiring the Americans out" might succeed after all.

Financial matters were in a deplorable condition. Congress had no authority to raise money by taxation to carry on the war. Sometimes the colonies responded to the call for money from Congress; oftener they did not. There were paper promises enough issued by Congress and known as continental currency, but they had sadly fallen in value. Washington, it is said, once remarked that it took a wagon-load of it to buy a wagon-load of provisions. Samuel Adams tells us that he paid two thousand dollars for a hat and a suit of clothes.

A tradesman, to show his contempt for it, papered his shop with continental currency. The current phrase, "not worth a continental," has survived all these years as a reminder of the deplorable condition of our finances at this time. No wonder the famishing and half-frozen soldiers in Washington's army, when paid off in the flimsy stuff, were mutinous at times, and that the desertions averaged more than a hundred a month.

234. Arnold the Traitor.—In the midst of all the trials of this "year of disasters," the country was startled by the disclosure of a plot of the blackest treason. The recklessly brave but unscrupulous Arnold proved himself a traitor of the deepest dye.

Born in Connecticut, he was early known as "a bad boy." From earliest childhood he was disobedient, cruel, reckless, and profane, caring little or nothing for the good will of others. While he was apprentice to an apothecary he enlisted in the colonial army, but soon deserted. Afterwards he set up as druggist in New Haven, but wasted the money he earned and ended the business by becoming bankrupt.

235. His Brilliant Military Career.—When the startling news from Lexington thrilled all the country, Arnold raised a company of soldiers and was appointed captain. Soon he became colonel and aided Ethan Allen in the attack on Forts Ticonderoga and Crown Point. Next he was sent to assist General Montgomery in the assault on Quebec, where he proved himself a valiant soldier. He received a severe wound in the leg while gallantly leading his men. For these useful services, Congress made him a brigadier-general.

Soon after this, Congress bestowed upon five prominent brigadiers the distinguished rank of major-general, but Arnold was not one of them. He felt slighted and became very jealous. Washington wrote him a kindly letter, which partly appeased his wounded vanity.

During the Burgoyne campaign, as we have read, Arnold won special renown for his splendid bravery at the battle of Saratoga, where he was again wounded. For his signal valor in this battle he was now made a major-general. But even this probably failed to satisfy him; for there were still five others superior to him in rank.

236. The Beginning of his Wicked Career.—As his wounded leg needed rest, Arnold obtained from Washington, in the summer of 1778, the command of Philadelphia, lately evacuated by the British. During his nine months there his conduct was bad. His manners were haughty and insolent. He lived with costly extravagance far beyond his means, drove a fine coach and four, and gave splendid parties. His associates were largely among the Tories, and he married a Miss Shippen, a bitterly disloyal young woman. His intimate friends were now for the most part the enemies of his country. Arnold's expensive habits of living soon brought him deeply in debt, and when the storekeepers urged payment of their bills, he contrived dishonest methods of obtaining money belonging to the government. Formal charges of misconduct were made; he was tried, found guilty, and sentenced to the very mild punishment of a public reproof by the Commander-in-Chief. This reprimand Washington performed as gently as possible, sparing his feelings by combining high praise for his past heroism with censure for his late misdeeds.

Arnold was angry. He had hoped to escape all censure. You may know how black a villain he was from the fact that, in his speech in court, defending himself, he spoke of his past services in battle and promised even more faithful devotion in future to his dear country, which he said he loved as his own life. It came out afterwards that even then he had been for months secretly exchanging letters with Sir Henry Clinton, and plotting how to betray his country! His letters were signed "Gustavus," and were secretly sent by his wife. The replies from Clinton purported to be from "John Anderson."

237. Secretly plans to betray his Country.—Arnold knew that of all things Clinton most longed to get possession of West Point; for it was the key of the river northward up to Lake Champlain, and it also controlled the crossing between New England and the Middle States. Arnold studied how to betray it, and by one bad act to satisfy both his revenge and his greed for money.

The first thing to do was to change the sullenness that had marked his behavior since the trial. He at once became cheerful, loudly patriotic, and so eager to help his dear country! Next he contrived to persuade some prominent officers to induce Washington to appoint him to the command of West Point. Not suspecting his treachery, Washington gave him the place. He took command in August, 1780.

238. Arnold and André meet, and plot Treason.—Now Arnold's plot began to ripen. But Clinton wanted to be very sure of what he was doing. He concluded to send a trusty officer to meet Arnold and settle the plan beyond doubt. So he selected the Adjutant General of his army, a brilliant young officer, Major John André, who knew all about it thus far, for he was the "John Anderson" who had, under Clinton's directions, answered the "Gustavus" letters.

On the morning that he started, André had a parting lunch with his fellow officers, with wine-drinking and song-singing—a right jolly time! Ah! if he could only have foreseen! André was an estimable young man, brave, educated, accomplished, a poet, an artist, and brought up in the best society of England.

André went up the Hudson in the sloop-of-war Vulture. After the moon went down, and it was dark enough for such a deed, a boat came silently from the west shore near Haverstraw, and took back from the vessel a tall young man wrapped in a black cloak. Arnold met him on the bank and led him into a thicket of fir trees. There, like two ugly spirits of evil, they crouched in the darkness, and talked over the details of the dastardly deed.

Arnold, eager for British gold, haggled for a higher price. They plotted the utter ruin of the patriot cause, till, at the earliest streak of dawn, boom! boom! sounded some cannon! The traitor was frightened! One of our shore batteries was firing a few shots at the Vulture, so that she had to drop down stream a few miles. André therefore could not return directly to the Vulture, but was obliged to remain hidden all that day.

The plans had all been arranged. Clinton was to send up a fleet with soldiers to West Point, and Arnold was meanwhile to have removed most of his troops from the fort on some pretense, so that Clinton's force could easily capture it. Arnold gave André some papers to carry to Clinton, maps of the fort, with instructions how to approach and take it.

Sir Henry had warned André not to receive any papers from Arnold nor to put on any disguise. André for some reason did not obey these orders. He may have suspected that, after all, some trap was planned to deceive the British, and thought best to carry back papers in Arnold's own handwriting. At all events, it was a fatal mistake for poor André.

239. Capture of André.—- André wore long riding-boots. Between his stockings and the soles of his feet he put these papers. He took also a pass from Arnold to carry him through the guards. The Vulture having dropped down the river, André crossed over and set out on horseback to go back to New York on the east side.

All went well until he reached the vicinity of Tarrytown. At this time the region was infested with "cowboys" and "skinners," who under the pretense of keeping up a partisan warfare for their respective sides used to steal whatever they could find.

On this morning several men from the American army had been sent out to look after the "cowboys." As André rode along, three of this party sprang from the bushes, leveled their muskets at him, and ordered him to halt. They were young men, and their names were John Paulding, David Williams, and Isaac Van Wart. One of them happened to have on the coat of a Hessian soldier whom he had captured. This may have misled André and prompted him to make a blunder.

"Gentlemen," said André, "I hope you belong to our side."

"Which side?" asked Van Wart.

"The lower party," answered André. "I am a British officer on urgent duty, and hope you will not detain me."

Then the three patriots ordered him off his horse. André saw his mistake. He showed them Arnold's pass, but they insisted on searching him. They examined his saddle, took off his coat and vest, but finding nothing wrong, were about to let him go, when Paulding said:—

"Boys, I am not satisfied; his boots must come off."

André objected: "his boots were very tight—he must not be detained—you'll suffer yet for what you are doing."

But off came the boots, and out came the fatal papers!

"Boys, this fine fellow is a spy!" exclaimed Paulding.

CAPTURE OF ANDRÉ.

André offered his captors his splendid gold watch, his horse, and a thousand dollars in money, if they would only let him off. The three common soldiers proved true to themselves and to their great cause and refused a bribe. Believing their captive to be a spy, they took him to their commander, Colonel Jameson.

240. The Arch Traitor makes his Escape.—This officer made the blunder of sending a messenger to Arnold with a letter saying a certain John Anderson had been arrested! The horseman found the arch traitor at breakfast with several of his prominent officers as his guests. His beautiful young wife was presiding with charming grace at the table.

Arnold, concealing his terror, left the table, kissed his sleeping babe, told his fainting wife he might never see her again, seized a horse, galloped to the river, sprang into a boat, and urged the oarsmen by their love of money and rum to row him to the Vulture. When the boat reached the vessel, the traitor was so mean as to hand over the poor oarsmen as prisoners. But the British captain generously sent them back.

Washington arrived at Arnold's house a few hours after he had escaped, and when the papers in Arnold's handwriting were shown him, his hand shook; he was overwhelmed with amazement and sorrow.

Turning to Lafayette, with tears running down his cheeks, and choking with grief, he cried out:—

"Arnold is a traitor, and has fled to the British! Whom can we trust now?"

It was only for a moment. The next instant Washington had recovered his iron self-control.

241. What became of Arnold.—Washington contrived an ingenious plan to capture Arnold, but it failed. The traitor got his reward; he was made a major-general in the British army and received thirty thousand dollars for his villany. But the gold turned to ashes in his hands. Everybody despised him. Men pointed the finger of scorn at him, saying, "There goes Arnold the traitor."

A member of Parliament, in the midst of a speech saw Arnold in the gallery, and, pausing, said, "Mr. Speaker, I will not go on while that traitor is in the house."

Washington had, all the years before, been Arnold's steadfast friend. He admired one who could fight with such energy, and who never knew fear. After the treason it is said that Washington could never mention the traitor's name without a shudder.

"What do you think of the doings of that diabolical dog?" wrote Colonel Williams, the gallant southern fighter, to General Morgan.

"Curse on his folly and perfidy!" said the noble-hearted General Greene. "How mortifying to think that he is a New Englander!"

242. André's Sad Fate.—The three faithful men who captured André were highly honored. Each received a silver medal from Congress, with a life pension of two hundred dollars a year. Their graves are marked by worthy monuments.

But poor André! what became of him? He was tried within a week by a court-martial of fourteen generals and condemned to death as a spy.

"We cannot save him," said the kindly old veteran, Baron Steuben. "Oh that we had the traitor who has dragged this gallant young officer to death, so that he might suffer in his stead!" André wrote a full and frank letter to Washington, urging that he was not really a spy. All Americans felt deep pity for him because of his youth, his virtues, his many accomplishments, his belief that he was serving his country, and because he had been the victim of a villain. But Americans could not forget that the British, four years before, had captured a brave young American officer, Captain Nathan Hale, and hanged him as a spy without any manifestation of pity or sympathy.

The officer who commanded the escort that brought André across the Hudson to the main army was a college classmate of Hale. As the young officers rode along on horseback, mention was made of Hale's sad fate.

"Surely," said André, "you do not think his case and mine alike!"

"They are precisely alike," answered the officer, "and similar will be your fate." Washington, who shed tears when he signed the death warrant, would gladly have saved André's life; but the stern rules of war and the good of the American cause left no room for mercy. His execution was put off one day, it is said, in hope that Arnold might be captured and made to suffer in his stead. André bravely faced the awful event, and on the morning of the day of his death conversed freely and even cheerfully. He was disturbed only about the mode of his death; he begged to be shot as a soldier, and not hanged as a spy; but the grim custom and rules of war forbade.

ON HIS DEATHBED ARNOLD CALLS FOR HIS OLD UNIFORM.

243. Arnold dies in Disgrace.—Arnold lived in London for more than twenty years after his foul treason. No doubt they were years of bitter remorse and self-reproach. His wife proved herself a devoted woman.

Arnold's children and grandchildren all felt keenly the disgrace that rested upon the family.

As the traitor came to his final sickness, his mind seemed to recall the days when he fought for his country with distinction. He thought of the steadfast friendship that Washington once cherished for him. After Saratoga, this friend had presented him with epaulettes and a sword-knot, and put them on with his own hand. The old uniform in which he had fought his battles, and which he wore on the day he escaped to the Vulture, had been carefully kept during all these years of disgrace.

Just before his death the desolate old man called for these sad reminders and put them on again.

"Let me die," said he, "in this old uniform in which I fought so many battles for my country. May God forgive me for ever putting on any other!"

Thus perished the man who, with the exception of Washington and Greene, prior to his infamous deed, had done perhaps more efficient service for the cause of our independence than any other American general. Think of the contrast between the deep infamy of an Arnold and the patriotic grit and unselfishness of those ragged, half-starved Pennsylvania soldiers who rose in mutiny during the next winter. Mad Anthony Wayne had led some of these men at the storming of Stony Point, and he was dearly beloved by them all; yet they would not obey even him.

As Wayne was speaking to them, two men, who had been sent by General Clinton to tamper with the mutineers and offer a bounty and high pay if they would enlist in the British army, were detected. The soldiers in their wrath turned these emissaries over to their general, and they were hanged as spies.

"Tell General Clinton," said these men who had not received a cent of pay to send home to their families for over a year, "that we are not Benedict Arnolds."

CHAPTER XVIII.
JOHN PAUL JONES: OUR FIRST GREAT NAVAL HERO.

244. The Colonies poorly prepared to cope with England on the Sea.—Now we must remember that the American Revolution, which lasted about seven years, and which resulted in our independence, was fought almost entirely on land. We were poor, and besides had but little or no experience in building men-of-war. The few vessels that had been built in this country were mostly sloops or schooners for fishing, or for trading.

In this lack of large sailing craft during the Revolution, we should have got on very poorly but for the generous aid of France. When Washington's forces closed in upon the enemy at Yorktown, he would not then have been able to capture the whole British army and so end the great struggle, but for the thirty-six French ships that arrived just in time to give us the assistance we so much needed.

In the first years of the war the colonies began to build a number of warships, but these were of little account compared with the navy of England. Such few vessels as we already had were hastily fitted up for naval service and armed with small cannon. These had to make up for their want of size by the boldness of their crews and the quickness of their movement. Privateering was then very common. This means that a vessel owned or officered by private persons has a commission from the government to go out and attack the enemy's vessels. Without this authority it would have been regarded as a pirate.

245. John Paul Jones begins his Remarkable Career.—The feeble colonies had then not only few vessels, but few officers to command them. There was one officer, however, John Paul Jones, who soon became widely famous as a naval commander of extraordinary courage and superb audacity. He was born in Scotland. When a boy of only twelve years he began to go to sea. In time he visited his elder brother, a farmer in Virginia. During the next few years he made a number of voyages to the West Indies, and became rich by his skill in trading.

When the war of the Revolution began, this energetic young Scotch sailor determined to take an active part in it. He entered the navy in 1775, when twenty-eight years old, and became lieutenant of the sloop-of-war Alfred.

On this vessel Paul Jones hoisted to the masthead the first American flag ever displayed over an American warship. It was a yellow silk flag showing a pine tree, with a rattlesnake coiled at its root as if about to strike, and the motto, "Don't tread on me." Our present flag, with its beautiful stripes and glowing stars, was adopted by Congress two years later.

The Alfred was the flagship of a little fleet of seven vessels. They soon captured two British vessels from the Bahamas, then went to Nassau, the capital of the islands, took the governor prisoner, and carried away nearly a hundred cannon with a large quantity of military supplies. On the way home they seized two more British vessels. On a later cruise, of forty-seven days, Jones took sixteen prizes.

246. John Paul Jones performs Daring Deeds on the English Coast.— Afterwards Paul Jones went to France, and sailing from Brest in his ship the Ranger, he swept the seas all around England, taking or destroying every hostile ship he met. He was so audacious as to sail into British ports, wrecking and pillaging everywhere. He entered the harbor of Whitehaven, England, surprised the forts, spiked the guns, and burned some ships at the docks. English commerce was crippled, insurance rates rose to a fabulous price, and merchants met with enormous losses.

The English were so alarmed that they sent out the well-armed sloop-of-war Drake to capture Jones and bring him in a prisoner. But the daring hero turned the game just the other way. He met the British craft in the Irish Sea, and after a severe battle of over an hour he captured her with more than two hundred prisoners and took the prize to Brest. All this pleased the French wonderfully, for they had had war with England.

In fact all Europe rang with the praises of John Paul Jones.

JOHN PAUL JONES.

247. Jones's Interview with Franklin; secures Help from France.— The American Commissioners in Paris, of whom Franklin was the leader, promised Jones a much larger ship; but they could not get the money to pay for it, and Jones was very impatient to be off to sea again. He went to the harbor of Lorient, on the west coast of France, to choose a ship. Week after week he waited for an order from Paris to buy the vessel, but none came.

One day, while in a restaurant, the young officer took up a copy of Poor Richard's Almanac, a very unique little annual, really the work of Franklin. Reading the bright sayings scattered over every page, he came upon this maxim: "If you would have your business done, go; if not, send!"

The truth of the homely saying came to his mind like a flash. He sprang to his feet.

"That was written for me," he said. "Here I am, sending to Paris, when I ought to go!"

He started at once. He appealed to the Minister of Marine, and then to King Louis himself. He pleaded his way to success. The king immediately gave him a forty-gun ship at Lorient. He went back and took command. The first thing Paul Jones did was to paint out the old name and give for a new one the French equivalent of Dr. Franklin's almanac name, Bon Homme Richard ("Poor Richard," or "Goodman Richard"); for he gave the credit of his sudden success to Franklin's wise maxim.

248. The Battle between the Bon Homme Richard and the Serapis.—
Our daring mariner soon sailed out with six other vessels, all flying the beautiful new American flag. The crew on the Richard numbered nearly four hundred men, a medley of sailors from almost every nation in Europe, and even including some Malays. He sailed up between England and Ireland, taking a number of prizes, then around the north of Scotland and down on the east coast of England.

Here, in the evening of a clear September day in 1779, his little fleet met, off Flamborough, the new British ship of forty-four guns, commanded by Captain Pearson. The Serapis, though a larger and better ship than the old Richard, tried to escape, but the Richard chased her and brought her to. It was just at twilight, and so near the land that crowds of people thronged the shores to see the contest.

As darkness settled down, the ships drew nearer. Just then the full moon rose slowly over the sea, and right in the range of its broad field of light were the dark shapes of the two hostile vessels.

Now they draw closer. On each ship rests a stillness like that of death. The men stand at their guns silent and thoughtful. The thousands on shore hold their breath. Silently up goes the British flag on the mainmast of the Serapis, and over the Richard waves the new banner of the "stars and stripes."

"Ship ahoy!" shouted Captain Jones through his speaking trumpet.

"Aye, aye!" was the reply from the English vessel.

"What's your name?" came ringing over the water.

"His majesty's ship Serapis! What's yours?"

"Bon Homme Richard!" replied the gallant Jones; "haul down your flag!"

The Englishman's answer was the flash and boom of a cannon shot that whizzed through the rigging of the Richard. Then raged the lightning and thunder of battle. Fast and furious was the roar of the big guns, now from this ship, now from that.

They drift nearer together; now their rigging is entangled; now they touch! Now the struggling crews fight hand to hand. Right and left the conflict rages, with pikes and pistols and cutlasses.

Jones is now here, now there, seeing all, controlling all, and mixing with the bravest, now training some gun, now pulling at some rope or cheering some lagging sailor lad. His strong will and sturdy pluck give new life to his men. They cheer as their shot begin to tell. The air is filled with the crash of cannon, the rattle of pistols, the orders of officers, the yells of the crews, and the groans of the dying.

The American flag is obscured with smoke, so that Captain Pearson, not seeing it, shouts, "Are you ready to surrender?"

Instantly comes Jones's defiant reply, "Surrender! I've not yet begun to fight!"

Then Jones lashed the ships together, while the cannon balls tore through the vessels, cut the masts, and scattered the wounded and dead all around. The Richard is leaking badly, but the fight still rages. Marines in the rigging bring down the enemy with incessant shots, and hurl grenades that fire the Serapis.

THE BATTLE BETWEEN THE BON HOMME RICHARD AND THE SERAPIS.

The flames spread; both ships are on fire! but still the big guns roar. Both vessels have been on fire three times, but the pumps are at work and the battle still rages. The scene is one of appalling, indescribable grandeur. Finally, at about ten o'clock, Captain Pearson sees there is no hope against such a foe as this, and so strikes his flag. When the haughty English captain gave up his sword to the brave Yankee sailor, he said: "I cannot but feel much mortification at the idea of surrendering my sword to a man who has fought me with a rope round his neck."

The gallant Jones received the Englishman's sword, and at once returned it, saying, "You have fought bravely, sir, and I hope your king will give you a better ship."

Thus ended one of the most desperate sea fights recorded in naval history. The Bon Homme Richard was a complete wreck and was fast sinking. Accordingly Jones took all on board the Serapis, which of course was then under his command, and in a few hours the American vessel went down in the deep sea, carrying with her the bodies of her dead. The victorious commander took the Serapis, with all his prisoners, into a Holland port.

249. Effect of this Grand Naval Victory; After-Life of Paul Jones.— This famous victory was a severe blow to England's naval prestige. The moral effect upon the nations of Europe of such a victory within sight of the English coast was something remarkable.

Franklin praised Jones, and Washington wrote him a warm letter of thanks. The French king invited him to his palace, and presented him with a superb gold-mounted sword. The empress of Russia gave him an honorary ribbon, and the king of Denmark awarded him a pension.

In America this victory brought universal joy, and Congress bestowed on the victor a large gold medal. The brave Captain Pearson was afterwards knighted by his king. On hearing of it, Jones said, "He deserves it; and if I fall in with him again I'll make a lord of him."

After a few years' further service in our navy, Paul Jones was offered a position of honor in the Russian navy. He accepted it and soon won a brilliant victory in the Black Sea over the Turks, who were frightened at his remarkable bravery.

Afterwards, when living in Paris, Jones became broken down in health. No wonder, for he had fought twenty-four naval battles! When he was taken sick, the queen sent her physician, to attend him. He died in Paris in 1792, at the early age of forty-five, thirteen years after his memorable victory. No one knows the place of his burial. At the public funeral a vast concourse filled the streets of the French capital.

General sorrow was shown throughout the United States at the death of John Paul Jones, the great ocean hero of the Revolution—indeed, the first heroic character in our country's naval history.

CHAPTER XIX.
BENJAMIN FRANKLIN: HIS HIGHLY USEFUL CAREER.

250. Benjamin Franklin, one of the most Useful and Influential Men of his Time.—Among the many men who acted a conspicuous part as "makers of our country," Benjamin Franklin holds a unique and interesting place. Combined with shrewd common sense and a practical philosophy was a genial and rare personality, which made him during his long lifetime a most useful and influential citizen.

Franklin did not fight and win battles like Washington and Greene, but he gained notable victories in diplomacy when the struggling colonies sorely needed them. For over sixty years he wrote hundreds of pamphlets, tracts, and newspaper articles, which moulded public opinion at critical times, and also served to increase the comfort and happiness of his fellow-men.

Most men who have attempted to write their own lives have made a sad failure of it. This busy man of the world, with no education save that which he was able to get in the "odds and ends" of time, told the story of his own life in a way that has commanded the interest and admiration of multitudes of readers for over a hundred years.

251. Franklin's Early Life; his Genius for Useful Inventions.—Benjamin Franklin, the fifteenth of a family of seventeen children, was born in Boston in 1706. His father was a poor man, who could afford his youngest boy only about two years of schooling. When he was ten, the lad left school to assist his father at his trade of making soap and tallow candles.

Nothing else pleased the boy so much as a book. He had access at this time to very few, and most of these were dull, but he read them eagerly. He read and re-read Bunyan's Pilgrim's Progress until he knew it by heart. He disliked his father's trade and longed to do something more agreeable. He even thought of running away to sea as one of his brothers had done.

252. Learns the Printer's Trade; how he learned to write Good English.—Finally the boy was bound out as an apprentice to his older brother James, to learn the printer's trade. This was more to the boy's liking, for it gave him a better chance to read. For three years young Franklin worked hard to master the business. In a short time he could set type as well as any of the Boston printers. He went on errands to the bookstores, and, making friends with the clerks, he was often able to borrow books to read. He would carry them home, sit up most of the night reading, and return them on the next morning.

In his story of his own life, Franklin gives a most interesting account of his finding an odd volume of Addison's Spectator, and how charmed he was with the style. He would read one of Addison's essays with great care, close the book, and then write it out in his own words. This was carefully compared with the original, and corrected and re-corrected until he had improved upon his first effort.

This and other similar exercises were long continued, and they gave the ambitious boy the command of a singularly clear and interesting style.

253. Writes for his Brother's Newspaper.—For three years the young printer worked steadily at his trade, without a moment of leisure except such as he took from his sleep or from his meals. He often sat up late and rose early, that he might have more time for study.

His brother James, for whom he worked, so prospered in his business that he began to print in 1721 a weekly newspaper. It was young Benjamin's duty to set the type and strike off the edition of a few hundred papers, and then carry the little sheet to the houses of the subscribers.

The boy read his brother's paper and soon had confidence enough in himself to write articles for it. He did not dare to let his brother know it, but slipped them under the door at night. They were printed and eagerly read for some time before their authorship was known.

254. Goes to Philadelphia; First Appearance in that City.—Young Franklin and his brother did not, however, get along well together. They quarreled, and the young printer at last sold some of his books and set sail for New York on a sloop. Unable to find work there, he was advised to go to Philadelphia. After many hardships and mishaps, he stepped ashore at the Quaker City one Sunday morning with one silver dollar and about a shilling in copper in his pocket.

Franklin was at this time a sturdy youth of seventeen. He was dressed in the peculiar fashion of the times. He wore knee breeches of buckskin, also a huge coat, the pockets of which bulged out with his spare shirts and stockings. He hastened to the first baker's shop and asked for threepenny worth of bread. The baker handed him three long rolls. He took one under each arm, and ate the third as he walked along the streets.

A young girl happened to see him as he passed her father's house, and she laughed aloud at the young man's comical appearance. The girl's name was Deborah Read, and she afterwards became the wife of Franklin. Hungry and tired, he ate his rolls, then walked down to the river for a drink of water, and at last went into a Quaker meeting and soon fell sound asleep.

FRANKLIN'S FIRST APPEARANCE IN PHILADELPHIA.

A good Quaker helped Franklin to get work at his trade as a printer. The young man soon proved himself a prize to his employer. He was strong, quick, frugal, of a studious mind, and, what was a rare virtue in those days, he never touched strong drink. Bright and sunny hours now came. He received good wages, saved his money, and made friends everywhere.

255. Goes to London and works at his Trade.—One of these friends was the governor of Pennsylvania. He advised Franklin to set up a printing office of his own. He urged him to go to London to buy a printing outfit, and promised him letters to people in England who, he said, would let him have all the money he needed. The young printer trusted too much to the pompous governor's promises and sailed for England, hoping to find the letters in the vessel's letter bag. But the governor had disappointed him; no such letters were ever written.

In due time Franklin found himself in the great city of London, where he did not know a single person. He at once showed what stuff he was made of. He quietly went to work at his trade and worked harder than ever. He kept up his studious habits, and spent all his spare time in reading good books.

256. Returns to Philadelphia; successful as a Printer and Publisher.—
After a stay of a year and a half in London, Franklin returned to Philadelphia, and soon after set up in business for himself as a printer. After a time he started a newspaper. He worked early and late, attending to every detail himself. He was not ashamed to carry material for his paper through the streets on a wheelbarrow.

Once he invited a rival in his business home to dine. Pointing to a loaf of bread from which they had eaten, he said, "Unless you can live cheaper than I, you cannot starve me out."

When he was twenty-four the prosperous young printer married Deborah Read, the young woman who had laughed at him years before as he trudged through the streets with the rolls under his arms. Deborah proved herself a real helpmate, thrifty and industrious. Attached to the printing office was a little shop which the young wife tended.

"Our table was plain and simple," says Franklin in his autobiography, "our furniture of the cheapest. For instance, our breakfast was for a long time bread and milk (no tea), and I ate it out of a twopenny earthen porringer, with a pewter spoon." In after years the thrifty couple indulged in some splendor, for in 1765 Mrs. Franklin, in a letter to her husband, alludes proudly to a papered room, horsehair chairs, a sideboard, and three carpets.

257. His Happy, Useful, and Prosperous Career in Philadelphia.— For twenty years Franklin lived a prosperous life as an active business man of the good Quaker city. He had become noted for his integrity, sagacity, and prosperity. His newspaper became known for its sparkling and timely editorials. The most intelligent and influential men of the city met in his office to discuss the questions of the day.

The same year that Washington was born (1732) Franklin issued the first number of his Poor Richard's Almanac, which soon gained great fame for its wise and pithy sayings. The popularity which this little work maintained for twenty-five years was astonishing. Its shrewd and quaint maxims soon became household words in almost every shop and home of the land.

Even with his increasing prosperity Franklin found time every day to devote many hours to his books. He became proficient in French, Spanish, Italian, and even Latin. He gave much time to music, and played with skill upon the harp, the guitar, and the violin.

This remarkable man now began to be at the head of many kinds of public and private enterprises, from treating with the Indians to plans for cleaning the streets. Honors, both public and private, were heaped upon him. He started a public library in Philadelphia, the first of its kind in America.

He invented the famous "Franklin fireplace," which proved very popular and is even in use to-day. The most trivial events would often suggest to him something that would secure beneficial results.

The story is told that Franklin saw one day in a ditch the fragments of a basket of yellow willow, in which some foreign goods had been brought into the country. One of the twigs had sprouted. He planted it; and it is said that it became the parent of all the yellow willows in our country.

258. Franklin's Famous Kite Experiment.—Franklin was a great student of the sciences, especially electricity. He wrote a pamphlet to prove that lightning and electricity are the same thing. The idea was sneered at, and people asked, "Of what use is it?" To which the genial philosopher replied, "What is the use of a child? It may become a man!" He hit on a plan to prove his theory.

FRANKLIN'S FAMOUS KITE EXPERIMENT.

This was the famous kite experiment which he tried in 1752. He made a kite of silk, fastened a piece of wire to the stick, and went out with his son to fly it during a thunderstorm. At the lower end of the hempen string was fastened a key, and below that a cord of silk, which is a non-conductor. He held the silk cord in his hand, and when a low thunder cloud passed, he saw that the fibres of the string rose, separated, and stood on end, exactly as the hair does on one's head when one is charged with electricity as he stands on an insulating stool.

When Franklin brought his knuckles near the key that he had tied to the string, sparks came from the metal, and he felt slight shocks.

This discovery made a great sensation in the scientific world. Franklin at once became famous, took high rank as a man of science, and was afterwards known as "Doctor Franklin." He now invented the lightning rod, which has been in use ever since all over the civilized world.

259. Entrance into a Broader Public Life.—From this time Franklin began to occupy more important positions in public life. In 1754 he was sent on a mission to Albany to enlist the chiefs of the powerful "Six Nations" to become allies of the English. On this journey he drew up a plan for the union of the colonies. It was almost like that by which they were afterwards bound together as a nation.

During the Braddock campaign Franklin in vain warned the haughty British general that "the Indians would surprise, on its flanks, the slender line, nearly four miles long, which the army must make," and would "cut it like a thread into several pieces." From his own purse Franklin advanced for this ill-starred expedition between six and seven thousand silver dollars.

The quarrels between the Pennsylvania Assembly and the Proprietors in England became so bitter that Franklin was sent to England in 1757 as the sole commissioner to make an appeal to the English government. He was cordially received abroad and highly honored by the most eminent scientific men of the time. He returned home after an absence of nearly six years.

Franklin was now fifty-seven years old. He had an ample fortune, perfect health, and a superiority to most men in personal appearance and dignity. He hoped to withdraw from public life and give the rest of his days to the study of science.

260. Franklin becomes a most Useful and Sagacious Helper to the Struggling Colonies.—Great and momentous events, however, were at hand. There was more important work for him to do. The struggling colonies, already taxed almost beyond endurance to carry on the war against the French and Indians, were allowed no representation nor voice in the matter of taxation. Franklin, with patriotic foresight and with keen force of logic, resisted the outrage. He declared it to be the "mother of mischief."

In 1764 Franklin was again sent by the Assembly to England, to present to the British court the protest of the people against "taxation without representation."

FRANKLIN AT THE COURT OF FRANCE.

From this time Franklin served the colonies in England as a most accomplished diplomatist, a vigorous writer, and a shrewd and sagacious agent. He failed to stop the passage of the notorious Stamp Act, but he fought the measure so vigorously by his writings and discussions that he aroused bitter opposition to it among the industrial classes, so that Parliament was compelled at last to repeal the obnoxious measure.

He was once brought before the House of Parliament and sharply questioned.

"Do you think," asked the prime minister, "the people of America would submit to pay the stamp duty if it was changed?"

"No, never," said Franklin; "the American people will never submit to it."

The colonists received with unbounded delight the tidings of Franklin's masterly diplomacy and the repeal of the Stamp Act. Bells were rung, bonfires blazed, and cannon were fired. "I never heard so much noise in my life," wrote Franklin's daughter Sallie to him; "the very children seem distracted."

Franklin now watched with honest shrewdness and a penetrating mind the many attempts of the British government to tax the Americans. Other colonies recognized his ability, and New Jersey, Georgia, and Massachusetts appointed him as their agent.

At last, when all attempts to induce the government to change its oppressive policy had failed and war was sure to follow, Franklin sailed for home. He reached Philadelphia about sixteen days after the battle at Lexington and Concord.

The morning after his arrival he was unanimously chosen a member of the Continental Congress, which was to meet in Philadelphia on the tenth of May. He now took a leading part in aiding his countrymen in their war for liberty. He was one of the five men, it will be remembered, chosen to draft the Declaration of Independence.

261. His Remarkable Service Abroad as a Diplomatist.—Shortly afterwards Franklin was chosen a special ambassador to France.

"I am old and good for nothing," said the philosopher; "but, as the storekeepers say of their remnants of cloth, 'I am but a fag end, and you may have me for what you please.'"

Two years afterwards, by his wisdom and his thorough knowledge of diplomacy, Franklin was chiefly instrumental in securing a treaty with France. By this memorable compact our independence was acknowledged, and we were recognized by France as one among the nations of the world.

The news of the treaty was received in America with unbounded joy. General Washington drew up his little half-starved army at Valley Forge to announce the event, and to offer prayers and thanksgiving to God. During the next three years Franklin rendered invaluable services in obtaining money, arms, and other means to aid his country in her life and death struggle with England.

At last, when Great Britain gave up all hope of subduing her American colonies, and was ready to make terms of peace, Franklin's diplomacy triumphed. Probably no other man in America could have guided the affair so wisely.

262. Franklin's Last Days.—Franklin was now an old man of seventy-eight. He was so feeble that he could not walk, and could only ride in a litter. Thomas Jefferson was sent over to France in 1784 as his successor.

Upon his arrival the French prime minister said, "You replace Doctor Franklin, I understand."

"No!" replied Jefferson, "I succeed him. No man can replace him!"

The long sea voyage homeward proved very beneficial to the old philosopher's health. He was chosen a delegate to the convention that met in Philadelphia in 1787 to frame a new constitution. Although he was now eighty-one years of age, he was regularly in his seat, five hours a day, for four months.

Three years later, at his home in Philadelphia, in 1790, the "grand old man "died, at the age of eighty-four. The whole nation mourned his loss. No man of that period, except Washington, was held in higher esteem and veneration the world over than was Benjamin Franklin.

CHAPTER XX.
EVERYDAY LIFE ONE HUNDRED YEARS AGO.

263. Our Country One Hundred Years Ago.—Let us now take a hasty glance backward for a century and note the vast changes that have taken place in the matter of daily living during this time. Very different was the country in which our forefathers lived from that with which we are familiar. To be sure, there was a fringe of villages along the coast from Maine to Georgia. Fifty miles back from the Atlantic the country was for the most part an unbroken wilderness.

A few hundred settlers, and perhaps a hundred log cabins, made up a village where now stands the great city of Cincinnati. Indians and buffaloes roamed over the rich plains of the West which to-day furnish grain for Europe. Only seven of the states then had well-defined boundaries. Thousands of the marvelous inventions and discoveries which have added so much to the comfort and convenience of life had at that time no existence.

264. Newspapers.—Forty-three newspapers managed to survive the war of the Revolution. Even the best of these were mean-looking, and printed on poor paper. For the most part, they contained but four small pages, and were issued not oftener than two or three times a week. As to quantity of printed matter, they could not sustain comparison for one moment with the newspaper of our time.

There was no such thing as an editorial page. All kinds of queer advertisements there were; as, for runaway slaves or stolen horses: tedious letters appeared, written to the editor from distant points: treatises on geography and morals abounded instead of news. To fill out space, the editor would occasionally reprint some standard historical work or book of travels.

That material which gives the modern newspaper its peculiar value and is now known under the general name of "news" was unknown. There were few or no facilities for gathering facts as to the happenings of events or the doings of individuals, communities, and nations; and certainly no pains was taken to forward such material for publication.

265. The Postal Service and Letter-Writing.—In the early colonial times there was no such thing as an official postal service. Up to the time of the Revolution there were certain means provided for carrying letters, but they were very meagre.

The postmen used to travel some thirty to fifty miles a day in good weather. Letters were sent from New York to Boston three times a week during summer, and twice a week in winter. Six days and even more were required to make the journey. One pair of saddlebags easily contained all the mail.

A DISCUSSION ON A FINANCIAL QUESTION OF THE TIMES.

If such were the scanty mail accommodations of the chief cities, we can imagine what they were in the small country towns. Sacks of letters and papers are now easily carried in one afternoon farther than they were then transported in five weeks. After the war, Washington had an extensive and important correspondence with the influential men of the country. In many of his replies he complained of the tedious delay in receiving his mail. Well he might, for his letters were sometimes longer in going from Mount Vernon to Boston than they would now be in reaching China.

In remote sections the post-rider was often a decrepit man or some crippled soldier. One old postman used to improve his time, as his horse jogged slowly along, by knitting woolen mittens and stockings. There was no special protection to the service. Letters and packages were opened and freely read or examined by the carriers. So common was this evil that the great men of this time used to correspond in cipher.

We may be sure that when it cost much to send letters, and the difficulties of forwarding them were so many, the letter-writers of those days took special pains to write long epistles, full of news. People learned most of the news of the day from distant places, whether it pertained to politics, society, or gossip, through faithful correspondents.

Imagine a busy merchant in one of our great cities writing a business letter, but giving most of the space to the results of the last election, or the doings of the state legislature. The telegraph, the telephone, stenography, and the typewriter of our day have revolutionized business communication and much of personal correspondence.

266. The Stage Coaches.—During the war of the Revolution, stages stopped running between distant cities, and horseback traveling was resumed. When peace was declared, the "coach and four" again took the road. Boston and New York were then the two great commercial centers of the country; yet during Washington's first term two stages and twelve horses carried all the passengers by land between these two cities.

The stage coach at this time was not much better than a huge covered box mounted on springs. There were no closed sides, glass windows, steps, or doors. It was not to be compared for one moment with the far-famed Concord coaches in after years. In summer an ordinary day's journey was forty miles, but in winter only about one-half of this distance.

The stage started early each morning—often at three o'clock—and its daily time limit was about ten at night. Often the passengers were forced to get out and help lift it out of the mud or a deep rut. If there were no unusual accidents or mishaps, it reached New York, from Boston, at the end of the sixth day. Even at this snail pace the good people used to wonder at the ease, as well as the speed, with which the journey was made.

It is no wonder, then, that a journey to any remote place became a serious matter. Prudent men, when ready to set out for a distant point, arranged their business affairs for any emergency, made their wills, and, after a formal dinner at the tavern, bade their family and neighbors a solemn farewell.

267. How Fires were put out.—The law at this time compelled every man to take an active part in putting out fires. He was obliged to keep at least four leathern buckets hung up at some convenient place in his house or shop, with his name painted on them, together with a big canvas bag. When an alarm of fire was raised, either by vigorous shouts of "Fire! fire!" or the ringing of the church bell, the good citizen seized his fire buckets and his canvas bag, and, guided by the smoke or flame, started for the scene of action.

There were no idlers at an old-time fire. Some rushed into the building with their canvas bags and filled them with such movable goods as could be readily carried in them. A double line extending to the water was formed of men, boys, and even women. One line passed the full buckets to those who were nearest the fire, while the other line returned the empty vessels to the well or river.

Some of the larger towns boasted of a "fire engine." This was merely a pump mounted over a tank, which the men kept full by pouring in water from the buckets. The rich householder was allowed to send his slave or servant to the fire with the fire buckets.

When the fire was out, the buckets were left in the road, to be picked up and carried home by their owners. Persons who neglected to keep their fire buckets in good order and in their proper places, or who failed to carry them home after the fire, were fined.

268. How Sunday was passed.—The observance of Sunday began at sundown on Saturday. The early part of the evening was devoted to family worship, and shortly after eight o'clock all were in bed. No work except such as was really necessary was done on Sunday. Most of the cooking was done the day before. Each member of the family, unless sick in bed, went to church. The farmer traveled on horseback with his wife on the pillion behind.

The singers sat in the front gallery. The boys and young men had seats in the left-hand gallery, while that on the right was occupied by the young women. We have read in a previous chapter something about the tithing-man and his duties. The short noon interval was devoted to eating a cold lunch.

No meeting-house in those days was warmed. Old and feeble women were allowed to use tin foot-stoves, filled with a few hot coals. In the bitter cold months of a New England winter it was no trifling affair to endure the actual suffering that accompanied religious worship on Sunday. The story is told of a good minister in Connecticut who in the depths of winter prudently preached in overcoat and mittens, but complained that his voice was drowned by persons stamping and knocking their feet together to keep warm.

269. The Minister and the Meeting-Houses.—The minister was always held in high esteem. He was usually the most important man of the village, and was looked upon with reverence not unmingled with awe. His authority was almost supreme. If a person spoke disrespectfully of him, or even laughed at his oddities, the offender was heavily fined. The advice of the minister was often asked, and sometimes given unasked, on matters of business as well as of religion. Fearless and resolute in what they believed to be right, the influence of the ministers of that time in public affairs was deservedly very great.

The minister's salary was but a pittance. It was never the same two years in succession, and was rarely paid in cash. Donations of corn, beans, turnips, and other farm products were usually given in place of hard money.

The sermon was the one event of the week. Every well person in the village turned out to hear it. Copious notes were taken, and its various points furnished topics for fireside discussion during the week.

270. How the Doctors healed the Sick.—The village doctor, together with the minister and schoolmaster, held a high social rank. There were only two medical colleges in the country, and these were not well attended. Medical books were scarce and costly. Even the best doctors could not boast of a medical library of fifty volumes.

A VILLAGE MAGNATE RIDING IN THE OLD-TIME CHAISE.

The future doctor served his time as a student with some well-known physician. He ground the powders, mixed the potions, rolled the pills, cleaned the bottles, tended the night bell, and otherwise made himself useful. If the young student had a good preceptor and was gifted with a keen observation and a retentive memory, he returned to his native town or went elsewhere fairly prepared to begin practice.

There were no drug stores in those days, and each doctor was his own apothecary. He ground his own drugs, made his own tinctures, salves, and plasters. Most of the medical preparations used then would not be tolerated to-day.

Then as now the country doctor used to ride night and day, year after year, whatever the weather or the condition of the roads, to attend the good people of his neighborhood. He received, as he richly deserved, the respect and affection of his patients for his life of hardship and self-denial.

271. How the Schoolmaster taught School.—Besides the doctor, minister, and lawyer, the village schoolmaster was socially and otherwise an important man. He was usually a student who was "working his way" through college, and who sought, by teaching winters and working on a farm in summer, to defray his expenses at Yale, Dartmouth, or Harvard.

In many of the school districts he was expected to "board round." That is, he lived with the parents of his pupils, regulating his stay according to the number of the children of the family who attended school.

AN OLD SOLDIER FIGHTING HIS BATTLES OVER AGAIN.

In those days there were large families and many children, and the young schoolmaster was a welcome guest. The best room in the house, the warmest corner by the fireplace, and the choicest food were reserved for him. During the long winter evenings he discussed theology and politics with the fathers, played games with the children, and escorted the girls to "spelling matches" and "quilting bees."

272. The Everyday Home Life.—Such conveniences and comforts as are now found in almost every home were then unknown. Cooking stoves, matches, refined sugar, sewing machines, and kerosene oil had never been heard of. The mechanic's home had no carpets on the floor, no pictures on the walls, no coal in the cellar, no water faucets in the kitchen. Fruits and vegetables, now so cheap in their season, such as tomatoes, oranges, bananas, celery, and dates, were either quite unknown or beyond the reach of scanty means.

The farmers of a century ago ate plain food and wore plain clothes. Their daily fare was usually salt fish, salt pork, beef, a few vegetables, and dried apples. The numerous farm implements, which have done so much to cheapen food and to bring thousands of acres into a state of high cultivation, were not yet invented.

The well-to-do farmer managed to pick up a great deal of general information and news of the day. He was noted for an inquiring turn of mind. He could tire out the weary visitor or stranger on the road with numberless questions on current social, political, or religious topics. At times he would unbend enough to play "fox and geese" with his children, or attend "apple bees" and corn huskings.

CHAPTER XXI.
WHAT OUR NAVY DID IN THE WAR OF 1812.

273. Outrages committed by the Pirates of the Barbary Coast.—A hundred years ago the ports of the nations lying on the northern coast of Africa—the Barbary States, as they were called, Morocco, Algiers, Tunis, and Tripoli—were infested by fierce pirates. They used to rush out with their swift vessels and capture the ships of Christian nations. After plundering them of their valuables, they would hold the crews as slaves, or sell them to slave dealers.

These pirates became for years the terror of Europe. Merchants paid annual tributes of large sums of money to the Pasha to save their cargoes from seizure. Even our own nation, in 1795, paid these sea robbers for the release of American sailors captured and held by them as slaves, and also for the exemption of our ships from attack. First and last we paid these robber states not less than a million dollars to buy their good will.

It is difficult to realize that there was once a time when the President of the United States negotiated treaties, the Senate ratified them, and Congress voted tribute money to keep the peace with pirates.

In 1801 a disagreement arose about our regular payment; and the Bashaw of Tripoli, whose greed it was hard to satisfy, had the impudence to declare war against the United States and cut down the flagstaff in front of our consul's residence.

274. The Gallant Exploits of Decatur and his Brave Men.—Although we had only a small navy, President Jefferson thought it best to put a stop to this blackmail business, and settle with the pirates in a different way. So he sent some war vessels to punish them, and they did it quite thoroughly.

During one of these encounters the United States frigate Philadelphia, one of our best, under the command of Captain Bainbridge, chased a pirate craft into the harbor of Tripoli, but unluckily ran on a reef. She stuck fast, helpless either to fight or to sail. She was captured, with all her crew, by the enemy.

But a few months afterwards, Stephen Decatur, a gallant lieutenant of only twenty-five, sailed from Sicily in a small vessel, the Intrepid, which had just been captured from the Moors. He boldly entered the harbor of Tripoli one evening about dusk, and sailed quietly along close to the Philadelphia. Then pirates did not suspect harm, as the Intrepid appeared to be a Moorish vessel. With its crew of seventy men concealed under the bulwarks, the little vessel was instantly made fast to the ill-fated frigate.

"Follow me, lads!" cried Decatur.

The men from the Intrepid sprang to their feet and climbed on board the Philadelphia. The surprise was complete. In ten minutes Decatur and his bold sailors had killed or driven overboard every pirate, then set the ship afire, leaped back upon the Intrepid, and escaped from the harbor amid a storm of shot from the batteries. Not one of our men was lost in the whole affair.

This heroic adventure, which made young Decatur a captain, became common talk in Europe. England's greatest naval hero, Lord Nelson, said, "It was the most bold and daring act of the ages." There is no single naval exploit to be compared with it for boldness, except Cushing's destruction of the ironclad Albemarle in the war for the Union.

275. Outrageous Conduct of the British toward American Sailors.—During the years soon after 1800, Napoleon Bonaparte was at war with almost all Europe, and especially with England.

The British navy was very large and in constant need of sailors. To get them, English men-of-war used to stop American merchant ships wherever they met them on the high seas. They would fire a cannon shot across the bows of the American vessel to compel it to heave to. British officers would then come on board, marshal the crew in line, and pick out sailors whom they claimed to be deserters from British ships.

Very likely the ones thus singled out could prove that they were Americans by birth or adoption. No matter for that! They were needed, and, as the men-of-war had the power to take them by force, go they must. In time this dastardly business became even worse. The British sometimes stationed their war vessels off the entrance of our largest harbors, ready to search our merchantmen as they sailed out.

Now all this bid fair to destroy our commerce. None of our ships were safe. Importing, exporting, our vast fisheries, important manufactures— many kinds of business—were on the verge of ruin.

In spite of our protests the British government kept up this practice for years, until it was said that more than nine hundred American vessels had been searched, and over six thousand American sailors kidnapped from them.

276. The War of 1812 begun.—Why did we endure these insults from England so long? Perhaps the principal reason was our small navy. The English war fleets then numbered over a thousand vessels, and ours less than twenty! These outrages could not, however, be longer tolerated. England even insisted that she had a perfect right to seize our ships and to carry off our citizens.

War was declared in 1812. In this war most of our land battles were more or less failures, but the brilliant success of our naval contests more than made up for them. In fact, whenever we speak of the war of 1812, we always think of the surprising series of victories won by our splendid though small naval force against England.

ISAAC HULL.

277. The Great Naval Battle between the Constitution and the Guerrière.—Only a few weeks after war was declared, our frigate Constitution, Captain Isaac Hull, met the enemy's man-of-war Guerrière, Captain Dacres, off the Massachusetts shore. The British vessel had been sailing proudly up and down our coast, challenging the Yankee craft to fight. The Guerrière in real British pride flings out a flag from the top of each "ocean spire." Her guns flash but the balls fall short.
"Not a cannon to be fired till I give the word," cried Captain Hull; "double shot the guns."
"May we not begin?" shouted his first officer as the shot came tearing through the rigging.
Another broadside from the Guerrière! The men are getting impatient. Captain Hull calmly waits until he can bring every gun to bear.
"Now, boys, give it to them!" he shouted at the top of his voice.
They did their work well. In twenty minutes the proud English frigate was a helpless wreck.
"I will not take your sword," said the gallant Hull to Captain Dacres as the British officer surrendered; "but I will trouble you for that hat!"
It seems that these two brave captains were personal friends, and Hull had made a bet with Dacres that his vessel would "whip" the Guerrière if there should ever be a war, and the loser was to forfeit his hat!
The Constitution was almost unhurt. The Guerrière, shattered and useless, was set on fire, and in a few minutes blew up. All that was left of the splendid vessel instantly vanished from sight forever. Hull took his prisoners to Boston, where he was received with enthusiastic welcome.
The news of this victory created equal joy in every section of the country. Its chief importance lay in the confidence it inspired among all the people,

demonstrating that a first-class English battleship was far from invincible. The British government was astounded. So were the naval authorities, some of whom had sneered at the Constitution as "a bundle of pine boards."

CAPTAIN HULL REFUSES TO ACCEPT CAPTAIN DACRES' SWORD.

278. Naval Battle between the Wasp and Frolic; Other Brilliant Naval Victories for the American Sailors.—A few weeks later the American sloop-of-war Wasp fell in with the British brig Frolic off Virginia. It was a sharp fight for three-quarters of an hour. Both vessels were nearly destroyed, when the Wasp came close to the Frolic and gave a tremendous broadside that carried away everything before it. Then the Wasp's crew boarded the Frolic and found not a sailor on deck—only the officers, who surrendered. The surviving sailors had gone below to escape the deadly fire. The very next week Commodore Decatur of the frigate United States attacked the British frigate Macedonian near the Canary Islands. It was a brisk fight of two hours, when the Macedonian surrendered with a loss of over one hundred men.

Decatur's victory produced a profound impression both in this country and in England. Congress recognized its importance by a vote of thanks and a gold medal to the commodore.

279. "Old Ironsides" and her Noble Record.—In the same month occurred the famous battle off Brazil between the Constitution under Commodore Bainbridge and the frigate Java. It was a furious contest for two hours. The enemy's ship had every mast shot away, and her hull was torn with shot. Her deck was covered with more than two hundred killed and wounded. The wreck of the Java surrendered, the survivors were taken on board the Constitution, and the hull was burned. This was the fourth brilliant naval victory gained within six months.

The Constitution has ever since been popularly known as "Old Ironsides," by which name her exploits have been celebrated from that day until this in oratory and song. Many years ago the government planned to break her up and sell her timbers. This prompted Dr. Oliver Wendell Holmes to write his famous poem beginning:—

Ay, tear her tattered ensign down!Long has it waved on high.

These stirring lines had a powerful influence upon the public mind, and the noble-vessel was saved. She may be seen now (1900), carefully protected, in the navy yard at Charlestown, Mass.

Slowly but surely the idea dawned upon many minds in Europe that a nation was springing up on the other side of the Atlantic that would sometime dispute with England, the "mistress of the seas," the supremacy of the ocean.

280. Battle between the Chesapeake and Shannon.—The year 1813 opened with hopeful prospects, but the scale turned less in our favor than during 1812. A brilliant young officer, Captain James Lawrence, was given in reward for his bravery the command of the Chesapeake, then lying in Boston Harbor. She was one of the finest frigates in our young navy, but had the name among the sailors of being an "unlucky" craft.

Lawrence had hardly taken charge of his new ship when he received a challenge from the British frigate Shannon, cruising outside, daring him to come out and fight. He hastily made ready for sea, collected such a crew as he could, part landsmen and part foreigners, and sailed out. This was really very unwise.

JAMES LAWRENCE.

The Shannon's crew were picked men, and had had long and careful drill, while Lawrence's men were fresh and unprepared. Lawrence was young, proud of his late victory, and full of courage. The hostile ships fought fiercely and with terrible effect. In a few minutes every one of the Chesapeake's officers was either killed or wounded.

While Lawrence was giving an order, a musket ball inflicted upon him a fatal wound. As he was carried below, his dying words were, "DON'T GIVE UP THE SHIP!"

—a stirring battle-cry, which has ever since been a source of inspiration to our navy.

The battle was soon over. The torn rigging of the Chesapeake was entangled with that of the Shannon, the enemy's officers leaped on board and raised the British flag. The Chesapeake was taken to Halifax, where Lawrence was buried with military honors.

281. Commodore Perry and his Brilliant Victory on Lake Erie.—The story of Perry's brilliant victory on Lake Erie has been told in prose and verse ever since it took place. The control of this inland sea between two hostile countries was very important. The British already had a little fleet of six vessels with sixty-three guns, to oppose which we had hardly anything in the shape of vessels or trained men.

A naval officer, Oliver Hazard Perry of Rhode Island, not quite twenty-eight years old and who had never been in action before, was appointed to take charge of the whole matter in behalf of the United States. First, he must have an armed flotilla to meet the enemy.

With remarkable energy the young captain put a large force of wood-choppers and ship carpenters at work for months near Erie, Pa., felling huge trees and building war vessels of the green timber. Soon he had launched nine, with fifty-four cannon—more vessels than the enemy, but fewer guns.

One beautiful September morning the British fleet was seen on the horizon.

"Sail ho!" rang out from the masthead of the American flagship.

"Enemy in sight!" "Get under way!" was the signal sent to each vessel.

Perry stripped his flagship, the Lawrence, for action. At her masthead he raised a blue battle-flag, upon which had been painted in large white letters the dying words of the brave Lawrence, "Don't give up the ship."

"My brave lads," said Perry, "this flag has on it the dying words of Captain Lawrence. Shall I hoist it?"

"Aye, aye, sir," shouted every man, and cheer after cheer echoed and reechoed through the fleet. This was the signal for battle.

The enemy's fire was directed mostly upon Perry's vessel, which fought the two largest British ships till the Lawrence was almost a helpless wreck—cannon dismounted, masts shot away, and most of the crew either killed or wounded.

Should Perry surrender? NOT HE!

Taking his motto banner, he sprang into his only open boat, with his little brother and four stout sailors, and standing erect with his battle-flag half folded about him, balls flying all around him, he was rowed through the thickest of the fight to another of his ships, the Niagara, half a mile distant.

A mighty shout went up from all our fleet at the sight of this heroic deed.

"Fire upon that boat," ordered the British commander.

The enemy at once poured a hail of cannon-balls, grapeshot, and musket bullets around the men in the open boat. Strange to say, not a person was hurt. Perry sprang on board of the Niagara, took command, sailed his vessels into the enemy's line, and thundered a series of broadsides right and left into five of their best ships.

OLIVER HAZARD PERRY.

In fifteen minutes from this moment the work was over! For the first time in history an American fleet had met a British fleet in a fair fight—and captured it!

The battle had lasted three hours. The victory was complete. Then with singular pride Perry returned to the shattered Lawrence and there received the enemy's surrender! When he was sure of victory, he wrote in pencil on the back of an old letter, resting the paper on his cap, and sent to General Harrison (afterwards President in 1841) that remarkable despatch, the first sentence of which has been so often repeated:

"WE HAVE MET THE ENEMY AND THEY ARE OURS!"

This victory, so astonishing for its daring act of valor, turned the scales of war. It saved the western states from further inroads by the British, and paved the way for General Harrison to recover what was lost in General Hull's surrender of Detroit.

282. Other Events of this War.—The next year, 1814, which saw the end of the war, was marked by events few but important. In the summer the British with their vast fleet blockaded all our most important ports, and sailing up rivers and into unprotected harbors, they plundered without mercy the defenseless cities and towns.

In August one of their fleet sailed up to Washington, the city being entirely unguarded. President Madison, the officers of the government, and many citizens fled, and General Ross marched unopposed into the city. Obeying instructions from his government, he burned the Capitol, the President's house, the Treasury, and other public buildings, with vast amounts of valuable books and records. This shameful act has always received the sharpest condemnation from the civilized world.

Next the British army marched to Baltimore, where the fleet bombarded Fort McHenry all day and all night, but without avail. The next morning Francis Scott Key, then a prisoner on a British ship, seeing the flag still flying over the fort, hastily wrote in pencil, on the back of an old letter, the stirring song that we all know so well, "The Star-Spangled Banner."

The British General Ross was killed, and his army hastened to the ships and sailed away.

In September the English, with an army of fourteen thousand veterans, tried to force a way from Canada to New York through Lake Champlain. Their army marched from Quebec, while the fleet sailed down the lake, and both were at Plattsburg together. But our gallant flotilla under Commodore McDonough utterly destroyed the British squadron, far superior to ours.

283. How General Jackson defeated the British at New Orleans.— Later in the year the British made a vigorous effort to capture New Orleans. More than ten thousand trained veterans, believed to be the finest troops in the world, were met by less than half that number of men under Andrew Jackson, afterwards President. The battle was short but decisive.

The British general repeated the fatal error of Bunker Hill in marching his soldiers to attack men who were behind breastworks, and who knew how to hit every time they fired. Jackson's wall of cotton bales was assaulted time and again, but the red-coat lines broke and ran before the withering fire of the backwoods rifles. The sharpshooters of the South-west had worsted British veterans who had defeated the best soldiers of Napoleon.

In less than an hour the enemy's leader, General Packenham, was killed, seven hundred of his men lay dead on the field, and the contest was over. The British lost over two thousand in all, the Americans only thirteen! Never had a British army met a more decisive defeat.

This battle, fought on the eighth of January, 1815, was really needless; for peace had been made in Europe about two weeks before.

284. Results of the War.—The war of 1812 was not fought in vain. It put an end at once to searching American vessels and kidnapping American sailors on the high seas. Foreign nations saw that we were determined to maintain our rights on the ocean, and have never thought it best since then to insult our country. This war also served to strengthen the American feeling of nationality.

CHAPTER XXII.
THE SETTLEMENT OF THE PACIFIC COAST.

285. The Great Rush Westward.—Shortly after the close of the Revolution, long processions of emigrant wagons, with their white canvas covers and their companies of hardy men and women, began to move westward on all the main roads through New England, over the highways of New York toward the lakes, over the Blue Ridge Mountains of Virginia, and through the valley of the Ohio.

Thousands of thrifty settlers followed just behind the pioneers and cleared the forests, bridged the streams, built villages, and tilled the rich valleys. Thousands left their homes in the Carolinas and went over the mountains to settle on the rich lands of Kentucky and Tennessee.

The hardships which these early settlers endured are beyond description. It was one long hard struggle for food, shelter, and life itself. This was only the beginning of that mighty stream of migration which flowed for the next half century or more beyond the Mississippi, beyond the Rocky Mountains, into the region of the extreme Northwest and to the shores of the Pacific.

The story of the marvelous growth of our country beyond the Alleghanies during the last hundred years reads more like a fairy tale than the plain truth.

286. Discovery of the Columbia River.—In 1792 Captain Robert Gray of Boston, in the ship Columbia, was coasting along the Pacific shores, trading with the Indians for furs, when he discovered a broad and deep stream, which he entered and sailed up for many miles, and named after his vessel. The discovery of this great river produced momentous and far-reaching results.

287. The Purchase of Louisiana by President Jefferson.—Now comes another important event. Our pioneers, who wanted to push on still farther, could not consistently cross the Mississippi River to stay there; for all that country belonged to France. This entire region of over a million square miles was then called Louisiana.

Our people were very anxious to obtain part of this land, because it included New Orleans. The possession of it seemed necessary for our growing commerce and for our future protection. Thomas Jefferson, then President (1803), was on the point of attempting to buy of France enough of this southern region to include the mouth of the river, when he learned to his surprise that the French would be glad to sell us the whole of that vast territory!

Napoleon was just then planning military operations on a great scale against England, and he was in sore need of "the sinews of war"; so he was glad to sell to this country this immense area for fifteen million dollars.

The addition of the Louisiana territory more than doubled the area of the United States.

288. The Wonders revealed by the Lewis and Clarke Exploring Expedition.—The next year President Jefferson thought it best to learn all about this wonderful addition to our territory, and so sent an expedition, under Captains Lewis and Clarke, to explore it. They started from St. Louis in May, 1804. What a remarkable journey it was!—more than two thousand miles up the Missouri River to its source, then across the Rocky Mountains, next down the Columbia River to the Pacific. They were the first white men who ever explored this vast domain, having traveled about six thousand miles.

On their return in September, 1806, they were welcomed with unbounded joy. The stories of their perilous adventures sounded like a fairy romance, and the book of their travels was read everywhere. The explorers brought back word that the Indians had immense quantities of valuable furs. Soon throngs of American hunters and trappers began to roam over the vast plains and through the forests.

All the way from the Missouri River to the Pacific a chain of trading posts, and stores for exchanging goods for furs were established. The wagons of the fur-traders and the winding caravans of emigrants that went under their protection soon made a pretty fair road. This was known as the Oregon trail, and in time it became the principal northern highway for Pacific travel.

289. How Dr. Whitman saved Oregon to the Union.—In 1836 a group of young missionaries, two of them with their brides, went from New England to Oregon, taking with them a wagon all the way from the Missouri to their new homes on the Columbia River. One of these was a doctor by the name of Marcus Whitman, whose labors and counsel became of great value to the company.

After they had been settled in Oregon some years Dr. Whitman discovered, one day in October, 1842, that the British were sending large bands of settlers down into Oregon, apparently to crowd American emigrants out of that rich country and to take complete possession.

"The country is ours! The United States is too late. England will have Oregon and you cannot help it," exclaimed an English subject to him.

"I will see," was the doctor's quiet reply.

The moment Dr. Whitman heard this he became alarmed at the danger. If the President at Washington could only be informed of the facts, the threatened loss might be averted. The National Capital was three thousand or more miles away; and yet to delay a year or two might mean the seizure of all this rich country by the British.

How to inform the government at Washington was the question. Could he himself do anything to save to his country this immense and valuable region?—one man, in midwinter, and across a continent? The problem haunted him—"Must I go?" He could not sleep. Difficult, almost impossible, as would be the journey, yet he heard the clear call of duty.

A firm and bold, resolve, quick as a flash, had taken hold of him. He rode home in haste.

"I am going to Washington to lay bare this scheme," said he to his wife. "I will bring settlers to Oregon."

"You cannot ever get there," exclaimed the young wife; "you will perish on the way."

"I must go; Oregon must be saved," said Whitman.

290. Whitman begins his Perilous Journey.—Twenty-four hours later Dr. Whitman, with one companion, and pack mules for the guide and their supplies, started on horseback on the perilous undertaking.

Over mountain ranges, through deep gorges and rugged forests, now drenched in storms, now buried in snow, and half famishing for food—their sufferings cannot be described.

WHITMAN'S FAMOUS "RIDE FOR OREGON."

They fed their horses on cotton-wood bark, while the men themselves lived on mule and dog meat. Two or three times they were really lost in the blinding snowstorms, and wandered about bewildered for days. Once only, Whitman gave up in despair, and then, worn out and bewildered, he knelt in the deep snow, and in a final prayer surrendered to God all earthly hopes. Then the party sank down and awaited a snowy burial. They were not, however, to die in the wilderness, but were rescued from death almost as if by a miracle, and after untold hardships for three months they reached St. Louis.

291. Dr. Whitman succeeds in his Grand Mission.—Dr. Whitman at last arrived in Washington and convinced President Tyler and Daniel

Webster, his Secretary of State, of the great value of Oregon and its importance to the Union. It is claimed that he thus saved to our nation, by his famous "Ride for Oregon," that entire region of country now known as Oregon, Washington, and Idaho, an area thirty-two times as large as the state of Massachusetts.

This heroic patriot afterwards went through the Eastern States and told the people of the wonders of the Pacific coast. He stirred up such an interest that when, in the following June, he started back for Oregon he had the satisfaction of leading a caravan of two hundred wagons, with nearly a thousand people. After that, emigrants thronged every year in larger and larger numbers, till the territory was soon beyond the danger of British invasion.

The dispute as to which nation had a right to Oregon was at last settled in 1846 by a treaty between the United States and England. By this treaty the boundary line was fixed, and our rightful claim to the vast Oregon country was confirmed for all time.

292. California becomes One of the United States.—During all these years, while so many eyes were turned towards Oregon, few thought much of California, for it then belonged to Mexico. The coast trade in hides and furs and the inland immigration from the United States had slowly changed the kind of population. Although it was still Mexican by name, yet by 1846, besides the Spanish, Mexicans, and Indians, there were about ten thousand other inhabitants, mostly American citizens. In that year war was declared between the United States and Mexico. Then the large body of Americans in California thought they had a right to declare their independence of Mexico.

At just this time John C. Fremont, an army officer and a famous western mountain explorer, was fortunately on the great plains, and was sent with an army expedition to explore a new route to Oregon. Being informed by special messenger of the war with Mexico, he changed his course and went to California. When he arrived there his small but courageous band, increased in number by patriotic residents and acting in harmony with our fleet, soon secured the independence of this great state.

293. The Discovery of Gold in California.—It appears fortunate and even providential that California came into our hands just when it did, for shortly afterwards a most remarkable event occurred. Captain Sutter, an early emigrant, had settled on the Sacramento River and built a sawmill.

In January, 1848, one of Sutter's laborers, by the name of Marshall, while digging a ditch for the mill, found shiny pieces of yellow metal which they suspected might be gold.

"I wonder what that yellow stuff is," said he. "I wonder if it is gold."

"I reckon it is brass," said one of his helpers.

"Let me try vinegar on it," said Marshall. It was tried and the vinegar did not affect the "yellow stuff."

The men about the sawmill threw down their tools and went to work searching for gold. Mr. Sutter laughed at the idea. But gold indeed it was, and there was plenty of it!

294. The Effect of this Great Discovery.—The news spread. Soon everybody about knew that pure gold was found and in wonderful quantities. What a rush there was to the "diggings"! How all sorts of people from all over the western coast crowded in! Doctors left their sick, ministers their pulpits, traders their shops, mechanics their tools, and farmers their fields, all half frantic with the desire to dig their fortunes out of the golden sands of California.

When the news of the discovery of gold reached the East, many people seemed to catch the contagion. Multitudes started at once for California. Thousands came by long wagon trains over the dreary plains. Hundreds died of starvation or were killed by Indians. Thousands went by the Isthmus, other thousands by Cape Horn. Vast numbers came from foreign countries. Even the crews and often the officers abandoned the ships that brought crowds to the Pacific coast and started for the gold "diggings."

295. The Mad Rush to the Gold Regions.—The rush to the gold fields began in 1848, but became enormous in 1849. Those who went that year are since called "Forty-niners." There were over eighty thousand of them! The crowds that thronged the gold regions dug up the country for miles around Sutter's mill. They tore up his beautiful valley and ruined his farm. But they soon learned that gold was also to be found in larger quantities along the streams, among the mountains, and in valleys.

Month by month new-comers swarmed in, and the excitement grew more intense. Some found prizes, nuggets of solid gold as large as an acorn or a walnut, and at times masses two or three pounds in weight. However much gold a man found, he was wildly eager to get more.

A great deal of suffering ensued from the scarcity of food and the enormous prices of everything needful. Potatoes sold for a dollar apiece, eggs at the same price, wood at fifty dollars a cord, and flour at a hundred dollars a barrel. Large butcher knives were found very useful for digging, and brought thirty dollars each. A dose of the cheapest medicine in an apothecary's shop cost five dollars, and a physician's visit a hundred dollars. Unskilled laborers were paid twenty-five dollars a day.

Money was not used at the mines, but in its place the ore itself, or "dust," at about sixteen dollars an ounce. Miners carried small scales, weighed their gold dust, and paid their bills with it.

At the rough log tavern: "What do you charge for dinner here?" "Half an ounce."

At the wayside store: "What's the price of these boots?" "Three ounces."

296. The Pony Express and its Remarkable History.—San Francisco, being the principal base of operations and the center of much of the immense travel to and from the mines, grew in a few years from a cluster of shanties to a large and wealthy city. The people of California now demanded more frequent and more expeditious transmission of mail matter than that by steamers and across the Isthmus.

It was finally decided to establish a horseback letter express between St. Joseph, on the Missouri River, and San Francisco, about two thousand miles. It was a daring and hazardous project. But the express began business in April, 1860, and made the through trip in ten days. Only letters were carried. The charge was five dollars each, afterwards reduced one-half. The company had sixty hardy riders and four hundred and twenty strong, fast horses, though it was nicknamed the "pony express."

THE "PONY EXPRESS" RIDER.

A rider started from each end of the journey at the same hour. There were stations every twenty-five miles for keeping and changing horses. On a postman's arrival at a station the bags were instantly slung on a fresh horse (for never more than two minutes must be spent at a station), and away went the new courier for the next station. The speed was by and by increased, until the long run was made in only eight days!

Ah! that was furious riding! What speed they made! In 1861 the pony riders took President Lincoln's message through in one hundred and eighty-five hours! It was dangerous riding too. Day and night, over sandy plains and lofty mountains, on, on dashed these bold riders.

The "pony express" was worth to the nation a hundred times its cost. Why? Because just at that time our Civil War was beginning to darken the land, and the South was making desperate efforts to entice the vast Pacific region to unite with the seceding states. This "pony express" line proved to be the first strand of a strong cable to unite the East and the West.

297. More Rapid Means of Communication between the East and the Pacific Coast urgently needed.—For many years before 1860 there was talk of the urgent need, and finally of the absolute necessity, of closer connection between the old East and the new West. There were plenty of reasons for a railroad; but in 1861 there came another overpowering reason that eclipsed all others. The war for the Union had begun, and it was a matter of supreme importance that the Pacific states should be saved in the Union. No step could lead more surely toward this result than to have a railroad for constant and swift travel.

298. The Railroad over the Rocky Mountains to the Pacific Coast rapidly built.—In 1863 the great work was begun. The government was wonderfully generous and contributed money and land freely, for it was felt that the railroad must be built as quickly as possible. The completion of the gigantic undertaking in 1869 at Ogden, Utah, was gayly celebrated. Two trains, loaded with passengers from New York and San Francisco, approached each other at this place. The last rail was laid, the last rivet clinched, the last spike, a spike of gold sent from California, was driven, when the locomotives moved up and saluted, amid the cheers of the enthusiastic throngs!

In seven years' time, from 1849 to 1856, the gold found in California was worth nearly five hundred millions of dollars! Imagine the effect of such an output of the precious metal upon the industries and commerce of our country!

California is still rich in its gold, but it is still richer in its wonderful climate and its marvelous scenery; in the wealth of its grain fields; its sheep and cattle; its orange groves and its vineyards. These make California the real El Dorado,—the real land of gold, and ensure the prosperity and happiness of its people.

CHAPTER XXIII.
LINCOLN AND THE WAR FOR THE UNION.

299. Abraham Lincoln; the Abiding Influence of his Good Mother.—
The early settlers in the Western states were generally very poor. It was the honorable poverty of the pioneer, who bravely begins with only his axe and a few tools, with which he builds his log cabin, clears the forest, and works his way to competence and comfort.

So lived in Larue County, in the state of Kentucky, about fifty miles south of Louisville, Thomas Lincoln and his wife Nancy, in a rude log cabin with no windows, a dirt floor, and only a flapping bearskin for a door! In this humble abode, which they called home, there was born to them on February 12, 1809, a son, Abraham.

The father was a strong and kindly man, and the mother was a woman rather above her lowly position in life, and well educated for the time and place. As her boy grew up she read to him stories from the Bible and taught him to read for himself.

In after years, when Abraham Lincoln had gained the people's ear, men noticed that he scarcely made a speech or wrote a state paper in which there was not an 'illustration or a quotation from the Bible. He had been thoroughly instructed in it by his mother. It was the one book to which she, being a woman of deep religious feeling, turned for sympathy and guidance. Out of it she taught her boy to spell and read, and with its principles she so familiarized him that they always governed his after life.

When Abraham was eight years old the family moved to Indiana, where, in about a year, his mother died. This was an unutterable grief to him, for he loved her most deeply and tenderly. Throughout his life he revered her memory, and when he was in his prime he said, "All that I am or hope to be, I owe to my mother."

300. How Lincoln learned to read Good Books.—Young Lincoln attended school only six weeks. He was a tall, gaunt lad, and his long, stout arms were very useful to his father on the farm.

Like Franklin, he had a hunger for books, and having none himself, he used to walk miles to some family to borrow them. Every evening he used to read by the log fire Pilgrim's Progress, the poems of Robert Burns, The Life of Washington, or Plutarch's Lives. Think of that boy sitting before the cabin fire, reading over and over the story of Washington; and then think of what he came to be.

When the family went to bed he used to climb, on a rude ladder of stout pegs driven in the logs, up to his bed made of hay, and there, by the light of his tallow candle, would read over and over his precious books. He bought a biography of Washington with three hard days' work at twenty-five cents a day. He carried the book with him to the field, and read it at the noon hour and while the horse rested.

LINCOLN READING HIS FAVORITE BOOKS BY THE FIRESIDE.

301. Some Things Lincoln did when a Young Man.—When Lincoln was about twenty-one, the family moved to Illinois. The young man was rugged and tall, six feet and four inches, but very strong. In feats of running, jumping, and wrestling he easily surpassed the best men in the county.

He was hired at ten dollars a month to go down to New Orleans on a flatboat loaded with farm produce. On the trip he saw gangs of slaves chained together, and he attended a slave auction, where men, women, and children were bid off like cattle. The painful sight sank deep into his heart, and he never forgot it. He was a soldier in the Black Hawk war, and was chosen by his comrades captain of the company, for all the men loved and respected him.

302. Makes up his Mind to become a Lawyer.—Young Lincoln grew rapidly in public esteem. People took kindly to him, for he was himself kind and unselfish. Though awkwardly tall and homely, there was a something tender and friendly about him, which made every one feel that he was honest and sincere.

As the years passed Lincoln kept on steadily educating himself by devoting every leisure hour to his books. He took regular studies, such as grammar, arithmetic, geometry, which he exceedingly enjoyed.

He was a thoughtful reader of a few of the great English classics. He could repeat numerous scenes from Shakespeare and many of the poems of Robert Burns. Whatever he read was read thoroughly—to understand it.

His need of money led the ambitious young man to study surveying, as Washington did—a very desirable attainment in a new country. He surveyed well Everything he did, he did well.

Visiting a courthouse one day, he heard for the first time the argument of a lawyer. He was absorbed and delighted. Never before had anything so captivated his imagination. From that day he made up his mind to be a lawyer. Too poor to waste any money on shoes, he walked twelve miles barefoot once to borrow a law book; and he came home reading it as he walked.

303. His Early Studies and Rapid Advancement in his Profession.—The struggling young lawyer now carefully studied the art of the clear and exact expression of thought. He attended that nursery of American oratory, the country debating club, and was a faithful student of the best method of speaking, making rapid progress by long and patient practice.

We no longer think of him as the boy of the log house, the homespun clothes, the coon-skin cap, and the bare feet, but rather as the brave young lawyer, studious, honest, persevering, self-reliant, and always faithful to duty.

After this Lincoln's advancement is rapid. His worthy traits draw to him many and strong friends. At twenty-five he is elected to the legislature. He discharges the duties of the office so well that two years later he is chosen again. Now an older lawyer invites him to be his partner.

He has become a man of note. People come from far to consult him. His growing fame daily widens. The people next call him to a higher place. At thirty-nine he is honored by being chosen a member of Congress. He fills the place with credit and honor. He is now the rising man of his state.

304. Slavery as a Menace to the Country.—There had always been one serious trouble in our republic—slavery. It began early. About a year before the Pilgrims came over in the Mayflower a Dutch ship brought twenty negroes from Africa to Virginia, and they were sold as slaves to the planters.

As years passed the traffic rapidly increased, and paid an enormous profit. Some of the colonists tried to stop this, but in vain; it was profitable. Soon slavery spread all over the country; mostly in the South, but somewhat even in New England. In the South, slaves were very useful in raising tobacco and rice, and, later, cotton and sugar cane.

At the formation of the republic all the Southern states came in as slave states. To this most of the Northern people, though they held slavery to be a great wrong, and feared that it would some day bring serious trouble, did not strenuously object, because it had long existed throughout the colonies. But as years passed the North strongly opposed the extension of slavery into new states or free territory. The South, however, had come to believe that slavery was right. When Missouri asked admission to the Union, the

South claimed that it should be received as a slave state. The North said, No! There was a great discussion over this question, which was finally settled in 1821 by allowing Missouri to come in as a slave state. After this it was understood that slavery should never be introduced north of the line of its southern boundary.

ABRAHAM LINCOLN.

305. Lincoln chosen President of the United States.—In 1854 an effort was made to bring in Kansas and Nebraska as possible slave states. This at once aroused a storm of indignation throughout the North. Mr. Lincoln stood forth as a champion of freedom, and Stephen A. Douglas, popularly known as "the little giant of the West," supported the claims of the South. They held public debates all through Illinois, being rival candidates for the United States Senate.

These great debates were listened to by thousands. Lincoln's speeches especially attracted much attention. They were printed and read in all sections. Many a voter said, "How plain he makes it all! He says it far better than I could." This contest raged in 1859. Douglas won the smaller prize of senator; but Lincoln, suddenly lifted into national fame by his splendid defense of freedom, was next year chosen President of the United States.

He was elected because of the firm determination of the North that, while they would not disturb slavery where it already existed, it should not extend any farther into free territory. This resolve was not unfriendly to the Southern people. It did not invade their rights as the North understood them. It was not intended as a threat to the people of that section; but they chose so to regard it and immediately took a hostile attitude.

In December, 1860, South Carolina seceded, then other states; so that before Mr. Lincoln began his duties as President the seven cotton states had seceded. Believing that they had a right to do so, they formed a government of their own and assumed a warlike attitude to the general government.

306. The Momentous Responsibilities of the Position.—We have traced the poor boy of the Western cabin step by step up to the highest office of the nation, to rule as the chief magistrate of thirty millions of people. It was not a nation in peace, but torn asunder, each half in deadly conflict with the other. Upon him were to rest the control of vast armies, of a great navy, the decision of questions of unspeakable importance, and the solution of most perplexing international problems.

Can this self-trained lawyer from the Western prairies bear all this sudden and tremendous burden, and bear it with courage, credit, and success? Surely no man of modern times ever faced a greater or more difficult task.

307. War begins; the Effect at the North and in the South.—The next month (April 12, 1861) after Lincoln's inauguration, Fort Sumter, in Charleston Harbor, was attacked by a circle of nineteen hostile batteries. After thirty-six hours of furious bombardment, Major Anderson, his powder and food being exhausted, his flagstaff shot away, his fort crumbling and on fire, felt that he could do nothing but surrender. He and his little force, carrying with them their tattered flag, were taken on board a Union ship to New York.

The shots fired at Sumter kindled another fire all through the North. A conflagration of patriotic zeal flamed up all over the loyal states. The people accepted instantly the awful challenge and sternly resolved to defend the endangered Union at every hazard.

Both sides had been deceived. Vast numbers through the North had not believed the slave states would really carry out their threat of secession. Vast numbers through the South had always believed the North would never fight, but at the last moment would consent to some sort of compromise.

Northern men felt that they had in no way wronged the South, that no act of theirs and no word of President Lincoln had given cause for precipitating the horrors of a civil war.

Southern men claimed that according to the Declaration of Independence all governments derive their power from the consent of the governed, and that the South had a right to withdraw its consent and establish a government of its own. Although there were some disloyal men all through the North, political parties vied with each other in the fervor of general devotion to one country and one flag. The President's call for seventy-five thousand volunteers was answered by the enthusiastic enlistment of the whole number.

In the South the excitement was equally great, but different in character. The masses went wild with passionate delight; but very many thoughtful people lamented the bombardment of Sumter as hasty, reckless, and ruinous. Some of the states were at first unwilling to secede, and finally went out reluctantly; but a belief that they were right swept them along, and, once out, they were as active as any.

308. Vigorous Efforts to preserve the Union.—Neither side was prepared for a long war, but the South was much better prepared to begin it than the North. Instantly every effort was put forth by the government to preserve the Union. Scores of warships blockaded the Southern ports to prevent cotton from being sent to England, and to cut off English ships from bringing in supplies, especially military stores.

The governments of Europe, except the Russian, were unfriendly to us. Four more states soon seceded, making eleven out of the fifteen slave states. Thousands of troops were gathered for the defense of the National Capital.

In July a Confederate army of about thirty thousand threatened Washington. A battle was fought at Manassas, only thirty miles southwest of the city. At first the Union forces had the advantage and seemed victorious; but just then heavy reinforcements of fresh troops came to help the Confederates, drove back the weary forces, and the day ended in Union disaster.

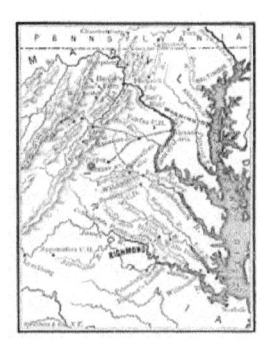

Click to enlarge.
MAP OF SEAT OF WAR IN VIRGINIA.

This battle of Manassas, or Bull Run, was a severe and unexpected defeat. It showed the scope of the tremendous conflict yet to come. There was not much more heavy fighting during the remainder of that year; both sides were busily making enormous preparations for the future struggle.

309. The Desperate Struggles of 1862.—In the early part of the next year (1862) each side had ready in the field about half a million of men. In the East, General McClellan, with a large army, set out in April from Washington for Richmond. He advanced within seven miles of that city, where was fought the battle of Fair Oaks. Neither side was victorious. The desperate seven days' battles soon followed, with result still indecisive. This, the so-called Peninsular Campaign, failed of its purpose.

In September the Confederate General Lee marched north and, invading Maryland, fought the bloody battle of Antietam. He was slightly worsted, and forced to retire into Virginia.

In the West, General Grant, the coming man, with the help of Commodore Foote's fleet of gunboats, captured in February Forts Henry and Donelson with ten thousand prisoners. Soon followed the desperate battle of Shiloh, in which Grant, reinforced by General Buell, repulsed the Confederates.

In April a great navy and army sailed up the Mississippi River, bombarded the forts below New Orleans, then passed up and captured the city. This was an important Union triumph.

The year had been one of many hard-fought battles, only a few of which we are able to mention. The general result was in the East lamentable failure, but in the West brilliant success, of the Union armies.

At the close of 1862, after a year and a half of fighting, the war had already lasted longer than either side expected when it began. At first both had hoped that after a few months the trouble would be settled by some kind of agreement or compromise. Each side was surprised at the vast number of soldiers, the immense military equipment, and the determined spirit shown by the other.

310. The Emancipation of the Slaves.—As the war went on, it was plain that the tens of thousands of slaves, although they did not actually fight in the Southern armies, were helping the South just as much as if they carried muskets. They built forts, toiled in gun shops and powder mills, and raised crops at home. This, of course, released thousands of whites from home duties and swelled the ranks of the Confederate army. It was a terrible and costly war. The final result even seemed doubtful. To save the Union the South must be crippled at every possible point. To set the slaves free was to weaken the South. Mr. Lincoln held that a sound principle of military law gave him the authority to abolish slavery. He proposed to do it primarily as an act of military necessity by virtue of his office as Commander-in-Chief of the army, just as when a general in active warfare destroys buildings or burns bridges to aid his army operations.

It was sound common sense, as well as a profound military policy, to seize the most favorable opportunity to strike at the real cause of the trouble. Public opinion was rapidly shaping itself to this end. Lincoln was one of the most clear-sighted and sagacious of men. He patiently abided his time for so momentous a step.

311. The Proclamation of Emancipation.—Finally, acting on his own judgment and that of his trusted advisers, Lincoln issued in September, 1862, his warning proclamation to the effect that if the Confederate States did not cease hostilities before the first of the next January, all slaves within the Confederate lines should be thenceforth and forever free.

The negroes very soon heard this wonderful news and many thousands of them eagerly awaited the coming of the day when "Massa Linkum would set 'em free." They looked upon the good President as the savior of their race.

On that famous morning, January 1, 1863, the prophecy was fulfilled. That New Year's Day will be forever memorable as the date of the great Emancipation Proclamation, an act by which four millions of slaves were brought from the night of bondage to the sunlight of freedom.

This was the monumental event of the war, perhaps the wisest thing President Lincoln ever did or ever could do. In after years it will perhaps be regarded as the greatest event of the century. Few men in all history have had an opportunity of doing a deed of so vast and far-reaching importance.

Emancipation was quickly followed by the enlistment of negroes, or "freedmen" as they were now called, as soldiers in the armies of the Union. During the year 1863 more than fifty thousand of them, and before the end of the war nearly two hundred thousand, had enlisted under the banner of freedom. They were good soldiers, and on many a battlefield they fought with an unflinching courage.

CHAPTER XXIV.
MORE ABOUT THE WAR FOR THE UNION.

312. Union Defeat at Chancellorsville.—Now let us return to our narrative of a few of the prominent military operations of the war. In May, 1863, the army of the Potomac, under General Hooker, moved southward from Washington. At Chancellorsville it was met by a Confederate force under Generals Lee and Jackson. The battle lasted two days, and was disastrous to the Union arms; in fact, the worst defeat of the war. It marked the zenith of Confederate success. In this battle "Stonewall" Jackson, so called from his splendid firmness, one of the ablest of the Southern generals, was mortally wounded.

"STONEWALL" JACKSON.

313. The Mighty Struggle at Gettysburg.—General Lee, proud of this success, now resolved to lead his army into the North. Sweeping past Washington and across Maryland, he pushed up into Pennsylvania, the whole country around being terrified at his approach, especially Baltimore and Philadelphia, both of which cities were threatened. Lee had now eighty thousand soldiers, the finest army the South ever possessed. The army of the Potomac, under the command of General Meade, whom Grant called the right man in the right place, followed closely. The two defiant armies met at Gettysburg, where occurred the most momentous battle ever fought on this continent. It lasted three days, July 1-3, 1863. The first day's fighting ended in favor of the Confederates. On the second day their desperate efforts to drive the Union forces from their positions were repelled, but with an enormous loss on each side.

GENERAL MEADE.

On the third day came the final test. The brave Confederate General Pickett led many thousands of soldiers over an open plain in a most desperate charge to break the Union center. On, on they came, their ranks now torn through and through by Union shot and shell, but still on they charged. Drawing nearer, up they rushed to the Union line with the familiar Southern yell, and with frantic fury dashed upon our firm-set ranks. Our men wavered with the mighty shock and for a moment fell back, but instantly rallied with the Union cheer.
In the furious onset and the hand-to-hand fight, friend and foe fell by thousands. But the charging battalions were shattered, crushed, driven back, melting away under the concentrated fire, and only some few fragments of all that vast column straggled back over the field of death.

GENERAL ROBERT E. LEE.

Lee was baffled, defeated; the Union was safe. The invaders, with that vast army that came with stately pride, went back to Virginia with sorrowing memories of the direst disaster of the war. Never again did a large Confederate force hazard a march into the North. After Gettysburg there was little hope of Confederate triumph.

314. Memorials of the Victory.—Gettysburg was a costly victory. Over that broad area of the three days' battles, strewn through wood and meadow, on field and hill, lay the bodies of thousands of soldiers. One-third of Lee's entire army, and about a fourth of the Union forces, had been killed or wounded. The arena of fiercest fighting in the third day's final charge is now marked by a suitable monument, which bears upon a bronze tablet an inscription that indicates the historical importance of the spot.

Upon opposite columns are also inscribed the names of the officers who led the surging columns of gray, and the names of those officers who held firm the impregnable walls of blue.

The whole field of battle, covering several square miles, is dotted with hundreds of similar memorials of many varieties. These monuments have been erected year after year by the survivors or by their friends. They indicate the positions held by regiments, brigades, and divisions, where desperate charges and equally desperate repulses occurred, or where gallant officers fell.

315. Lincoln's Masterly Address at Gettysburg.—In November, 1863, the central portion of the battlefield was set apart as a National Cemetery and dedicated with solemn ceremonies. The most important of these was the notably eloquent address by President Lincoln, which has passed into history as an event hardly less memorable than the great conflict itself. Perhaps in no language, ancient or modern, are any words found more comprehensive and eloquent than this brief speech.

Time has tested the strength of this short, simple address. After more than a quarter of a century it is still as familiar as household words.

GENERAL U. S. GRANT.

316. Success of General Grant in the West.—Let us now read about a few of the great events of the war in the West during the first half of the year 1863. Here General Grant was the central figure of important military operations. He had already become prominent by the brilliant campaigns we have mentioned. His remarkable career furnishes one of the many examples of great men coming up from obscure and unpromising conditions of life.

He was born in Ohio in 1822, and received a military education at West Point. He was a successful officer in the Mexican War, having been engaged in nearly all the battles of the war, where he manifested conspicuous bravery. Returning from Mexico, he engaged a while in farming, but with discouraging results. Evidently it was not his vocation.

When the Civil War opened, Grant was employed at a small salary in his father's leather store in Galena, Illinois. He at once offered the governor his services, and was appointed a colonel of an Illinois regiment. He rose rapidly to conspicuous positions.

317. Capture of Vicksburg.—General Grant, after defeating the Confederates at the battle of Shiloh, and driving them south to Corinth, followed them to Vicksburg. This was a stronghold from which they seemed to defy every effort to dislodge them.

The city stands on a high bluff some two hundred feet above the Mississippi, and as there were heavy batteries all along the river front and on the hillsides, Grant could not attack the city with his gunboats. On the north there were miles of swamps and creeks, so that he could not approach on that side. On the east the city was heavily fortified with cannon.

President Lincoln and the country expected General Grant to capture Vicksburg. What could he do? Witness his superb generalship!

He first protected against cannon shot a number of gunboats and steamers by means of bales of hay, and planned to run them past eight miles of batteries one dark night in April. This movement was so perilous that officers would not order their men to go, but called for volunteers. So many were eager to go that lots were drawn for a chance. One soldier refused one hundred dollars for his place.

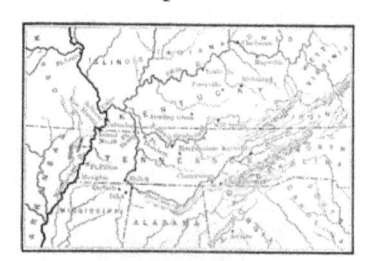

Click to enlarge.
MAP OF MILITARY OPERATIONS IN THE WEST.

Soon as the watchful Confederates sighted the first boat of the grim procession, they opened a deafening cannonade, and started a series of bonfires that lighted up all the miles of that voyage of death. Some of the transports were destroyed, but enough got through to answer the general's purpose.

Next Grant ferried his army across the river some miles below Vicksburg, and fought and defeated General Pemberton's troops, which had moved down to meet him. Then, learning that General Johnston was coming to attack him, he marched up between the two armies. On his east side he met Johnston's army and defeated it. Thence he turned west and drove Pemberton again, and the next day routed him once more and drove his entire army into Vicksburg.

Commodore Porter's gunboats now threw huge shells into the doomed city from the river and Grant's army bombarded it on the east. It was an awful siege. No building was safe. The people lived in caves dug in the sides of the hills. Food was so scarce that mules, cats, dogs, and rats were devoured. At last, after seven weeks of siege, Pemberton, on July 4, surrendered his entire army of about thirty thousand men, the largest force captured during the war.

These two great victories, at Gettysburg and at Vicksburg, one in the East, the other in the West, both won at the same time, gave new hope to the Union cause. The Confederacy was at last cut in two, for the Mississippi River was open in its entire length, and its waters, in Mr. Lincoln's words, "flowed unvexed to the sea."

From this eventful Fourth of July in 1863 the strength of the Confederacy began to decay. There was little hope for its final success after this time. All its future contests only delayed the inevitable end.

318. Two Other Important Victories in the West.—In September occurred the severe battle of Chickamauga, where the Union army would probably have been utterly defeated but for the valor of General Thomas, who thus won for himself the name of the "Rock of Chickamauga." Late in November the Union army was shut in at Chattanooga by the ever alert Confederates, and was relieved only by General Grant's skillful planning and hard fighting.

GENERAL THOMAS.

This battle was fought on a cold, drizzly day. The fog, settling on the valley and sides of Lookout Mountain, up which our brave boys climbed, covered the lower part of the advancing army so that only the upper lines were visible. This brilliant victory is popularly known as "the Battle above the Clouds." These movements ended the army operations of 1863.

319. Sherman's Famous March to the Sea.—The year 1864 saw two great movements, both planned by General Grant, who had now been called by President Lincoln to come to Washington and take control of all the armies of the Republic. One was his own advance against Richmond, and the other General Sherman's famous "March to the Sea."

GENERAL W. T. SHERMAN.

General W. T. Sherman, a brilliant officer and General Grant's dear comrade and lifelong friend, had driven his opponents southward and captured Atlanta. General Hood then very boldly but injudiciously led a Confederate army up to Nashville, where General Thomas attacked and utterly defeated him.

Meanwhile Sherman had begun his celebrated march to the sea. Having burned the mills, foundries, and workshops at Atlanta which had been of great value to the Confederates, he started in November with an army of sixty thousand on a three-hundred-mile expedition to the Atlantic! They marched on three and sometimes four parallel roads, foraging on the country, destroying railroads, burning bridges, and devastating a belt of territory from forty to sixty miles wide. Our army was followed by thousands of negroes, enjoying their new freedom.

In December Sherman reached the sea and telegraphed to President Lincoln the capture of Savannah as a Christmas present! Resting there, he then marched his conquering legions north, through both Carolinas, up to Goldsboro, having met and defeated Johnston's army at several points along the way. He was now able to aid General Grant, whose campaign against Richmond we must now consider.

320. Grant's Advance on Richmond; Lee's Surrender at Appomattox.—Early in May, Grant had started with a hundred and twenty thousand men on his advance against Richmond. He pushed his work with great vigor, fighting almost daily, but after every battle flanking Lee's right, and thus working constantly southward. It was a series of bloody battles, and the slaughter was enormous; but such is war. He continued slowly advancing all summer, and in the fall of 1864 began the siege of Richmond.

Finally, in April, 1865, General Sheridan had cut the last of the railroads supplying the Confederate capital. Then with Grant's army on one side and Sheridan's on the other, the Confederacy quickly collapsed. Jefferson Davis fled and a panic seized upon the people in the doomed city, while fire and havoc ran riot. The Union army soon marched in and restored order.

GENERAL SHERMAN ON HIS MARCH TO THE SEA.

One week later Lee surrendered his whole army at Appomattox. General Grant treated his fallen foes with great generosity, requiring only the oath of officers and men not to fight further against the United States. The victorious general permitted all the men to keep their horses, to enable them, as he said, "to do their spring plowing on their farms."

321. The Story of Sheridan's Famous Ride.—Read's stirring poem, "Sheridan's Ride," has always been a favorite, for it records in verse the gallant deed of one of the most brilliant generals in the war for the Union. In the early fall of 1864 Grant sent General Sheridan with a large force of cavalry to lay waste the Shenandoah Valley. Sheridan did the work so well that it was said, "If a crow wants to fly down the valley, he must carry his provisions with him."

GENERAL SHERIDAN.

The story runs as follows:—
One morning in October the Confederates approached under cover of a fog and surprised the Union forces at Cedar Creek and put them to flight. Sheridan was then at Winchester, twenty miles away, slowly riding back to join his army. A messenger met him with the bad news. On his famous black horse he dashed forward at full speed down that "good broad highway, as with eagle flight," towards the line of battle. As he came nearer he met the first of the fugitives and rallied them with fierce and forcible words. At once they were as eager to fight again as they had been ready to fly.
A brave nucleus of the army which had not shared in the surprise was fighting with determined pluck to prevent disaster from becoming disgrace. Men said, "Oh for one hour of Sheridan!" All at once a deafening cheer was heard above the roar of musketry and artillery as the tired men recognized the long-looked-for Sheridan. The news flashed from brigade to brigade along the front with telegraphic speed. As the gallant general, cap in hand, dashed along the retreating lines, a continuous cheer burst from the whole army.
The entire aspect of affairs seemed changed in a moment. Further retreat was no longer thought of. "This retreat must be stopped!" shouted Sheridan to his officers as he galloped down the lines. The line of battle was speedily re-formed; the retreating army turned its face to the foe.
The ranks of the Confederates swayed and broke everywhere before the charge of the Union cavalry and the impetuous advance of the infantry. They were completely defeated, with the loss of many prisoners, and nearly all of their guns.
Sheridan's ride to the front, October 19, 1864, has passed into history as one of the most thrilling events that have ever given interest to a battle scene. Stripped of all poetic gloss, the result achieved by Sheridan's superb generalship, after reaching his shattered army on the field of Cedar Creek,

still stands, with few if any parallels in history, as an illustration of the magnetic influence of one man over many, and as an example of snatching a great victory from an appalling defeat.

SHERIDAN RALLYING HIS TROOPS AT CEDAR CREEK.

322. Death of Lincoln.—Wild was the delight of the country when peace came. There were public meetings, processions, bonfires, every possible display of universal joy!

Suddenly, like a total eclipse at noonday, came the darkness of a great sorrow. Abraham Lincoln, the great and good President, whose heart had bled for the nation's suffering, who had never held a trace of bitter feeling towards the South, was shot down by an assassin!

Instantly the nation was plunged into the deepest sorrow; joy ended in grief, delight was turned to mourning. Ninety thousand Union soldiers had been slain, but this last sacrifice overshadowed all. Never before was a great nation shrouded in a sorrow so deep. Thousands mourned, as for the loss of a personal friend.

The people hardly realized till his death the greatness of this man, the hero of the mighty struggle by which the Union was saved. From that day to this, the admiration and love, not only of the nation but of all mankind, have been increasing for the great and kind-hearted man, the wise leader, the blameless President,—Abraham Lincoln.

323. The Cost of the War.—The cost of the four years' war was something tremendous. At the close of the strife the total debt was about three thousand millions of dollars! This, however, was but a small part of the loss.

The cost in human life can never be estimated in money. The area fought over was so large that there was fighting somewhere almost every day! The number of battles, great and small, was more than two thousand! The total Union loss of men killed in battle and of those who died of wounds and disease was not less than three hundred and sixty thousand. The number of enlisted soldiers on the Union side was over two and a half millions.

324. Grand Review of Troops at Washington.—At the close of the war a grand review of Union troops was held at Washington. These comprised the army of the Potomac, commanded by General Meade in person, and Sherman's army fresh from its march to the sea. These battle-scarred veterans, perhaps one-fifth of all the Union soldiers who had tramped and fought for years, now passed in review, bearing aloft the tattered and shot-torn flags around which they had rallied on many a battlefield. The two days were beautiful and the sight was superb.

The National Capital was full of strangers in holiday dress, and every house was decorated with flags. For two days the two armies marched in close column around the Capitol, down Pennsylvania Avenue, past the President and cabinet, who occupied a large stand prepared for the occasion in front of the White House. On the second day it took six hours and a half for Sherman's magnificent army of sixty-five thousand sunburnt veterans to march in solid columns in review before the President.

This grand review was a fitting conclusion to the war. The million men who were still in arms at the close of the war, old comrades of camp and field, shook hands and parted, each to his home, where mother or sister or wife or children or other dear ones awaited the long-absent soldier.

325. The Country after the War.—The war proved beyond all question that the American Republic is a nation, not a league, and it rid it also of human slavery. It took, of course, a long time for the bitter feeling on both sides to die away. More than a generation has passed since the great Civil War desolated our fair land. The people of to-day have little cause to recall its sufferings and horrors.

How dear to the hearts of the American people are the familiar ceremonies of Memorial Day! What more impressive object lesson could our children have than to see the gray-haired veterans marching with thinner ranks and more faltering steps, on this sacred anniversary!

CHAPTER XXV.
OUR NAVY IN THE WAR FOR THE UNION.

326. Our Navy at the Beginning of the War.—For a number of months before the breaking out of the war the Southern leaders of the secession movement had been quietly but skillfully preparing for it.

A large part of the soldiers had been sent off to the frontier posts. Rifles, cannon, and all such supplies had been taken months before from Northern stations and sent South. Our navy had been purposely scattered all over the world. More ships were abroad or useless than were at home fit for service. The whole number available after the attack on Fort Sumter was only thirteen.

All through the South most of the southern-born officers of the government who were in control of Federal property, as custom houses, post offices, arsenals, forts, navy yards, and ships, abandoned their trust, or turned all these properties over to the seceding states.

It was in reference to such a piece of transfer that the Secretary of the Treasury, John A. Dix, sent to New Orleans that famous telegram which thrilled the whole North:—

"IF ANY ONE ATTEMPTS TO HAUL DOWN THE AMERICAN FLAG, SHOOT HIM ON THE SPOT!"

Great was the peril. More vessels must be had, and that at once. The seventeen warships in foreign ports were called home, scores of steamers were bought and dozens were built as quickly as possible.

327. Urgent Need of Vessels to blockade Southern Ports.—One of the most urgent needs for a navy was to blockade the Southern ports. This was to be done by stationing well-armed ships near the mouth of every harbor to seize any vessel trying to get out with a cargo of cotton, or to capture any ship coming in with supplies. "Running" this blockade was a profitable but dangerous business.

But we can judge whether our gallant navy did its duty in watching the eighteen hundred miles of Southern coast line, if we remember that during the four years of the war the Union blue-jackets captured or destroyed over fifteen hundred blockade runners—more than one a day.

328. Naval Operations on the Western Rivers.—The Confederates had fortified many cities and important bluffs along the Mississippi River and its branches, and had built many heavy gunboats. Our government had at first not a single gunboat to meet them. Something must be done very soon. In less than a hundred days there were built at St. Louis, from the keel up, with powerful engines, heavy armor plate, and cannon, eight powerful gunboats, all ready for action. These ironclads, with some mortar boats, did effective service at the capture of Forts Henry and Donelson, of Columbus, Memphis, and Vicksburg, and all along the rivers.

329. How New Orleans was protected against an Attack by the Union Forces.—While the Union ironclads were fighting farther north along the Mississippi and other large rivers, Commodore Farragut was doing valiant work below New Orleans. This city was protected by two strong forts.

Just below the forts there stretched from each bank towards the middle a big boom of logs. The space in the middle of the river between the ends of the booms was filled with hulks of old ships, first firmly anchored, then heavily chained to each other, and lashed to the booms with huge cables, making almost a bridge. Above this formidable barrier was a fleet of iron rams and gunboats.

Besides all this, there were a number of fire rafts, loaded with cotton and hay, ready to be set in a blaze and float down on any Union craft that would dare to come up. How was it possible for the Union vessels to force their way up the river in the face of these obstructions?

ADMIRAL FARRAGUT.

330. Farragut prepares for the Attack.—Farragut had about fifty vessels all told: frigates, ships, sloops, gunboats, and mortar vessels. He anchored the mortar boats around a point of land nearly two miles below the forts, and dressed them with evergreens and foliage of trees disguising their position. Then the great thirteen-inch bombs burst inside and around the forts all day, all night, for six days.

Meanwhile two small gunboats went one night up to the chained hulks to break the barrier; and though detected and fired on, the officers worked calmly and persistently. They contrived to get a gunboat through, then steamed up the river, turned and rushed down on the cable with such force as to break it! Daylight showed a wide opening for the Union fleet.

331. The Grand Work done by Farragut and his Fleet.—The next morning at two o'clock, April 24, 1862, the fleet steamed up. The forts fired and the ships fired, but the fleet kept moving in the darkness. Soon one passed through, then another, the swift ones dashing ahead.

But the flagship Hartford, on which was Farragut, having passed through, turned aside to avoid a blazing fire raft, when she ran aground! Then the Confederates, seeing the Hartford stuck fast, pushed a fire raft up against it. Instantly the flames flashed along the rigging and the ports, the big guns of the fort meanwhile pounding her. But the gun crews kept working their cannon as steadily as if on practice, and the rest fought the flames, and soon subdued them. The flagship was saved. Other ships passed up, all fighting, some surviving by hairbreadth escapes; a few were lost.

When the morning sun rose, the astounding work had been done, the gates of fire had been passed, and the Union fleet under Farragut was triumphant. New Orleans was captured and the control of the river secured nearly up to Vicksburg.

332. The Merrimac and the Monitor.—When the war for the Union began, and just before the Confederates seized the navy yard at Norfolk, the commanding officer there contrived to burn or sink all the ships; but the best one, the Merrimac, was soon raised and rebuilt as a powerful ironclad.

When the fine old frigate had been remodeled her entire appearance was changed. She had no longer the appearance of a ship, but seemed like a house afloat. The story is told that an old sailor on board the Cumberland, who first sighted her, reported gravely to the officer of the deck, "Quaker meeting-house floating down the bay, sir."

In anticipation of what harm it might do, the government engaged Captain Ericsson, a Swedish inventor in New York, to build as quickly as possible, after his own plans, an ironclad, a new and very odd-shaped kind of warship—the now famous Monitor. The construction was pushed day and night without an hour of delay.

333. Attack of the Merrimac on the Union Fleet.—Before long the dreaded Merrimac was finished, and on March 8, 1862, the ponderous black monster steamed slowly out to attack the Union ships in Hampton Roads. She made straight for the fine frigate Cumberland, the solid shot of whose broadside fell like pebbles into the sea from the slopes of the huge ironclad. On, on came the ponderous monster, and crashing into the wooden side of the Cumberland, opened a hole "wide as a church door." The sinking ship went down with her flag flying and her guns booming to the last!

Next the Merrimac attacked the Congress, whose captain and three-fourths of her crew were killed or wounded. Hot shot were used, which soon set the Congress in a blaze. Then the ironclad, as if she had done enough for one day, went grimly back to Norfolk, intending to continue her destruction the next day.

Everywhere in that region is alarm. The shores are thronged with anxious thousands. The city of Washington is almost in a panic. The grim monster may steam up here on the next day, and hurl its exploding shells into the Capitol or the White House. Philadelphia, Baltimore, and all the seacoast cities of the country are exposed to destruction. What is to be done? Can the danger be averted?

334. Timely Arrival of the Monitor.—That very night, as if by a special providence, the Monitor arrived from New York! Early next morning, when the naval Goliath of yesterday came out in his iron armor, victorious and confident, a young David stood up to defy him!

A strange craft indeed was the Monitor. Her rail was but little above the water, and nothing was to be seen on her deck but a kind of round iron box in the middle, a pilot house forward, and a small smokestack aft. At a mile's distance she might be taken for a raft. Indeed, the Confederates well described her when they called her a "Yankee cheese-box on a raft."

THE FAMOUS CONTEST BETWEEN THE MONITOR AND THE MERRIMAC.

335. Famous Battle between the Monitor and the Merrimac.—It was a Sunday morning, and the sun rose in a cloudless sky. The batteries on both sides of the bay were crowded with men waiting for the coming contest. At the first sign of life on board the Merrimac, the Monitor began her preparations for the battle.

Slowly the Confederate ram came down the bay. She opened fire on the Minnesota, which was still aground. The frigate responded with a mighty broadside, but the cannon balls rattled off the iron flanks of the huge ram like so many peas. Clearly everything depended upon the little Monitor.

The battle now began, and the huge shells and heavy shot crashed like loudest thunder. It was a strange, an awful battle. At times the two vessels were in actual contact. The dense smoke, the deafening roar of explosions, the shouts of officers' orders, the crews often hurled off their feet by the terrific blows smiting the iron armor—all made it beyond description fearfully sublime. The Merrimac's plates were split and torn. One shot, entering her port, did terrible havoc.

Just as Lieutenant Worden of the Monitor was looking through the slit in the turret to take aim, a shell struck outside and filled his face and eyes with powder and iron splinters! He was insensible for some time.

When he came to himself, his first question was, "Have I saved the Minnesota?"

"Yes," was the reply, "and whipped the Merrimac."

"Then I don't care what becomes of me," he answered.

After more than three hours of this frightful combat, the humbled Merrimac steamed back to Norfolk, the victorious little Monitor giving a series of farewell shots as she sailed away.

Thus ended this marvelous battle, the first in the world's history between ironclad vessels. All Washington retired to sleep that night with a sense of relief, for it seemed as if the nation had been saved.

The brave Worden shortly after the famous battle went to Washington. President Lincoln was at a cabinet meeting when he heard of the lieutenant's arrival. He rose hastily and said, "Gentlemen, I must go to that fellow."

When Lincoln entered his room, Worden was lying on a sofa with his eyes and head heavily bandaged.

"Mr. President," said he, "you do me great honor by this visit."

"Sir," said Mr. Lincoln, with tears in his eyes, "I am the one who is honored by this interview."

336. Confederate Privateers attack Union Merchantmen.—When the North began blockading the Southern ports, the South of course used all its energies to break the blockade by aiding ships to pass in or out, and also to destroy our commerce wherever it might be found.

The first craft that went out on this errand of destruction was an ocean steamer then at New Orleans. It had been speedily altered into a warship and named the Sumter. She slipped through the blockade in June, 1861, and did a lively business capturing and burning our merchantmen.

Then the South, as it had no navy of its own, had to seek aid abroad. England seemed to be very willing that her shipbuilders should furnish ships for the use of the Confederacy in seizing and destroying Union vessels.

The first of the cruisers secretly built in a British shipyard to destroy our commerce was the Florida. She burned or sank over forty vessels before she was captured.

337. The Famous Alabama makes Sad Havoc.—The Alabama was the most famous of the Confederate cruisers. She was built under false pretenses and with a false name, in an English port, of English material, armed with English cannon, and manned by English sailors.

The Alabama, once fairly at sea under Captain Semmes, skillfully avoided our men-of-war sent to capture her, and continued in her two years' cruise till she had burned or captured sixty-seven of our merchant ships.

338. The Alabama destroyed by the Kearsarge.—At last the Alabama went into the harbor of Cherbourg, in France. Captain Winslow of the United States warship Kearsarge, then searching for her, heard of this and at once challenged her, and then waited outside. On the nineteenth day of June, 1864, the Alabama was compelled by law to leave the port. The battle began, and was watched by thousands from the shores.

The Kearsarge swept around in great circles, compelling the Alabama, about half a mile distant, to do the same. The men on the Alabama fired fast and wild. Their shots flew over, or fell short; but the Kearsarge fired carefully and with true aim. Nearer drew the Kearsarge, circling still. Its two eleven-inch guns made frightful havoc, tearing great rents in the Alabama's sides. She was sinking, and started for the shore. Winslow now steamed in front and headed her off. Then down came the Confederate flag.

Soon the far-famed and dreaded cruiser sank to her watery grave. The names Winslow and Kearsarge long rang through this country with plaudits of enthusiastic praise.

"I would rather have fought that fight," said brave old Admiral Farragut, "than any ever fought on the ocean."

339. England pays for the Damage done by the Alabama.—After the war England refused for years to make compensation for the damage the Alabama had done to our commerce. But seeing that the same course might some day injure herself, and sensible of the injustice, she at last consented to make amends. In 1872 a Board of Arbitrators met at Geneva, and agreeably to its decision "John Bull" promptly paid $15,500,000 to "Uncle Sam" to distribute among those who had suffered by the depredations.

340. Preparations for the Capture of Mobile.—In the summer of 1864 a prominent Southern port, Mobile, was yet uncaptured. Its defenses were strong. Two splendid forts stood sentry at the gateway. Long lines of piles narrowed the channel to about three hundred feet, and a triple row of torpedoes threatened any approach. In the harbor the Confederates had a small fleet of gunboats and one tremendous ram, the Tennessee.

Admiral Farragut determined to capture Mobile. He had four monitors and fourteen wooden ships. All the preparations were made with the utmost care. The officers and men of the fleet regarded the admiral with staunch loyalty and absolute trust. The attack was made early on the morning of August 5.

341. Farragut's Crowning Victory at Mobile.—The fleet passing through the channel, rained shot and shell so furiously upon the forts that the Confederates could not well serve their guns. But our finest ironclad, the Tecumseh, was struck by a torpedo, and she sank with over a hundred of her brave men!

Her captain, the gallant Craven, was at the time in the pilot-house with the pilot. As the huge ironclad lurched heavily over and began to sink, both rushed to the narrow door, but there was only room for one to pass at a time. Craven stepped to one side, saying, "After you, pilot." The pilot leaped to a place of safety, but the noble captain went to the bottom in his iron coffin.

The fleet now fought a desperate battle with the Confederate ironclads. The armored vessels were soon sunk or scattered. The Tennessee tried to ram our ships, but with little success. Then our ironclads gathered around our "wooden walls," steamed straight for the ram, and there was fought one of the most desperate naval fights of the war.

Sharpshooters fired into the ram's ports, our ships successively poured in a terrific fire, and hammered at close range with huge solid shot and fifteen-inch bolts of iron, till the white flag went up, and once more the stars and stripes waved triumphantly over the harbor of Mobile.

Thus ended the battle of Mobile Bay,—one of the most brilliant naval contests of modern times,—Farragut's crowning victory. Three hours elapsed from the time the first gun was fired until the great ram hauled down the Confederate flag.

The port of Mobile was thenceforward closed against blockade runners, and the last channel of communication between the Confederacy and the outside world was cut off.

342. Farragut in the Rigging during the Battle.—During the battle Farragut stood in the main rigging; but as the smoke increased he gradually climbed higher, until he was close by the maintop. The shots were flying thick and fast. There was great danger that he would lose his footing, and so the captain sent aloft one of the men with a rope who lashed him to the rigging so that he might not fall if wounded.

FARRAGUT LASHED TO THE RIGGING.

When Farragut saw the danger from the approaching Tennessee, as he stood tied to the rigging, he said to his signal officer, who was lashed to the other mast:—

"Can you signal, 'For Heaven's sake'?"

"I can signal anything," replied Kinney.

"Well, signal to all the fleet, 'For Heaven's sake, go for the ram!'"

The fact that the admiral was fastened to the main rigging during the greatest sea fight perhaps in our history gave him a unique reputation throughout the country. Farragut was amused and amazed at the notoriety of the incident.

When a picture of the scene in one of the illustrated papers came to hand a few days after the battle, the admiral said to one of his captains in conversation, "How curiously some trifling incident catches the popular fancy! My being in the main rigging was a mere incident, owing to the fact that I was driven aloft by the smoke. The lashing was the result of your own fears for my safety."

343. Cushing plans to destroy the Ironclad Albemarle.—One of the large sounds, or inland gulfs, on the coast of North Carolina was the scene of a great deal of blockade running during the war. The place needed constant watching by our ships.

But the chief cause of anxiety was a monster ironclad, the Albemarle, that the Confederates had built up the Roanoke River. She had sunk or disabled several Union gunboats. She had gone up the river to refit. The entrance to the sound was so shallow that none of our large warships could pass in.

Could anything be done to check the Albemarle? Lieutenant Cushing, only twenty-one, but a most daring naval officer, said, "Yes, there could!" His plan was to steal carefully up by night, seize the huge ironclad and bring it away, if possible, or else blow it up. The river was guarded on both banks, and the ram itself was watched by special sentries. No matter for that; he would go. He obtained a noiseless steam launch, and rigged a torpedo on the end of a long spar, turning on a hinge at its side. The crew of the launch consisted of fifteen men, with Cushing in command.

CUSHING'S BRILLIANT EXPLOIT.

344. Cushing's Plan Successful; Destruction of the Albemarle.—One dark rainy night Cushing steamed in his little torpedo boat up the river. They passed all the river guards undiscovered. A camp-fire on the bank near the ironclad showed to him, as he stood in the bow of his boat, the dark outlines of the monster. He steamed on softly. Just then a dog barked! Then guards sprang up and fired. The big bell on the ram clanged its alarm, lights flashed on the water and shots hissed all around the launch.

The brave young officer saw that the ram was surrounded by a large raft of huge logs. Instantly his resolution was formed. He steamed off some distance to get a long run, then turned and rushed for the Albemarle. Shot whistled around him. On came his little craft, bumped upon the logs, crashed over them, and pushed up under the huge ram. Cushing now lowered his torpedo spar, calmly guided it into its place, pulled the fatal cord—crash! a roar of thunder!—and all was over. The great ironclad was a terror no longer.

345. Cushing reaches the Fleet in Safety.—Each man had to save himself as best he might. Cushing leaped into the water. After about an hour's swimming he reached the shore and fell exhausted upon the bank. He crept into a swamp for some distance, tearing his feet and hands with briers and oyster shells.

Next day he met an old negro whom he thought he could trust. The negro was frightened at Cushing's wild appearance and tremblingly asked who he was.

"I am a Yankee," replied Cushing, "and I am one of the men who blew up the Albemarle."

"My golly, massa!" said the negro; "dey kill you if dey catch you; you dead gone, sure!"

Cushing gave the negro all the money he had to go into the town and learn the news.

After a time the negro came back, and, to Cushing's joy, reported the Albemarle sunk. At last the intrepid officer found a boat and paddled for eight hours until he reached the Union squadron. After hailing one of the vessels, he fell into the bottom of the boat, utterly exhausted by hunger, cold, fatigue, and excitement.

Lieutenant Cushing, to whose intrepidity and skill the country was indebted for this and many other bold exploits, was engaged in thirty-five naval combats during the war. What a record for a young man of twenty-three! He died at thirty-two, the youngest officer of his rank in the United States Navy. One of our finest torpedo boats, which did good service during the Spanish-American war, is well named "The Cushing."

CHAPTER XXVI.
THE WAR WITH SPAIN IN 1898.

346. The Downfall of Spain on this Continent.—For half a century or more after the time of Columbus, Spain was the greatest military and political power in the world. Her ships and her sailors carried the proud banner of Castile to every shore and clime then known.

The vast domain claimed by Spain on this continent by right of discovery and exploration comprised the fertile islands of the West Indies, the greater portion of Central and South America, and all that part of our own country west of the Mississippi. In territory, in wealth, in power, the sovereignty of Spain became the mightiest in the world.

How are the mighty fallen! The once powerful empire has crumbled into dust. The year 1898 saw its overthrow on this side of the Atlantic and in the Philippines.

347. Spain's Cruel Policy towards her Colonies.—For the most part Spain ruled her colonies with shocking oppression. Her policy was to extort all possible gain from them to her own selfish profit. She retained to the last the barbarous methods of less civilized centuries. Finally, after long years of oppression, the South American colonies began to cut loose from her tyrannical sway.

In a few years Spain was stripped of all her possessions in America, excepting only her islands in the West Indies.

348. Cuba rebels against Spanish Oppression.—One would naturally suppose that these disastrous losses would have taught Spain to govern her only remaining American colonies, Cuba and Porto Rico, with more wisdom. But not so; she kept right on as before, growing worse, if possible, still clinging to the old policy of cruel oppression and merciless extortion.

Some thirty years ago a rebellion began in Cuba which lasted ten years. In vain Spain spent millions of money and sent thousands of soldiers to subdue it. Hundreds of Cubans were cast into prison to die of fever and starvation, and their property was confiscated.

349. Cuba again rebels against Spain in 1895.—In 1895 the long-suffering Cubans rose in rebellion again. Their army was larger, better furnished, and they gained possession of a much more extensive portion of the island.

Now Spain became really alarmed. She sent to Cuba a hundred and twenty thousand soldiers. They melted away, mostly from sickness and mismanagement, like frost in the morning sun. It was all in vain; for it was now plain that Spain could never conquer the Cubans, and just as evident that the Cubans unaided could never win their independence.

The war had already been barbarous enough, when the Spanish General Weyler set in operation his inhuman concentration plan. This meant the gathering up in the country districts of thousands of helpless old men, women, and children, and driving them to the towns and forts, where they were shut up like cattle in large enclosures, surrounded by a deep ditch and a barbed wire fence.

Along the line of the fence were frequent guardhouses, where soldiers with loaded guns prevented escape. The poor outcasts were crowded into wretched palm-leaf huts, with foul water and scanty food. It is said that in the island about four hundred thousand helpless people were herded in this way. They died by thousands.

350. The Barbarities in Cuba excite Great Indignation in this Country.—Now, all these horrors in Cuba aroused a great deal of indignation in this country and excited profound sympathy for the sufferers. Shiploads of provisions were sent by the Red Cross and other societies to relieve the starving thousands.

The feeling throughout this country at last came to be intense. For years and years past our people had watched the long struggle with the keenest interest. For years our presidents had protested to Spain against the useless warfare.

Now, when the real state of affairs in Cuba in 1897 became known, our government sent word to Spain that this slow starvation of helpless men, women, and children was not war, but savage barbarity, and must be stopped. In reply, Spain asked for some delay and promised milder measures.

351. The Battleship Maine blown up in Havana Harbor.—In order to protect American interests in Cuba, the battleship Maine was sent to Havana in January, 1898.

A calamity now occurred that shocked the world. On the evening of February 15 this magnificent ship, while at anchor in the harbor of Havana, was destroyed by an explosion. Two officers and two hundred and sixty-four American sailors were hurled to instant death!

The awful disaster sent a thrill of horror and indignation through our country. A court of inquiry was instantly appointed by President McKinley to investigate the matter and ascertain the cause. Meanwhile the country waited for forty days, with surprising patience, for the report, which came during the last of March, stating that the Maine had been blown up from the outside by the explosion of a submarine mine. Subsequent evidence before the Senate committee showed that the mine had been exploded by men who wore the uniform of Spain.

352. War declared against Spain.—Public feeling in our country grew more intense every hour. The President continued to do his utmost to avert war by peaceful and diplomatic methods. Thinking people knew well enough that such efforts would be in vain. It was evident that Spain would never grant independence to Cuba. It was also evident that the American people (from the moment they heard of the blowing up of the Maine) had made up their minds that the only real solution of the problem was to put an end forever to Spanish rule on this side of the Atlantic. This of course meant war.

Congress took the responsibility and declared war against Spain on April 21, 1898.

353. Dewey acts promptly and sails for Manila from Hong Kong.— The first step of our war with Spain was to send Commodore Sampson with a fleet to blockade the large seaports of Cuba. All eyes were turned to this island; for every one expected the war to begin there; but instantly the scene of action was shifted to the other side of the globe.

ADMIRAL DEWEY.

The first day of May saw one of the greatest naval victories in the history of the world. Our government had telegraphed orders to Commodore George Dewey, then at Hong Kong, China, in command of our Asiatic squadron, to sail at once to the Philippine Islands and "capture or destroy" the Spanish ships.

Dewey had taken part in important naval battles in our Civil War, and was an experienced and skillful officer. In anticipation of war, his fleet was ready for action on an hour's notice.

After his instructions arrived from Washington, Dewey promptly sailed for Manila with six warships and two tenders. He delayed outside the harbor till the moon had set, and then steamed silently through the three-mile-wide channel. He was entering in the dark a bay he had never seen. He knew it was planted with torpedoes, and that he was going to attack a Spanish fleet of ten ships, besides large forts with heavy guns.

A wonderful task! but Dewey was a wonderful man. He understood his business. He had been trained under the eye of the great Admiral Farragut and had fought long and hard in the war for the Union.

354. The Remarkable Naval Victory at Manila.—Dewey's fleet arrived before sunrise in front of the forts and the line of Spanish ships. The battle at once began. Our vessels kept moving on the curve of a long ellipse or flattened circle, and every time each came around it poured a series of rapid and accurate shots directly into the enemy. They answered furiously, but not deliberately. Round and round wheeled our ships in a slow and deadly circle. Our men could see the walls of the forts crumbling, some ships all ablaze, and others shattered and sinking.

After two hours of these tremendous circuits Dewey stopped firing and moved his ships about three miles out of range to rest his men, give them breakfast, and look after his ammunition. The men, in fine spirits, ate their morning meal, and rested. It was a stoker on the flagship Olympia who said that below "the temperature is nearly up to two hundred degrees, and so hot that our hair is singed."

Before noon Dewey returned, circled nearer still, and fought even more fiercely. In an hour and a half more the work was finished. One ship was riddled, then reeled and sank; then another; one was broken midway and went down; now one was in flames, then a second, and so on till the entire Spanish fleet, besides gunboats and transports, were sunk or burned up or shot to pieces!

BATTLE OF MANILA.

How did our ships stand the contest? Only two or three were hit at all, and none seriously injured. Our six had destroyed thirteen Spanish vessels and silenced their forts. The Spaniards had lost six hundred and thirty-four men, killed and wounded. We had only one man killed and seven slightly wounded.

355. The Nation's Grateful Appreciation of Dewey's Victory.—Thus was fought, on May Day, 1898, at Manila, perhaps the most surprising naval conflict the world had ever seen. In three and a quarter hours the naval power of Spain went down in the blue waters of the bay, and the splendid fame of George Dewey echoed round the globe. Congress gave him a vote of thanks and a gold medal; and he was made Admiral, the highest officer in the American navy.

Many years ago Admiral Farragut said to the father of the hero of Manila, "Doctor Dewey, your son George is a worthy and brave officer. He has an honorable record, and some day he will make his mark."

Never before in the history of our country was there projected a series of patriotic demonstrations grander in their purpose or finer in their execution than those which greeted Admiral Dewey on his return to this country, in the fall of 1899, from the scene of his famous victory.

When Dewey sank the Spanish fleet in Manila Bay, he opened a new era in the history of our country. From that day the United States received more distinct recognition among the nations responsible for the political affairs of the world.

356. Preparations to meet the Spanish Fleet.—Now let us return to the scene of war in our own country. On the last day of April the Spanish fleet, under Admiral Cervera, left the Cape Verde Islands, sailing west; there were four armed cruisers and three torpedo-boat destroyers; all good new ships and in prime condition. The alarming question was, Where will they strike? The good people of our great eastern cities began to imagine what would happen if these powerful warships should come sailing into our harbors.

Every effort was promptly and vigorously made to defend exposed points with forts and torpedoes. Events proved that it was needless. No ship of that Spanish fleet came within five hundred miles of any American city. Yet it was evident that Cervera's fleet must be captured or destroyed before our coast could be safe, or military operations could be prudently begun in Cuba.

Extraordinary efforts were made to ascertain the exact location of the hostile squadron.

Finally it was found that it had slipped on May 19 into the bay of Santiago. Our fleet at once gathered around to blockade the entrance, to make it impossible for any vessel to pass in, and to attack Cervera's ships should they attempt to come out. Among our blockaders were the splendid ships New York, Massachusetts, Brooklyn, Texas, Iowa, Indiana, and the Oregon that had sailed around Cape Horn from San Francisco, fourteen thousand miles in sixty-seven days.

RESCUE OF HOBSON BY THE SPANISH ADMIRAL.

357. Hobson's Brilliant Exploit.—Admiral Sampson did not deem it advisable to steam in and attack Cervera, as the channel was thickly planted with mines. So our semicircle of ships watched and waited. At night our strong search-lights blazed into the mouth of the harbor and lighted it with a fiery glare.

If the narrow neck of the harbor could only be somehow obstructed, so that Cervera's ships would either be completely "bottled up," or would have to creep out to sea by daylight, the naval power of Spain would be crippled. So thought Admiral Sampson, and he selected Lieutenant Hobson for this daring deed. It meant going right into the midst of the enemy's batteries and torpedoes.

A large steamer, the Merrimac, was taken and loaded down with coal; and a crew of seven men were selected to go with Hobson. Strange fascination of mingled courage and patriotism! Hundreds of sailors begged the chance to go!

It was all carefully planned; and about two hours before dawn, on June 3, they started. As they drew near, the Spanish made the water boil and hiss with their shots. But on they went to the chosen spot, balls and shells striking all about, howling and shrieking in their ears and tearing their ship.

Coolly but quickly they sank the Merrimac, sprang to the raft they had prepared, and were clinging to it when the firing ceased and a little steam launch came up with Cervera in it! The Spanish admiral reached out and helped lift in Hobson and his seven comrades! He took them ashore, praised them for their daring, gave them dry clothing, fed them, and soon after exchanged them for some Spanish officers who had been captured by our men.

358. The Army does Brilliant Service at Santiago.—It was plain that the Spanish ships would never come out until they were driven out. So during the last week in June an army of about twenty-five thousand men, under General Shafter, landed a few miles east of Santiago to coöperate with our fleet in capturing the city. Our forces, losing no time, moved on through tropical jungles, exposed to the enemy's sharpshooting from trees. It was a deadly advance towards log forts on the steep heights, impeded by the annoying tangle of barbed-wire fences.

On the first and second days of July our gallant troops captured the two forts, El Caney and San Juan, which overlooked Santiago, and drove the enemy in hot haste into the city.

359. The Remarkable Naval Victory at Santiago.—Then Cervera's hour had come! On July 3, a beautiful Sunday morning, the eyes that for more than a month had watched with sleepless vigilance that narrow opening between the rocks, saw at last the bow of a Spanish warship. It slipped out and turned sharply to the west; then came another, and a third, and so on till all six had passed. They at once opened a fierce but ill-directed fire upon our fleet.

The men on our vessels were mustering for Sunday morning inspection when the enemy was seen. "The enemy is coming out!" was signalled from ship to ship, and on each deck rang out the command, "All hands clear ship for action!"

Every man was ready to do his duty. Every ship was stripped for action. Instantly our ships were after the Spanish squadron, firing as they followed. What a sight was that! There was never before one like it! Two lines of hostile ships rushing along the coast, tearing the ocean to foam, each a volcano pouring out smoke, and more than a hundred big guns hurling shells and shot which strike with awful crash upon the iron walls of the enemy's ships!

ADMIRAL SAMPSON.

On they dashed, mile after mile. One of our huge shells fell midway of the Pluton, which at once went down with an awful plunge. The Furor, riddled with shot, fled to the shore and broke in pieces on the rocks. Furious was the chase for the other four; nearer and nearer, till our ships came up. Then the Maria Teresa, the flagship, with huge holes torn in her, and set on fire by our exploding shells, escaped to the beach, a sinking, burning wreck.

Next the Oquendo, half her men killed, and her sides all split open, also fell helpless on the beach. In forty minutes these four ships had gone to their doom.

ADMIRAL SCHLEY.

Still beyond was the famous Vizcaya, doing her best to escape. But the Brooklyn, Commodore Schley's flagship, gained on her and poured shells into her, so that with the Oregon now rushing up in a burst of speed which astonished all who saw her, her race was soon run, and she, too, went to her grave on the strand, a shattered, blazing hulk.

Yet one more, the Colon, newest, fastest, and best of the squadron, was now about four miles ahead; but our ships gained steadily upon her, and in less than two hours she hauled down her flag and ran ashore forty-five miles from Santiago.

360. After the Battle at Santiago.—The sun that shone in the morning upon six of Spain's finest ships looked down at noon upon a row of half-sunken wrecks along the coast.

At the risk of their lives our men rescued their foes from the mangled hulks, the burning decks, and the surging water.

"Don't cheer, boys," cried one gallant captain, "the poor fellows are dying."

Another captain said in his report, "So long as the enemy showed his flag, our men fought like American seamen; but when the flag came down, they were as gentle and tender as American women."

The Spanish loss, according to their own accounts, was three hundred and fifty killed or drowned, and about one hundred officers and one thousand six hundred and seventy-five men prisoners, including the brave Admiral Cervera. Their loss in value was over twelve million dollars. Upon our side only one man was killed, and three were wounded, all on the Brooklyn. Not one of our ships was badly injured. Evidently the Spanish gunners could not shoot straight!

So ended this famous naval engagement. Never, perhaps, has the world seen two such instances of the utter destruction of an enemy's naval force as in the battles of Manila and Santiago.

361. The Campaign in Porto Rico.—The surrender of all Cuba soon followed. Then General Miles was sent with nine thousand troops to Porto Rico, the only remaining island on this side belonging to Spain. He landed near Ponce, on the southern coast. The city surrendered without a shot and welcomed our army. The Spanish troops fled on the approach of our soldiers.

General Miles in a proclamation assured the inhabitants that they should enjoy the rights and immunities of American citizens. As he moved inwards, other cities along his line of march surrendered, and the Spanish forces made only occasional resistance to our progress. Just before an expected battle news of peace came from Washington. All fighting ceased, and this fertile island came into our hands with little bloodshed.

362. End of the War.—Meanwhile our government was making energetic preparations to send a powerful fleet under Commodore Watson across the Atlantic and to carry the war to the Spanish coast. We may be sure that Spain, and even some of her neighbors, did not like the prospect. There had been enough of rapid, crushing, and unbroken defeats to satisfy even the Castilian point of honor.

When it became evident that Watson's fleet would be ready in a few days to carry the war to the very doors of Spain, the representatives of the great nations of Europe said things had gone far enough. Diplomatic pressure was applied to poor Spain. She was politely but firmly told that she must make peace at once, and on any terms.

The French Minister at Washington was authorized by Spain to sign a preliminary document, or protocol, embodying in precise language the conditions on which our government would negotiate peace. This document was signed at Washington on August 12, and hostilities ceased.

The formal treaty of peace was signed in Paris December 10, 1898. By the terms of this treaty Spain agreed to give up its sovereignty in Cuba, to cede to the United States Porto Rico, a few small West India islands, and one of the Ladrone group; also to cede to this country the Philippines, after payment by us of twenty millions of dollars as "reimbursement for insular expenses."

363. Our Nation's Future.—The immediate results of this short-lived Spanish war were full of deep meaning to our nation. No one now can safely say what the distant outcome will be. It is certain to be far-reaching and momentous.

Our country has rapidly advanced to its position as one of the foremost nations of the world in wealth and in power. Let us trust it may also lead in good government, in national honor and righteousness. Let us earnestly hope that in the long years before us our sacred Union shall still be preserved, unbroken,—forever one great Union of prosperous and happy states.

APPENDIX.

BOOKS FOR REFERENCE AND COLLATERAL READING IN THE STUDY OF AMERICAN HISTORY.
This book is designed to be used before the formal text-book on American history is begun in grammar-school grades. It is intended also to serve as a convenient basis for more extended work both on the part of the teacher and of pupils. Hence the reading of the preceding chapters is only one part of the proposed plan. A systematic course in supplementary reading should be added. The following plan is suggested, but it may be modified, of course, to meet the needs of any particular class of pupils.

> NOTE.—The whole subject of reference books on American History is treated thoroughly in Montgomery's Student's American History [see "Short List of Books," page xxiv in Appendix, and "Authorities Cited," page xxx in Appendix], Montgomery's American History [see "Short List of Books," page xxxiii in Appendix], and Fiske's History of the United States [see Appendix D, page 518, Appendix E, page 527, and Appendix F, page 529].

REFERENCE BOOKS FOR TEACHERS.

Two books are of special value to teachers. These are Channing and Hart's Guide to American History [Ginn & Company, Publishers, price $2.00], and Gordy and Twitchell's Pathfinder in American History [Lee & Shepard, Publishers, complete in one volume, $1.20. In separate parts, Part I, 60 cents; Part II, 90 cents].

These two works are replete with suggestions, hints and helps on collateral study, numerous references, detailed lists of topics, and a wide range of other subjects which make them indispensable to the teacher of American history.

SCHOOL TEXT-BOOKS FOR READING AND REFERENCE.

Pupils should have easy access, by means of the school library or otherwise, to a few of the formal school text-books on American history. In connection with this book Montgomery's Leading Facts of American History and Fiske's History of the United States are especially valuable. The following books are perhaps equally serviceable: Eggleston's History of the United States; Steele's Brief History of the United States [usually known as "Barnes's History"]; Thomas's History of the United States and Mowry's History of the United States. These books are useful in reading for additional topics, for dates, maps, illustrations, reference tables, and for "filling in" subjects which do not come within the scope of this book.

TOPICS FOR COLLATERAL READING.

For ordinary school work the text-books to which we have just referred will furnish enough and suitable material for these topics. When, however, standard works on history are of easy access, through the school or public libraries, it is well even for pupils of the lower grades to read sparingly by topics from such works. These topics should be carefully selected by the teacher. They should be brief and call only for a few pages of reading.

In the succeeding pages references have been given only to a very few standard works, such as those by Fiske, Parkman, Irving, and McMaster, and such other books as can ordinarily be easily obtained.

REFERENCES FOR READING.

Pupils should also have easy reference to books from which topics may be read or which may be read sparingly by select passages indicated by the teacher. Many of these books have been suggested more on account of their interesting style than for strict historical accuracy. Read the designated works not as a whole but only by topics or selections. They will do much to awaken and maintain a lively interest in American history.

OUTSIDE READINGS.

While the study of this book is in progress it is well for the pupils to limit their miscellaneous reading to such books as bear directly upon our subject. Under this head we have suggested many productions which belong to the "story-book" order. Wholesome books of fiction and semi-fiction may certainly do much to stimulate and hold the attention of young students of American history. With this topic, as with all other topics on collateral reading, the teacher should exercise a careful supervision.

FOR READING OR RECITATION.

The work should be enlivened by reading occasionally, before the class or the school, poems or prose selections which bear directly upon the general topic under consideration. We have referred only to a very few such extracts from good literature. Other selections will readily suggest themselves.

USE OF A TOPIC BOOK OR NOTEBOOK.

The teacher and pupil should appreciate the scope and usefulness of a Topic book or Notebook. By this is meant a blank book with semi-flexible or board covers, of a convenient size, and of at least 48 pages. Into this blank book should be written carefully with ink brief notes as the several chapters of this book are read or studied. It may well be a kind of enlarged diary of the pupil's work.

Make brief notes of the various books read in whole or by topics; topics not treated in this book but discussed in the class, such as King Philip's

War, the Mexican War, etc., and references to new books to be reserved for future reading and other subjects which will readily suggest themselves.

This notebook should be well illustrated. The basis should be the inexpensive photographic copies (sold for about one cent each) of famous pictures illustrating important events in American history. Catalogues giving the exact titles, cost, and other details are sent to applicants, free of expense.

Portraits, maps, facsimiles of documents and autographs, etc., are often easily obtained from book catalogues, guide books, advertising pages, and secondhand text-books.

All this illustrative material should be pasted in the notebook at the proper place, neatly and with good judgment, allowing plenty of space for margins. Such a compilation is, of course, a matter of slow growth. It should be carefully preserved as a pleasant reminder of school days.

> NOTE.—Think of enriching your notebook with photographic reproductions of such works as Stuart's "Washington"; Faed's "Washington at Trenton"; Trumbull's "Surrender of Cornwallis" and "Signing the Declaration of Independence"; Benjamin West's "Penn's Treaty"; Leutze's "Washington Crossing the Delaware"; Vanderlyn's "Landing of Columbus"; Johnson's "Old Ironsides" and Overend's "An August Morning with Farragut."

Milton Keynes UK
Ingram Content Group UK Ltd.
UKHW031146311024
450535UK00004B/149

9 789362 923813